Prioritizing Urban Children, Teachers, and Schools through Professional Development Schools

Prioritizing Urban Children, Teachers, and Schools through Professional Development Schools

Edited by

Pia Lindquist Wong

and

Ronald David Glass

PRESS

Published by State University of New York Press, Albany

For information, contact State University of New York Press, Albany, NY
www.sunypress.edu

Production by Kelli W. LeRoux
Marketing by Anne M. Valentine

Library of Congress Cataloging-in-Publication Data

Prioritizing urban children, teachers, and schools through professional
    development schools / edited by Pia Lindquist Wong and Ronald David
    Glass.
        p. cm.
    Includes bibliographical references and index.
    ISBN 978-1-4384-2593-1 (hardcover : alk. paper)
    1. Laboratory schools—California—Sacramento—Case studies. 2. City
children—Education—California—Sacramento—Case studies. 3. School
improvement programs—California—Sacramento—Case studies. I. Wong,
Pia. II. Glass, Ronald David.

    LB2154.S23P75 2009
    371.04—dc22   2008034703

10 9 8 7 6 5 4 3 2 1

Contents

Figures and Tables

Acknowledgments

The history of the struggle for social justice recounts the tireless efforts of diverse individuals and groups, some on the front lines and some in the background. All of these collective efforts are critical for justice to be achieved, just as the work of a large web of teachers, candidates, university professors, students, parents, and community members has been crucial to the Equity Network professional development schools whose stories are told in this volume. The chapters highlight our work to address compelling inequities in our regional K–16 public education system. Here we would like to acknowledge, with gratitude and admiration, the work of those whose names will not appear in this book but without whose efforts the Equity Network would not have been possible.

Victoria Lemus, administrative support, and Fely Lambating, budget manager, were essential staff members to the Equity Network. Victoria came to us having just completed her B.A. in Spanish. In her interview she said she "just really needed a job." She got so much more than a job and did so much more than was required. She designed and wrote newsletters, created online surveys and analyzed results, maintained the project's Web site, arranged travel for groups as large as fifty, and kept many of us organized, particularly the project director. She is now a teacher at the Met High School. Fely saw our work through two successful audits and her remarkable management of this complex project ensured that our many initiatives ran smoothly. Victoria and Fely were unflappable in the face of confusion and conflicting institutional imperatives, and brought order to our sometimes chaotic but important projects. Both worked with remarkable efficiency, accuracy, and grace, and earned high praise from the broad web of institutions and individuals connected to the Network who were dependent on them.

We would also like to recognize the significant support that we received from a wide range of university colleagues. In particular, we recognize Elizabeth Kean as an important mentor to all of the faculty members working on this project and as a courageous and original thinker who led the initial establishment of the Equity Network. Debbiesiu Lee and Angela Clark-Oates, doctoral students at Arizona State University, generated an extensive search of the professional development school literature.

Many university and school administrators provided key support, and some deserve special mention: Catherine Emihovich and Michael Lewis, past deans for the CSU Sacramento College of Education; Robert Pritchard and José Cintrón, current and past department chairs for Teacher Education and Bilingual/Multicultural Education, respectively; Charlotte Chadwick, Donna Cherry, Dennis Mah, and Tamra Taylor, site administrators who helped build and sustain a strong foundation for the Network; and Pamela Costa and Deb Bruns, district administrators who shared the Network vision. We also acknowledge the support of Tom Alves, executive director of the San Juan Teachers Association. Our thanks too to Meredith Linden for excellent formatting and indexing work.

Finally, all the contributors to this volume offer their deepest gratitude and appreciation to their own families, who undoubtedly are breathing a collective sigh of relief that this book is finally complete. Those of us who heed Paulo Freire's exhortation to make this world "less ugly, less cruel, and less inhumane" can only persist in this work with the love of family and comradeship of friends.

Pia Lindquist Wong and Ronald David Glass, Editors

Introduction

The Equity Network

The Contextual and Theoretical Frameworks for Urban Professional Development Schools

Pia Lindquist Wong and Ronald David Glass

Context

Beginning in 1998, a group of relatively new faculty at California State University Sacramento's College of Education began discussions about innovations in teacher education that ultimately led to the creation of the Equity Network. The Equity Network aimed to provide outstanding teachers for low-income, racially, culturally, and linguistically diverse (LI/RCLD) pupils as well as learning environments that prepared these pupils to fully participate in our democratic society. This is our story—it is sure to resonate with the experience of others who daily face similar difficulties in making U.S. public schools achieve their promise. We hope our story will help inspire renewed national commitment to equity for those children left behind once again by our educational system.

Our pilot attempts to reform our own teacher education practice focused on closer collaboration among stakeholders in the K–16 system.[1] These laid the groundwork for establishing the Equity Network of professional development schools (PDSs) in 2001.[2] Ten elementary schools, one middle school, and one high school have been the consistent core set of Network PDSs, although one additional elementary school was added within the last three years and one high school dropped its membership, but was replaced by another. These schools are located in five districts within the greater metropolitan area of Sacramento: one large urban district, two large urban fringe/suburban districts, and two small urban fringe/suburban districts. Approximately 140 teachers participate to some degree in the Network, though the most active core group numbers about 60.

1

All of the schools serve predominantly LI/RCLD pupils, with especially high concentrations of these pupils in the elementary schools. Two teachers' associations (Sacramento City Teachers Association and San Juan Teachers Association) also participate in the Equity Network along with a community partner, Sacramento Area Congregations Together, an interfaith affiliate of the PICO National Network.[3]

The Equity Network was designed to address the concrete conditions faced by too many LI/RCLD children in our community. Chronic poverty, limited health/dental care, poor housing conditions, underresourced schools, and unsafe neighborhoods—intensified by racism and other forms of oppression—make the call for high standards a sham because the basic structures—inside and outside of classrooms—needed to reach such ambitious goals either have never been present or have recently been eroded for these pupils. The reality faced by pupils in the Equity Network parallels that faced by pupils in typical inner-city situations, but, in Sacramento, this is not always so apparent.

Take a drive through one of Sacramento's many tree-shaded neighborhoods or glistening new subdivisions, and images of the 1950s Cleaver family of television's *Leave it to Beaver* come readily to the imagination. Fathers and sons, uncles and nephews can be seen fishing for salmon and trout on the banks of the Sacramento and American rivers bounding the city. Scrapbooking sessions and Bunko games occupy many mother-daughter pairs. Residents from all corners of the city proudly display Sacramento Kings banners, some even rivaling the largest banner flapping from the city's highest radio control tower. Unmoved by the tastes of their highbrow San Francisco Bay Area neighbors to the west, readers of Sacramento's alternative weekly newspaper voted Red Lobster as the best seafood restaurant in town and Denny's as the best breakfast spot—bistros, sushi, and nouvelle cuisine are just beginning to get a foothold in Sacramento.

Actual data about demographics in the Sacramento Valley reveal the tension between the surface appearance of smalltown life and the underlying realities of economic and demographic shifts. In September 2002, *Time* identified Sacramento as the most racially integrated city in the United States, where "everyone is a minority. . . . [But] racial tensions still exist." Sacramento is indeed rich with cultural diversity. Historic Chinese and Japanese communities with roots dating back to the 1840s gold rush and railroad-building era of coerced labor mix with new immigrants from Southeast Asia; Russian and Ukrainian enclaves establish new services that complement generations-old Mexican groceries and *panaderias*. Signs of revival can be seen in historically African American neighborhoods that were split apart by freeways and urban renewal's penchant for bulldozers. Enter almost any school in one of the metropolitan area's four large districts and you will encounter pupils who speak a range of primary languages and bring a variety of home cultures to the classroom. In the central city district, there is no ethnic majority: whites, Latinos/Hispanics, African Americans, and Asians are almost equally represented among pupils. Their teachers, however, will not reflect this diversity since over 80% of them are white women, many of whom grew up in surrounding suburbs that share little in common with America's "most integrated city."

Sacramento also embodies the economic contrasts that define California. New subdivisions compete with commercial wine grape vineyards to replace the diverse agricultural tracts that made California the breadbasket of the nation and gave rise to César Chávez's historic organizing efforts. Median prices for new homes, fueled largely by Bay Area exiles' demand, have doubled in the last ten years. A median home in Sacramento costs over $300,000[4] and the preponderantly civil service occupation base strains to keep up. Despite a veneer of prosperity, Sacramento sits at the northern end of the San Joaquin Valley, a region known historically for its agricultural productivity, but identified more recently for its chronic and widespread poverty and high rates of public assistance, earning it the dubious distinction of "the new Appalachia" (Doyle, 2005). Similarly, urban counterparts of this new Appalachia remain somewhat hidden beyond the tree-lined streets and quaint downtown Victorian homes that can obscure the inner-city realities that challenge this capital city of the country's largest state and the world's eighth largest economy. Countywide, 46% of public school pupils qualify for federally subsidized meals. In the central city district, 62% of pupils qualify for such assistance. Moreover, California still ranks near the bottom nationwide in per pupil funding, a fact that is glaringly apparent in Sacramento's central city schools that are characterized by overcrowded classrooms with few of the material, personnel, and technology resources common in suburban settings. Poverty and the problems associated with it are no strangers to Sacramento's children, and the tensions—racial, economic, linguistic, and cultural—easily threaten the promise that this highly integrated metropolitan area offers.

Sacramento's LI/RCLD communities are rich with cultural and linguistic resources that could be a boon to classrooms and schools. The challenge emerges from both the inability of educators to connect with these resources and the economic realities that shape the choices and outcomes of many immigrant and minority families who struggle with structural barriers and roadblocks to success. Both the promise and the challenge are molded in turn by the increasing emphasis on standardization and accountability, introduced first by the state in 1998 and intensified by the federal No Child Left Behind Act of 2001. In characteristic fashion, political and school leaders "celebrate diversity" with numerous proclamations, while pushing policies and practices that result in standardization and conformity to dominant norms.

The tension that results strains school-community relations, and LI/RCLD pupils continue to bear the brunt of the negative consequences from the full force of state and federal government policies. The educational programming for our state's most diverse pupils has become increasingly narrow.

Standardization and Accountability versus Engaged Pedagogy

All except one of the districts connected to the Equity Network have adopted scripted curricula for language arts and mathematics. These are virtually the only subjects taught in these districts, though in the handful of schools also serving significant numbers of middle- to upper-middle-class pupils, the curricular picture looks more enriched. As an outcome of standardized testing and the resultant grading of schools, Equity Network PDSs teach language arts, by mandate, for 3.5 hours per day. One hour is devoted to math. Thirty minutes are reserved for English language development, a bare minimum necessity considering that over one-third of the pupils are English learners (i.e., technically, native speakers of a language other than English) and another quarter have nonstandard English as their home language. Once recess and lunches are accounted for, there is less than one hour of instructional time left in a typical day. In Equity Network schools, this hour may be used to "catch up" on one of the multiple required elements of the language arts curriculum or to squeeze in P.E., art, social studies, or science. The latter two subjects have essentially been dropped from the curriculum, though teachers have tried to "integrate" social studies and science content into appropriate themes in the language arts curriculum. Despite an absence of adopted curriculum, science is slowly reappearing in the schools only because it is now to be tested in the 5th grade.

In addition to an almost exclusive focus on language arts and math skills and content, many of our partner districts and schools emphasize the importance of "fidelity" to the curriculum, which is monitored by "coaches" who provide "instructional support" but also keep track of the accelerated pacing schedules for lesson delivery. "Fidelity" means that only the materials provided by the publisher are used in instruction; that stories in the publisher's anthology are not swapped out (e.g., one could not substitute a story about Diego Rivera for one about Pablo Picasso, despite the grounded relevance of Rivera for our region); that instructional strategies besides those indicated in the teacher's manual for a particular lesson not be used even when they have proven effective with one's pupils (reader's theater, e.g.); that the teacher "move on" to the next lesson on schedule even if pupils demonstrate misunderstandings about the current lesson's content; and so on.

Strict "fidelity" is most carefully monitored in schools where accountability targets have not been reached, which includes most of the Equity Network schools. Already disadvantaged by many factors, these schools are put in a double bind by the federal Adequate Yearly Progress (AYP) accountability structure due to their high proportions of English learner (EL) and low-income pupils (Kim & Sunderman, 2005). Repeated failures to meet AYP result in increased monitoring and decreased curricular options.[5] The policy theory is that if test scores do not improve after implementing a highly scripted curriculum, the cause cannot be tied to the curriculum since "research" has proven that its "proper implementation" results in score increases. Thus, the "cause" is ascribed to "poor-quality teaching." Administrators and policymakers blame "resistant" teachers whom they view as either willfully undermining the curriculum program or lacking the competence to implement it appropriately.

From our vantage point of working with schools in the program improvement process (which in California operates largely on the notion of increased "fidelity" to the curriculum and larger, more sustained doses of that same curriculum), we note the following net outcomes: (a) a curriculum that is often frustrating and unengaging to teach; (b) teachers whose professional knowledge is increasingly undermined and devalued—first by administrators and "expert consultants" and eventually by the very teachers themselves who lose confidence due to repeated "failure" as evidenced by low test scores; (c) removal of the teacher from instructional decisions about the pupils she or he teaches; (d) intensified focus by teachers on the "causes" of low test scores, whether blaming pupil limitations and family deficits or, conversely, blaming themselves, rather than structural flaws in the system; (e) slow and uneven gains for pupil achievement; (f) growing discouragement among low-scoring pupils, particularly as they progress through the grades; and (g) teachers whose professional practice is increasingly narrowed as they have less and less opportunity and support to create curriculum and to teach subjects other than language arts and mathematics. This last point has particular implications for teacher preparation models that use field experiences; incredibly, many candidates will earn a credential having never observed an authentic social studies or science lesson taught with children in a classroom.

Establishing professional development schools—in which a central goal is to develop professional learning communities that deepen theoretical and practical knowledge and effectiveness—during these years of increasingly rigid accountability systems has meant weathering enormous tensions and challenges. Equity Network university faculty and K–12 teachers were committed to the professional development and action research components of the PDS model, but were seriously constrained in implementing the results of such efforts, given that "experts" and "coaches" were the only ones with authority to alter the curriculum or schedule. We observed that pupils were more engaged during instructional activities that offered choice and pupil-relevant purpose, but we could generally only squeeze such lessons in for one hour a week at the most. We identified significant opportunities for our immigrant parents to become involved in school activities, but it required deviations from the "script," which could not be managed in all of our PDSs.

We have not naively wished that accountability and standards would disappear, nor have we disdained the notion of transparency about the work of schools. However, the prevailing understanding of accountability and standards has imposed severe limits on our group's capacity to respond to classroom conditions and make full use of its ongoing collaboration across institutional boundaries. Of course, the constraints have spawned ingenuity as well. We learned the state's content standards better than we might have and now can use them to legitimize any number of pupil-centered, multicultural education projects! This has been an important first step in effectively countering the narrow, scripted curricula that dominate the schools. In addition to concrete alternatives for enriched and enhanced instructional projects, our partnerships afforded support to those teachers who *did* question the benefits of the accountability and standardization regimes but had no research-supported alternatives. These challenges also acted as a "reality check" for academics for whom the clampdown of accountability was initially a researchable policy question rather than a concrete school and community reality that confounded teaching and learning in myriad ways. For most, this "reality check" provided an opportunity to engage more deeply with the schools—for the benefit of the pupils in them, but also to advantage our candidates, who needed a sophisticated understanding of their professional context if they were to become the educational equity advocates we hoped they would. But, despite these benefits, the potential of our work has been seriously hampered by the policy context that established a system that neutralizes or negates the experiences, knowledge, and voices of key actors—notably teachers, pupils, and parents.

Of course, our situation was no different from that of any group attempting to question the dominant order or resist trends viewed as harmful to LI/RCLD pupils and the teaching/learning process. At times, we may have wished that we were establishing our PDSs during the heyday of California's pupil-centered policy era (Chrispeels, 1997). Nevertheless, the consolidation of our partnerships at this particular time was significant and responsive to concrete conditions in our local community. The Equity Network afforded higher status for the teachers in LI/RCLD schools because of their collaborations with university faculty. University faculty became better informed about the constraints to teaching and learning imposed by external standards and accountability. With both groups working together, we were able to provide more grounded and effective strategies for innovation than we might have if we had remained working separately and independently.

Our response to these specific sets of challenges in local schools became increasingly guided and informed by the principles of "engaged pedagogy" (Glass & Wong, 2003), a framework that drew from the critical pedagogy of Paulo Freire (1970), bell hooks (1994), and others, and from anthropological approaches to education (e.g., Gonzalez, Moll, & Amanti, 2005). Our actions in classrooms and schools and at the university were also shaped by a sociopolitical critique of the U.S. educational system, informed by a range of intellectuals including Anyon (2005), Kozol (1991), Lipman (2004), Valenzuela (1999) and West (2000). Putting into practice the fruits of theories that were themselves grounded in particular struggles for more just and democratic schools, Equity Network educators understood that our projects were allied with a history being borne into the future through our labors.

Our vision of engaged pedagogy puts pupils—their lives, voices, perspectives, historical and cultural backgrounds, and emerging cultural formations—at the center of teaching and learning efforts. From this center, teachers who aspire to engaged pedagogy employ dialogical and praxis-oriented methods, pay close attention to pupils' identity development, and tap the wealth of resources available in communities and from other adults who know these pupils. In addition, these teachers use critical reflection and continuous professional development to nurture their own self-actualization and professional growth. They ultimately use their engaged pedagogy to create classroom reform, based on curriculum and pedagogical innovation, whose success may lead to broader school reform. Finally, teachers practicing engaged pedagogy participate in a community of learners that includes the next generation of teachers as well as other educators from university and community settings.

The Professional Development School (PDS) Model

We envisioned the practice of engaged pedagogy across contexts—K–6 classrooms, middle and high school classrooms, professional development efforts, and university classrooms. The PDS model was a logical approach, given the possibilities for comprehensive and systemic change that it offered, and the fact that a central target for change was our own teacher preparation programs and not just K–12 schools. PDSs emerged in the early 1990s as a promising model for transforming K–16 systems. As with any educational reform, the PDS effort builds on successful practices from earlier reforms, but adds enhancements and new orientations. Lab schools, partnership schools, service learning, and other efforts all influenced the conceptual development of PDSs. At the same time, there are distinct elements of the PDS model that suggest a theory of action and a conceptualization of systemic change that is not present in these other reforms. The National Council for the Accreditation of Teacher Education (NCATE), through its published standards (2001), has been instrumental in advancing the thinking around PDSs and in guiding implementation of the model. The solid support of other organizations, notably the Holmes Partnership, has also strengthened the quality of work and the depth of the analysis of outcomes (Abdal-Haaq, 1998; Teitel, 2000).

A review of the literature on PDSs reveals agreement about four primary goals for PDSs (Darling-Hammond, 1994; Holmes Group, 1995; National Council for the Accreditation of Teacher Education, 2001). They include the following:

1. Enhance pupil learning.

2. Improve field experiences for candidates.

3. Engage K–16 educators in continuous and targeted professional development.

4. Use action research to inform teaching and learning in schools.

Advanced PDSs also tend to include participation from legislative/political bodies, community organizations, and teachers' associations.[6]

PDSs operate on a theory of action and change in which improvements to teaching occur along the learning-to-teach continuum, from pre-service subject matter and pedagogy fundamentals to advanced in-service professional development and learning. Such improvements require significant involvement from the K–16 teaching community. In the preparation phase of the teaching career, curricula and practica should be informed by the grounded expertise of classroom teachers and university instructors who actively participate in schools, by careful examination of the theoretical and empirical knowledge bases for the field, and through field experiences structured to introduce the novice to the complex world of the classroom, the school, and the community as well as the multilayered demands on the education professional in that complex world. These premises are not unique to PDSs; however, the conditions for addressing them make PDSs distinct.

In an ideal PDS setting, K–12 teachers work side-by-side with university instructors to develop the teacher preparation curriculum, from the content covered in coursework to the activities included in student teaching. University instructors *and* K–12 teachers provide instruction, guidance, and mentoring to candidates, thus creating a cohesive apprenticeship experience for these future teachers with explicit instruction on key values and practices needed to be effective. Moreover, this kind of collaboration shows great promise for firmly rooting a dynamic theory–practice exchange that is often lacking in conventional teacher preparation approaches (Melnick & Zeichner, 1998; Thompson, Bakken, & Mau, 1998; Zeichner, Grant, Gay, Gillette, Valli, & Villegas, 1998).

The PDS also makes possible thoughtful, purposeful teacher professional development cycles that deepen educators' content and pedagogical knowledge, strengthen their leadership skills, and broaden their ability to analyze, diagnose, and intervene in classroom issues, and beyond—but do so in ways that are grounded and responsive to the particular teaching context and the teaching/learning issues emerging from it. The PDS creates conditions under which this professional development also occurs in a community of learners—from explicit efforts to reflect on new teaching knowledge generated by mentoring candidates, to structured professional exchanges among K–16 educators, to new instructional opportunities (university courses, conference presentations, in-services for other teachers) facilitated by the partnership.

The pre-service preparation and ongoing in-service learning and development are rooted in a conceptualization of teaching that challenges dominant discourses and historical practices in teacher development. In the PDS vision of teaching, one is developing a craft (Shulman, 2004) and to be successful there must be a dynamic nexus between formal knowledge, the knowledge resulting from reflection upon action (Freire, 1970), knowledge constructed with colleagues and peers (McLaughlin & Talbert, 2001), and knowledge distilled from the context (Gonzalez, Moll, & Amanti, 2005; Hammond, 2001). Capacity in and knowledge of the teaching craft are continually (re)constructed, individually and in a community, with inputs from pupils, the professional community (K–16 and beyond), research literature, and the broader school context.

Such a vision of teaching makes sense particularly in relation to the vision of student learning that is at the heart of a PDS. The investment in educator learning and capacity is made specifically in order to provide learning experiences that are content-rich and demand high-quality thinking and production from pupils (in our case LI/RCLD pupils). Such learning experiences accelerate skill development, but are often mismatched with school expectations for our population. At the same time, these powerful learning experiences will reflect and integrate the funds of knowledge (Gonzalez, Moll, & Amanti, 2005) present in their communities but often ignored or disparaged in conventional schooling. This approach to pupil learning is also linked to a view of schooling as part of a larger struggle for social change and social justice. Rich learning experiences for LI/RCLD pupils coupled with high expectations for achievement can be one part of a larger push for equal opportunities and fair outcomes for these pupils. Until now, these dreams have been largely unfulfilled. The vision of pupil learning in our PDSs sits squarely on building the capacity to reverse this cycle of inequality.

In the ideal format, a strong collaborative partnership that links schools, universities, teachers' associations, community groups, and political actors provides the support needed to achieve these visions of teaching and learning that are at the center of PDS work. When pulled together, the K–12 system and the university system have the human and intellectual resource base needed to address the most vexing educational issues of our time. The challenge of the PDS is to bring these institutions together, despite the many structural and cultural barriers in the way. Through the collaborative work on these common goals, the partners are all forced to rethink fundamental modes of operation and basic orientations.

For teachers, the PDS provides an opportunity to think deeply about the teaching profession and mold its future—but this requires a critique of its present condition and the role of in-service teachers in the profession's formation. The PDS encourages participating teachers to view themselves as model practitioners and as advocates for the profession and for public schools. In this process, K–12 teachers grapple with translating practice and experience into theories and models, and they expand and deepen their own professional practice and knowledge base in order to appropriately guide and inform candidates. For university educators, the PDS redefines the role of the professor from one who researches school improvement from a distance, or guides student teachers and graduate students in their practice, to one who engages directly in school improvement. It overhauls the skill set and knowledge base needed at the professoriate level, and requires considerable strategic thinking since this kind of work is typically not recognized in the promotion and tenure process at the university. In addition to reconstructing university and school roles, institutional structures, practices, and resources must be re-aligned to facilitate these collaborations (Glass & Wong, 2003).

The Equity Network members viewed the PDS model as a strategic means for embracing responsibility for both pupil learning and teacher preparation within the K–16 system (K–12 public schools and undergraduate and teacher preparation programs). We also saw it as a reasonable vehicle for producing strong structures to support engaged pedagogy in specific schools serving LI/RCLD communities in our region. While our account will reveal that we were not always successful in meeting all the standards of high-quality PDS work and engaged pedagogy, we were emboldened by a vision of K–16 collaboration in which the various partners could pool their collective resources to address the twin goals of improved pupil learning and enhanced teaching, with each partner institution contributing its distinctive expertise and prioritizing efforts in these areas based on local context and dynamics.

We attempted to work from premises of shared responsibility, collaboration across domains, and critical inquiry. Our projects aimed at enhancing the educational experiences and outcomes for LI/RCLD pupils in the partner schools and at more effectively training candidates to replicate this work as teachers. And, we understood that our own professional development as educators (both K–12 teachers and professors) was central to our efforts.

The Equity Network: Structure and Operations

Because the Network crosses so many different jurisdictions and has operated for most of its existence primarily at the grassroots or school level, it has followed a more organic course of development and has not pursued a standardized agenda or required adherence to any particular program or curriculum for membership. Most of the PDS schools had been university training sites and were ready, at the time of the federal grant award, to focus and intensify that partnership. Though these organic evolutions undoubtedly made the establishment of PDSs easier, a different strategy might have produced better "reportable" outcomes. All of our PDSs have historically contended with huge test-score gaps among their various pupil subgroups. Many of them were part of the state or federal program improvement/accountability programs from the outset and continue in these programs today. However, our commitment to working in typical urban schools—where the problems seem intractable and the context is messy and complex—was shared across members of our faculty group who wanted to use the university and grant resources equitably and to focus support on the schools that were most in need and could benefit the most.

Thus, we strove to adhere to the principles of PDS work more than to conform to rigid pre-set implementation standards. We pursued the four PDS goals of improving pupil achievement, enhancing the student teacher field experience, engaging in continuous and targeted professional development, and using action research to inform our activities (Darling-Hammond, 1994; Holmes Group, 1995; NCATE, 2001). As we pursued these goals, we maintained a fifth principle: namely, to draw heavily on the expertise, experience, and knowledge of the local learning community—pupils, teachers, administrators, and community members—while purposefully integrating university actors (student teachers and instructors) into this learning community. As a result, each of our PDSs has evolved in a unique way that reflects its local context, and some of what is specifically done at one PDS may not be done at all at another. Though each PDS has distinct projects that involve student teachers, or candidates, and university instructors in activities to enhance pupil learning, all require additional and creative projects from candidates related to understanding and interpreting their urban school context, and all have action research and other kinds of professional development activities that bring K–16 educators together to deepen and improve their professional practice.

Because of the resources of the U.S. Department of Education Teacher Quality Enhancement grant, we were able to offer each PDS a small discretionary budget to facilitate projects with pupils, candidates, and teachers. Each year, the PDS team at each site developed a request for funds, with specific requests tied to activities that furthered one or more PDS goal; however, all goals had to be addressed in the set of proposed activities. In addition, after the first two years, the PDSs were also required to implement evaluations to capture the effects and/or the outcomes of the proposed activities. These site-level assessments included such measures as pre/post tests of tutoring projects by candidates, analysis of English language development from lab reports based on small group science projects conducted by candidates, and pupil impressions of poetry days and other special curriculum projects. These data complement Networkwide data, including an annual survey and writing prompt for PDS teachers, and the disaggregation of College of Education graduate exit surveys into PDS and non-PDS responses. These various data sources and others inform the accounts in this book.

In addition to school-based projects, the Network conducted numerous activities that drew from all the PDSs: a cooperating teacher (CT) course in which CTs learn effective strategies for observing candidates and collecting evidence for assessments using standards-based tools (e.g., the California Standards for the Teaching Profession, CSTPs, for practicing teachers and the Teaching Performance Expectations, TPEs, for candidates); teacher research groups; lesson study teams; and various workshops and institutes (e.g., Grant Wiggins's Understanding by Design workshop (Wiggins & McTighe, 2005), science education and English/academic language development, etc.). The Equity Network is also a member of the Holmes Partnership, makes presentations at its annual conferences, and has had participants in the Leadership Development Institutes offered by the Holmes affiliate, the Urban Network to Improve Teacher Education (UNITE). Finally, Network educators have made presentations at such conferences as the Holmes Conference, NARST, SACNAS, AERA, and ICTR.[7]

The Equity Network Governance Council, which has representation from each PDS and district, two teachers' associations, Sacramento Area Congregations Together, and the university (faculty, departments, and college) used its fall meeting to review these requests for funds and determine levels of funding. A midyear progress report and a year-end report completed the basic documentation cycle, and provided a concrete record of activities at each PDS over the year. In the spring, the Governance Council met again to review data generated by the PDS activities and to analyze key Networkwide indicators.

Each PDS has one or more assigned liaisons from the university, affectionately known as LENS faculty (LENS = Liaison for Equity Network Schools), who received release time from the College of Education to perform PDS work; altogether fifteen faculty members served as LENS faculty. It is significant to note that they came from two departments (Bilingual/Multicultural Education, and Teacher Education), which, prior to this effort, had not established any sustained, unified efforts. LENS faculty members participate in various ways at the PDSs, including teaching their teacher education program methods courses at the sites, integrating course activities with the site curriculum and projects, providing in-service professional development in their content area, facilitating the site steering committee, and so on. The LENS faculty remained relatively constant over the five years, with only two leaving (one to take an administrative position within the college and another to pursue campus-based activities). The LENS faculty meet monthly to share information and resources, provide professional and moral support, and to plan and strategize our work at the schools, in the districts and within the college. The result is a solid core of faculty members involved in an ongoing dialogue about partnerships, K–16 collaboration, school reform, urban schools, LI/RCLD pupils, and our innovative approach to teacher preparation.

More recently, faculty members from the Colleges of Education and Natural Sciences and Mathematics collaborated to offer science education professional development to Equity Network teachers.[8] We developed a summer institute with five major strands: content knowledge, effective lesson design (Marzano, Pickering, & Pollock, 2001; Wiggins & McTighe, 2005), educational equity strategies in science (Lee & Fradd, 1998), English/academic language development strategies in science (Merino & Hammond, 2002), and an introduction to the lesson study process (Lewis, 2002; Lewis, Perry, & Hurd, 2004). Ongoing professional development is also provided through academic year lesson study teams facilitated by a university faculty member. Teams use the lesson study process to develop "research" lessons that deepen teachers' content and pedagogical knowledge, develop their assessment repertoire and ability to analyze pupil work, and enhance the science learning of their pupils. Not only have we built a common body of work across the Network PDSs (currently two-thirds have lesson study teams and all but the high school site have sent teachers to the three summer institutes), but also we have integrated more content area university faculty into the life of the PDSs.

In Table 1, we note a variety of projects that will be more fully elaborated in subsequent chapters. In addition to describing them, we will analyze their impacts and relation to broader Network aims.

Table 1. Equity Network PDSs: Key Activities

School Name/Type	Key Activities
Bidwell Elementary	Curriculum mornings jointly run by candidates and teachers, incorporating contemporary innovations in different content areas
Bowling Green Elementary	Site-based science methods course culminating in a community health fair addressing key health issues for LI/RCLD pupils and their families
Florin Elementary	Lesson study teams and science education
FruitRidge Elementary	Lesson study teams
Golden State Middle School	Middle school certification program with two content blocks (science/math/technology and language arts/social studies/multicultural education) that were integrated into curriculum and service learning projects at the school
Greer Elementary	Teacher capacity-building for candidate evaluation, including new candidate evaluation protocol and service learning projects for candidates, including before-school tutoring lab
Howe Avenue Elementary	Teacher expert program with monthly guest lectures on topics identified by candidates
John Reith Elementary	Cooperating teacher mentoring course, lesson study teams and community outreach programs
Kingswood Elementary	Cycles of inquiry—discrete teacher research projects focused on pupil learning needs and on-site math methods course with a weekly one-on-one tutoring lab for methods application and improvements to pupil learning and candidates' practice
Language Academy (Elementary)	A community study conducted by teachers, candidates, parents, and pupils, leading to community-based generative themes that guided dual immersion curriculum development
New Technology High School	Team teaching and curriculum development for project-based learning
Westfield/Elkhorn Village Elementary	Teacher research groups and the implementation of findings, particularly related to English learners and their academic and social integration into the school community

Though it is tempting to represent the Equity Network as an orderly package that has systematically reached all of its lofty goals, this would not only be off the mark from a truth-value perspective, but it would minimize the important learning that has occurred due to oversights, mistakes, and missteps. Our shortcomings have been equally as important as our achievements in the difficult and deep learning that all Network members have benefited from as they have strengthened their commitment to using partnerships to improve the education and thus the life chances of LI/RCLD children in Sacramento.

Sacramento State College of Education: Transforming Institutional and Professional Cultures

The creation of the Equity Network was significant for the College of Education in many ways. With the exception of special education and bilingual certification, the college as a whole and its largest department (Teacher Education) had not previously articulated a philosophy or set of priorities to provide overall programmatic focus. It was as if the college prepared the "average" teacher for "average" pupils; however, this approach was disconnected from the actual "average" reality in our local districts as well as the research emerging about the specific knowledge, skills, and dispositions needed for urban educational settings (Murrell, 2001; UNITE, 2004; Villegas & Lucas, 2002; Weiner, 1999; Wilson & Corbett, 2001). The Equity Network explicitly focused on settings serving LI/RCLD pupils exclusively, and did so in tight partnership with the urban schools and districts where these pupils were concentrated. In addition to prioritizing urban communities, the Network represented the first formal college structure that brought school/district personnel and university faculty members together for substantive deliberations around school and university programs and policies. Further, the Network crossed college and university borders, bringing faculty with long-established track records working in LI/RCLD settings together with those exploring nascent interests, and forging professional bonds across departments and colleges whose prior experience with successful collaborations was limited. In many ways, the borders separating arts and sciences colleges and departments from education departments were as difficult to cooperate across as those separating the university from the schools and communities.

Equity Network faculty members came primarily from the Teacher Education and Bilingual/Multicultural Education departments and entered the initial conversations about teacher preparation innovation from different vantage points. Several, having just finished doctoral programs in which inventive school-university partnerships already existed, were attracted by the chance to recreate these ventures. Others were anxious to implement changes to a teacher preparation process that they viewed as fundamentally flawed. Still others had done advocacy work in LI/RCLD communities and saw the Network as a way to further this work from their position as a university faculty person. Each faculty member came to the Network with a different set of orientations and commitments. For some, the political and equity dimension of PDS work in LI/RCLD communities was paramount. For others, the primary draw was increased and improved collaboration and the opportunity to enhance K–12 instruction and student teaching experiences. For several who were committed to these general factors, the most compelling attraction was the sense of community offered by the cross-departmental grouping. These varying purposes were problematic at the outset, but less so as time went on.

One can also see in the variety of motivations and aims some reflections of race, gender, and status positions. Five of the fifteen LENS faculty were men; one was Latino and the rest white. Three of the ten women were women of color, a Latina, a Chinese-American, and a Filipina. Initially, most LENS faculty members' expertise was in social-cultural foundations and multicultural education, though gradually content experts joined in, with more science methods than language/literacy methods instructors. For the first three years, only three of the fifteen faculty members had earned tenure and promotion to the rank of associate professor; all have now earned tenure. Our own positions within the education system and within the racial and gender order of the dominant society impacted the ways in which we understood, interpreted, and acted on the issues central to the Equity Network's purpose as well as our capacity to connect with the various actors at the school site—pupils, teachers, administrators, and family/community members. The educational challenges in LI/RCLD communities are so persistent that one must be equally persistent in using a critical perspective to disentangle causes from effects, structures from anomalies, and broad trends from individual exceptions. Our collaborative work required all of us to interrogate carefully the myth of an educational meritocracy and come to understand how we achieved success in a system that sets many up for failure. For the white, monolingual faculty members, confronting the privileges accorded to middle-class, European culture in the norms and structures of schooling as well as in the transmitted knowledge base eventually deepened a critical consciousness that allowed for significant connections at the PDSs. For faculty of color, it was necessary to analyze the events and circumstances, often related to social class, that fueled our success, while so many of the friends we began school with experienced failure. Moreover, connecting to the richness of our own heritage required us to learn more about the role of advocate in these LI/RCLD communities. Each of us had to engage in honest and critical reflection that involved uncovering knowledge, rejecting knowledge once thought to be valid, and constructing new knowledge; through this, we found our commitment to educational equity and democracy strengthened.

Disentangling issues of race, culture, language, and social class within an academic setting can be disquieting and unsettling (Jacobs, Cintrón, & Canton, 2002). But even as we tackled the complex issues of our own positionality, we had to interrogate some mainstream intellectual constructs. We discovered that our own formal education had closed off certain questions. For example, does the agricultural knowledge exhibited by immigrant communities with a history of farm labor "count" as "science"? Are the "fundamental" questions of mandated science curricula—how does wind work, what is matter—really "fundamental"? Are other questions like "how can science help us think about and address high rates of diabetes and heart disease in our community" equally, or even more, "fundamental"? Is math made more useful by designing problems related to balancing presumed future checkbooks, or by understanding what educational, social, economic, and political fairness and equality might look like in our community? If we read formal poetry *and* hip-hop lyrics, if we read classics of the canon *and* contemporary literature produced in LI/RCLD communities, wouldn't pupils and teachers develop a more enriched understanding of language and its power as well as a new appreciation for the complexity of the human condition? As academics, we consistently grappled with such questions precisely because they were raised while developing meaningful, grounded PDS projects. Even though our state content standards privilege the scientific concepts of states of matter and properties of wind, our PDS pupils were much more likely to be engaged by inquiry into pollutants spread by wind throughout their communities and what they could do to keep their and their parents' respiratory systems functioning well.

Questions of for what and in favor of whom knowledge is taught (Freire, 1970) overlaid issues of the power and privilege accorded to members of our LENS group due to race, gender, and language. Without a commitment to equity issues, none of us would have sought out the Equity Network in the first place, but our own experiences with and understandings of these complex issues in our own lives as well as in the realities of LI/RCLD communities were quite varied. Confronting such truths about privilege, power, oppression, and injustice can evoke shame, outrage, and denial, and sometimes induce a disempowering despair. Unless white academics, in particular, are willing to face honestly the systemic discrimination that privileged their own schooling histories, thereby troubling the myth of meritocracy that has no doubt shaped their own sense of achievement and self-worth, they may fall prey to the prevailing ideologically tinged claims about LI/RCLD children's "underachievement" stemming from a range of individual, family, and cultural deficits. For white men and women, the daily realities of racism and discrimination faced by people of color may move them to resistance and action, but it is more likely that they will simply experience these violent acts as titillating stories that produce momentary feelings of outrage and wonder. When committed whites begin to grasp the truth that racism constitutes a continual assault on people of color that erodes their identity and self-worth, they begin to understand that their own sense of worth is also at stake. Developing a commitment to an embodied engagement in the struggle against discrimination and oppression within the educational system requires ongoing and difficult work on the part of all faculty members, but in particularly disturbing ways for white faculty members given the dominant ideologies that permeate the schools serving LI/RCLD communities.

For faculty of color, the issues are somewhat different. Like our white colleagues, we must question the system that helped us achieve academic success, and try to understand the complex interplay of ideological frameworks that make race and ethnicity both a help and a hindrance. Often times, our class privilege provided the opening we needed to take advantage of educational opportunities, and we must also come to terms with how our class privilege as academics interferes with our relations with the LI/RCLD school communities, despite our racial, ethnic, and linguistic solidarity with them. As we fully (re)connect our own experiences with the struggles, successes, and systems that shaped us all, then we can more accurately and adequately represent the issues confronted in our PDSs. We must find ways to succeed in a context that often negates our knowledge and experiences, while not falling victim to ideological biases and assumptions that can seem to be conditions of our professional advancement.

These struggles are all the more significant as one realizes that they are ongoing, thrust to the fore repeatedly by unanticipated conversations, events, and actions that are inevitable in PDS work with LI/RCLD communities. As we grappled with these issues of positionality, we aligned our PDS efforts with our rooted experiences growing up in the working class, working with communities of color as activists and advocates, witnessing racial discrimination in the South and in Appalachia, and remembering our ancestors' stories woven by Spanish, Chinese, and Tagalog mixed with English. We learned to listen more carefully to the experiences and voices of the PDS teachers and pupils, connecting them to a new reading of the research literature. We came to depend on the honestly and thoughtfully shared rich backgrounds and knowledge of our faculty group. These practices helped to bring each of us closer to a form of engaged pedagogy that melded our own heightened consciousness and clarified commitments to the deep potential in our PDSs. Ultimately, our ongoing critical analysis and determination to connect with the PDSs' communities produced a clear and grounded vision that we needed to create meaningful learning experiences amidst the pressure for standardization and accountability.

Our confrontation with the race and class limits of the education system had multiple fronts. Whether or not we had long-standing connections to local schools or were just beginning to forge such bonds, the Network faculty's commitment to collaborate fully with the schools paved a path directly from the university into the heart of Sacramento's LI/RCLD neighborhoods. LENS faculty members typically spent a minimum of one entire day per week at their sites. Their presence quickly enmeshed them in casual, everyday connections with teachers, pupils, and families. They also gained firsthand knowledge of school programs, resources, and processes that provided a counterpoint and contrast to their prior school experiences in more affluent and less diverse settings. LENS faculty members had to examine critically their own experiences and positionality in order to work effectively and develop meaningful projects in PDS relationships centered in communities struggling against poverty, racism, sexism, and linguicism.

Windows opened into the lives of pupils in the PDSs by virtue of one LENS faculty member's roots in Appalachia, another's working-class childhood, and another's experience of living abroad and fumbling with a second language. These insights emerged through the supportive relationships of the LENS group and enabled new roles and skills to solidify. We became advocates, intermediaries, and shields in order to address the needs and interests of the LI/RCLD pupils and their teachers, both in the collaborative PDS work and in other arenas such as policymaking and program development. We used our positions of power—whether related to university status, race, gender, or language—to positively affect teaching and learning in LI/RCLD communities. A strength of our learning community was its ability to support deeper engagement in arenas where we felt most comfortable and competent, while also pushing us to revisit assumptions, stretch our understandings, and shape new strategies to resist forms of oppression and domination in schools. That the LENS faculty members consistently modeled the principles of engaged pedagogy is a testament to their embrace of the difficult work of developing a reflexive, critical consciousness.

Though Network faculty members generally worked in the PDSs and the LI/RCLD communities from a position of power and privilege, the reverse was true in the university setting. Only two of the LENS faculty members had tenure when the Equity Network was formed. During the initial years when they were annually reviewed in the formal university processes, department and college committees questioned both their role and its importance. Senior faculty members voiced concern about the overt commitment to "failing" LI/RCLD schools, and questioned whether they were appropriate places to invest faculty time or to prepare candidates. Some expressed skepticism about spending so much time in one school and suggested it compared unfavorably with results obtained with traditional forms of professional service at multiple sites.

The LENS faculty members began to educate the college leadership and department colleagues about the nature of PDS work. As PDS projects solidified, clearer positive outcomes resulted that could be more readily "counted," not only by university committees but also by school and district colleagues who were facing similar questions. All LENS faculty members eventually earned tenure and promotion. Moreover, it became accepted in the college—sometimes wholeheartedly, sometimes begrudgingly—that it was important for the college to prioritize LI/RCLD schools, concern itself with the teaching and learning experiences of LI/RCLD pupils, and create structures to involve LI/RCLD communities and educators in decision-making processes about our programs. These accomplishments are as much a tribute to the successes at our PDS sites as to our skill and courage in reshaping university structures and standards.

Organization of the Book

This book chronicles our efforts and our learning as we established the Equity Network. The first section, "Toward Improving Urban Children's Lives," examines the scope and potential of PDS projects meant to impact the concrete conditions of children's lives, with full and humble appreciation for the severe limitations of school-based work that seeks to affect broader social and economic conditions. We feature several exceptional projects that connect classroom and school reform with the social and economic struggles waged by LI/RCLD families and communities. Each chapter details how pupils gained a critical understanding of the conditions of their lives and the social, cultural, and historical forces that shape their communities and schools. Each project integrated community funds of knowledge with the mandated core curriculum, not merely as an exercise in learning, but as integral to efforts to make a concrete difference in pupils' realities—whether in their classrooms, at school, or in their communities. Though this work is perpetually incomplete—poverty, oppression, and lack of opportunity seemingly have no limits—these projects nonetheless demonstrate that educators (pre-/in-service teachers, administrators, and university faculty), pupils, and families together can be a substantial force for educational equity and change. Chapter one, "Floating Boats and Solar Ovens," and chapter two, "Science for Social Responsibility," describe extraordinary PDS collaborations that resulted in transformed science curriculum for pupils and for candidates. In both cases, the science curriculum was reoriented toward community issues and developed in accord with more rigorous standards; it was also more deeply integrated than previously, particularly with regard to pupil-led inquiry. Moreover, both collaborations drew heavily on community funds of knowledge in the conceptualization and implementation of the science activities. Chapter three, "Education of the Community, by the Community and for the Community," focuses on the establishment of the Language Academy of Sacramento, a Spanish/English dual language immersion independent charter school serving a predominantly immigrant and low-income population, and the community-based, problem-posing curriculum development process used at this school.

Section two, "The Power of Connections: Recreating Teacher and Teacher Educator Roles," examines how new structures for decision-making and knowledge transfer resulted in "better knowledge," broader realms of influence, and more empowered stakeholders. The research on teacher preparation exhorts universities to make teacher education a central mission of the institution and not only of colleges/schools of education, thereby requiring faculty across disciplines to collaborate and to focus on preparing future generations of teachers (Goodlad, Soder, & Sirotnik, 1990; Holmes Group, 1995; Sarason, 1993). These proposals also envision faculty members and universities as important players in K–12 school reform and teachers and administrators as key actors in teacher preparation programs. New knowledge and skills are necessitated by these changes, and although history shows us that those responsible for implementing change must be a part of constructing it (Elmore & McLaughlin, 1988; Fullan, 2001; Tyack & Cuban, 1995), the road map for developing new roles and changing institutional structures has not been well drawn. In fact, much of the creative work of transforming institutions necessarily must be done with no maps at all—here the road is only made by walking it (Horton & Freire, 1990). Section two provides vivid examples of teachers and university faculty members who stretched beyond traditional boundaries to work together toward meaningful reforms in the Network PDSs. We found that leadership for reform is not about being in front or on top, but that it emerges from disciplined inquiry and experimentation that connects across roles and boundaries. Each chapter illuminates key questions: How do people come to know better (more deeply, critically) what they already know in order to function in the PDS? What kinds of new knowledge, skills, and dispositions are needed? How do PDS participants experience working across domains?

PDS teachers and administrators respond to the questions in chapter four: "Connecting Teacher Educators Across Roles, Domains, and Knowledge Bases." "Beyond the Classroom: Candidates Connect to Colleagues, Children, and Communities" (chapter five) focuses on how PDS candidates moved beyond initial conceptions of teaching as occurring just in one's own classroom, to more sophisticated conceptions based on forging connections with other classrooms, teachers, instructional support staff, and most important, their pupils' families and communities. "Structural Shifts and Cultural Transformations: University Faculty Members and Their Work in PDSs" (chapter six) views these broader connections from the faculty members' perspective. The PDS work resulted in new roles being formally recognized within the College of Education structure. The struggles required to make connections across the seemingly rigid boundaries of department, college, university, district, school, classroom, and community produced new forms of collaboration and leadership. These portend major changes for teacher education at our institution and in our region.

Section three, "The Politics of Transforming Institutions and Institutional Relationships," considers the complex and politically charged nature of institutional reform, particularly when it shapes clear alternatives to institutional relationships that are segmented, territorial, and exclusive. We examine the multiple layers of institutional transformation that can potentially occur with PDS work as well as the palpable power dynamics and political struggles involved. The chapters in section three detail challenges and setbacks we have encountered as our PDS work has caused critique and destabilization of traditional structures. In some cases, we have had to learn from mistakes and situations that posed more challenges than we could overcome. In other cases, we have created new structures for decision-making and program development that emerged from teacher authority and knowledge grounded in action research and collaborative inquiry.

"Perspectives on Negotiation and Equilibrium in the Politics of Knowledge" (chapter seven) blends the views of teachers and faculty members as they reflect on the start-up phase of three PDSs. In this polyvocal account, we clarify how one's role in making institutional change shapes one's perspective. "Not Starting from Scratch: Applying the Lessons from a Thwarted PDS Effort" (chapter eight) charts the evolution of our efforts to establish a high school PDS. This chapter provides rich examples and ideas, but also offers cautionary lessons about how meaningful reforms can become insulated and consequently misunderstood, and about the importance of constantly expanding the base of support for reforms. "Bridging the Disconnect: the Promise of Lesson Study" (chapter nine) examines a Networkwide lesson study initiative that involved faculty members from the Colleges of Education and of Natural Science and Mathematics and teacher teams at ten PDSs. We explore the multiple layers of meaning and action in lesson study, a project that is simple and elegant in its emphasis on collaboration around the design and teaching of a research lesson, but that is also complex and subversive in its potential to transcend traditional norms of isolation in teaching and more current tendencies, particularly in urban settings, that deprofessionalize teaching.

Our final chapter, "Making History by Creating New Traditions," highlights our most significant insights from our attempts to improve the lives of urban children, our efforts to connect and reconnect various actors and power brokers in K–16 education such that new knowledge, skills, and dispositions emerge that better serve LI/RCLD pupils and their teachers, and our negotiations with the politics of institutional transformation. We celebrate instances of success—improved learning for LI/RCLD pupils, enriched professional learning for urban teachers, and concrete gains for university programs—while also extracting important lessons from instances of unmet potential, where programs imploded, partners talked among themselves but effected little structural change, or key actors became diverted from the PDS work. We articulate promising future directions, and conclude by offering ideas for a new professionalism that builds on Equity Network successes and identifies the strategic actions required to overcome the Network's limits. We also suggest ways to create stronger networking and inclusionary measures within LI/RCLD communities so that democratization of education and the policymaking process is more fully realized, strengthening both LI/RCLD pupils' education and their communities.

Description of the Writing Process/Project

This book expresses the voices of many Equity Network educators and represents their varied experiences and diverse perspectives. We highlight many different dimensions of urban PDS work. This multiplicity has enriched the writing process rather than bogged it down. Our participatory writing effort has proven an appropriate capstone and helped to consolidate the Equity Network PDS work. Audience reaction at several of our national conference presentations and our own review of the literature helped us realize that our stories made a contribution. At a writing retreat in February 2005, we developed an outline of "snapshots" (brief cases about particular aspects of the work) and "movies" (full chapters that probed deeply into complex PDS issues), and we allocated writing duties. The themes for each section represented the primary pillars of our work—improving the education and life chances of LI/RCLD pupils, strengthening connections across stakeholder groups and institutional units, and rethinking educational institutions and the reform process itself.

While the writing has primarily been done by the university LENS faculty members, several chapters represent intensive collaboratives with full-time teachers who have made room in their lives to write, edit, rewrite, and write some more. PDS teachers and administrators and non-PDS university instructors read drafts and provided commentary at critical feedback sessions. Finally, two of us took responsibility for editing the manuscript to develop a more consistent narrative flow and a more integrated analytical framework. We are confident that the book captures much of the depth and range of our experiences and our learning, and we are hopeful that it contributes to efforts beyond our own to make schools serving LI/RCLD pupils and communities reach their full promise.

Notes

1. With support from a grant from the Stuart Foundation, Dr. Elizabeth Kean led a team of faculty members in the College of Education in developing pilot projects with local schools and districts around innovative practices in teacher education.
2. Considerable impetus and support for the Equity Network came from a federal Teacher Quality Enhancement grant (P336B000002) awarded to the College of Education in fall 2000. Additional support from a California Post-Secondary Education Commission grant (ITQ-01-064) has funded science education projects for the Equity Network.
3. The PICO National Network works from faith-based organizations to focus on community and family development. It uses grassroots community organizing strategies to pursue goals of "safe neighborhoods, quality health care, housing opportunities, and good schools." More information can be found at www.piconetwork.org.
4. Kleinheinz, 2007.
5. Several studies, especially those completed by the Harvard Civil Rights Project, identify factors that compound the challenges for Equity Network-type schools as they attempt to meet the mandates of NCLB. Among these factors are the methodologies used to calculate AYP. Most districts compare the scores for particular grade levels across years rather than scores of student cohorts as they progress through the system. The former methodology does not take into consideration changes in curriculum, teaching staff, and other school factors. In addition, high rates of student mobility, typical for such schools, are not taken into account when AYP is calculated. Finally, the California Department of Education has set one of the highest standards for AYP, though the state admittedly has one of the most challenging public school populations to educate because of high proportions of English learners and high rates of students living in poverty.
6. Of note are comprehensive partnerships in Columbus, Ohio, where the school district, city government, teachers' association, and the Ohio State University sustain a sophisticated collaboration that includes an educational foundation supported in part by the city's sports arena, graduate education courses offered at OSU by union professional development experts, and other agreements. The relatively new Milwaukee Partnership Academy also is an example of municipal leadership, private industry, local colleges and universities, school districts, and teachers' associations partnering to improve student learning and enhance teacher preparation and development.
7. Presentations at the Annual Meetings of the American Educational Research Association (AERA) have described PDS work with candidates, curriculum projects at the PDSs, and our assessment efforts. Presentations at the National Association

for Research on Science Teaching (NARST) featured a science/technology project at a Network middle school PDS. Network teacher research was presented at the International Conference on Teacher Research (ICTR) and the work of bilingual teachers in the Network was described at the meeting of the Society for Chicanos and Native Americans in Science (SACNAS).

    8. The Sacramento Science Projects for Educational Equity is supported by a grant from the California Post-Secondary Education Commission and provides resources for a summer institute and facilitation and material support for academic year lesson study teams. These professional development opportunities target Equity Network PDSs exclusively.

Section One

Toward Improving Urban Children's Lives

Ronald David Glass and Pia Lindquist Wong

Features of the Urban Landscape for America's Children

Thus far, we painted a picture of urban schooling that was lamentably bleak despite significant numbers of caring teachers doing their best to make a difference. Regrettably, many structural features of life outside of school also provide little cause for optimism for many urban children. If these children did not have a great variety of familial and, often, religious countervailing forces bolstering them, an even greater number would never beat the odds against them. Educating LI/RCLD pupils, especially those in underresourced urban settings, poses persistent challenges only superficially indicated by test-score gaps between these pupils and those from the majority culture in middle- to high-income settings. Across the nation, educators and policymakers have focused effort and resources on improving educational opportunities so that test-score gaps across pupil demographic groups would be narrowed. The system's report card is mixed.

Urban districts have historically served a large number of pupils, and they have operated under unwieldy bureaucratic structures that respond slowly to issues and problems. Standardization through elaborate rules and procedures offers a semblance of efficiency and control, but the bureaucracies are almost always impersonal, inflexible, and cut off from the communities they serve. Pupils, teachers, and community members usually feel anonymous within these systems and unable to make their concerns heard (Weiner, 1999). Moreover, the quest to impose uniform operations and instruction in these large urban systems runs directly counter to the diversity of the pupils.

Urban districts typically serve a much higher proportion of LI/RCLD pupils than suburban districts do. And, within the last 30 years, the capacity of urban schools and districts to respond effectively to their situations has been increasingly diminished because of inadequate funding, particularly on the general fund rather than the categorical funding side of the ledger (Timar, 1994; 2004). Typical urban schools must cope with crumbling infrastructure, insufficient curricular materials and basic supplies, minimal academic programming, and severely limited enrichment opportunities (e.g., *Williams v. California*).

Urban districts also occupy a distinct position in local economies as an important entry-level employer for local residents seeking jobs as cooks, clerks, janitors, and campus security personnel. As a major employer of neighborhood residents with limited formal education, urban districts confront additional constraints and complexity in their decision-making processes. Community employment and development needs in urban districts can often distract from a focus on pupil's academic and social needs, unlike the situation in suburban districts (Carnoy, Hannaway, Chun, Stein, & Wong, 1995).

Urban school districts serve 23% of all U.S. public school pupils and 40% of the nation's pupils of color (Fredericks & Dickson, 2003). The Council of Great City Schools reports that urban districts were "majority-minority districts" in which, on average, over three-quarters of pupils were pupils of color, compared with nonurban districts where pupils of color number less than a third of the student body (Casserly, 2006). Such racial and cultural diversity is accompanied by linguistic diversity; in urban schools, twice as many pupils (17%) are English learners as in their nonurban counterpart schools. Further, urban pupils are predominantly low-income with 63% qualifying for federal lunch subsidies, compared with just under 40% nationwide. This parallels the prevalence of family/household poverty; 83% of urban school systems have poverty rates above their state averages.

Numerous studies have demonstrated high correlations between family income and pupil achievement (Desimone, 1999; Lee & Burkam, 2002). In fact, it is widely recognized among the public and not just among scholars that poverty and cultural background affect (but need not determine) children's success in school. Because it generally requires focused additional resources (human and material) to mitigate the effects of poverty, it is noteworthy that the nation's urban districts, with their high concentrations of LI/RCLD pupils, are consistently underresourced. Nearly a third of urban districts nationwide spend less per pupil than their statewide averages. Since 1995, per pupil expenditures in urban districts have grown at a slower rate than nonurban expenditures (Casserly, 2006).

Disparities in per pupil expenditures also translate into other inequities that impact both opportunities to learn and schooling outcomes. Average school size in urban districts is almost 50% higher than in suburban districts, and these school settings are more likely to be inadequate: schools in which pupils of color comprise 50% or more of the student body are more than twice as likely to be overcrowded as schools in which pupils of color are less than 20%.

Along with problems of overcrowding, pupil–teacher ratios are higher in urban settings. Where LI/RCLD pupils predominate (75% of enrollment), 31% of teachers have 25 or more pupils in their classes. Where white pupils predominate (less than 10% LI/RCLD pupils), only 22% of teachers contend with class sizes above 25 pupils (Children's Defense Fund, 2004a). Moreover, various studies have shown that predominantly LI/RCLD schools are more likely to employ beginning teachers and teachers with lesser or inadequate educational credentials (degrees, certifications, or other specialized training relevant to their teaching assignment). The disparities in the background of teachers at high- versus low-poverty secondary schools can be quite significant (Ingersoll, 1999): for example, 27% of mathematics and 51% of physical science teachers at low-poverty schools nationally lack a major or minor in their teaching field, while those numbers rise to 43% and 65% in high-poverty schools. In some states, both urban and rural pupils in high-poverty schools are four times more likely to have teachers without a major in their teaching field than pupils at wealthier schools.

Compounding this teacher quality disparity, and in part related to it, LI/RCLD pupils have unequal access to high-quality curriculum. Because tracking persists, there is still a substantial gap in the course-taking patterns between whites and Asians compared to African Americans and Latinos. For example, whites and Asians outstrip by as much as 20% the proportions of their African American and Latino peers taking advanced placement and college preparatory classes and taking and passing advanced placement exams (Children's Defense Fund, 2004a).

The educational consequences of these unequal opportunities to learn are predictable. Only one-third of urban school districts nationally indicated that test scores in all grades improved from 2002 to 2003. Only one in nine urban districts had half of their pupils per grade exceed their state's average test scores. Among the nation's 4th graders, 41% of whites are reading at grade level compared to 15% of Latinos and 13% of blacks (Children's Defense Fund, 2004b). Similar and worse disparities exist when scores for mathematics are examined. Social class was also linked with low test scores: only 15% of 4th graders eligible for federally subsidized lunch demonstrated grade-level writing competence whereas 42% of the other pupils achieved that target.

Test scores increasingly impact promotion and retention practices. Pupils of color are retained at a much higher rate than white pupils: 9% of white pupils get retained compared to 18% of African American and 13% of Latino pupils. These practices have continuing negative consequences later in pupils' educational careers: African Americans and Latino/as aged 16–19 are almost twice as likely as white teens of those ages to not be attending school. According to the National Center for Education Statistics, 86% of the pupils in low-poverty schools who graduate in the top quarter of their high school class go on to four-year colleges, contrasted with 58% of the top graduates at high-poverty schools. Similarly, 48% of young adults from high-income families graduate college by age 24, compared to only 7% of young adults from low-income families (Carey, 2004). This situation is likely to worsen as college fees and tuition increases outpace financial aid programs (with loans rather than grants comprising the highest proportion of aid awarded), making college attendance even more dependent on family wealth rather than on individual achievement or effort (College Board, 2005).

California's Urban Children

Californians have yet to reverse a decades-old trend of inadequate support for the growth and development of our most precious but also most vulnerable population group, our state's children. In California, 27% of the population in 2000 was under 18 years old, higher than the national average of 25.7%. Though indicators are positive at the start of life regarding infant mortality and birth weights, state performance falls off significantly after the child is born, as evidenced by California's high rate of children in poverty. Ironically, the state's residents have median incomes $7,000 higher than the national median and average home values $100,000 higher than the national average, but they are particularly miserly when it comes to providing for public education (U.S. Census Bureau, 2006).

In early, preschool years, more than 60% of the state's children attend center-based child care programs (generally considered to provide higher quality care and preparation for school), though participation rates differ by racial group, with white children more likely to be enrolled (Bridges, Fuller, Rumberger, & Tran, 2004). Access to these programs is limited both by overall enrollment capacity and also by costs. The Children's Defense Fund calculated that a family with two parents earning minimum wage would have to pay 55% of their income to have one child participate in a center-based child care program (Foster, 2005). Equally disturbing is the reality that 15% of the state's children do not have health insurance and more than a quarter of toddlers have not received needed immunizations (Foster, 2005). California children are also increasingly subjected to mental and emotional strains caused by violence and inadequate housing in their neighborhoods. In 2002, over 400 California children under the age of 19 died from firearm-related injuries, and 83% of these deaths were determined to be homicides (Children's Defense Fund, 2002). The Youth Violence Scorecard gave urban areas in California a grade of "F" due to high levels of children under age 17 hospitalized with injuries caused by physical assault (Gettelman, 2002). Runaway housing prices and rents result in high proportions of low-income families that must allocate over 50% of their income to meet housing costs, significantly more than the 30% maximum recommended by financial analysts. Moreover, in many parts of the state, low-income housing is scarce, with almost three low-income families vying for every unit of low-income housing available. In addition, in most urban areas, those receiving state and federal assistance cannot afford the average rental rates and, in some cases, the public subsidy falls short by as much as $300 per month. The lack of affordable housing leaves many low-income families with poor choices—to live in overcrowded or substandard housing, the fate of well over 10% of California's urban families (Riches, 2004).

The financial picture for the California K–12 public school system is notoriously austere: the state ranked 47th in the country in 2004 in K–12 per pupil expenditures (Foster, 2005). This inadequate funding was the subject of the 2001 *Williams v. California* class action lawsuit initiated by pupils and families across the state who charged that the state failed to provide them with equal access to instructional materials, safe and decent school facilities, and qualified teachers. This case was settled in 2005 and resulting legislation has required increased scrutiny and resources to address the plaintiffs' charges, but persistent and deep structural inequities make adequate funding a perennial issue. Sadly, substandard working conditions resulting from 30 years of disinvestment in public education (McCombs & Carroll, 2005) and a hyperpoliticized policy environment often make pupils and their teachers among the least "special" of the interests considered in public spending priorities.

K–12 School Reform and Teacher Preparation

For too long, these challenges facing K–12 teaching and learning have been treated in isolation from those facing the university system. Widespread school reform initiatives often had little university support or intervention. Teacher preparation program improvements at the university level usually only superficially consult practitioners. In our case, the College of Education (CoE) historically focused on teacher preparation with only minimal attention to the specific issues related to working with LI/RCLD pupils. Since this same bias is embedded in the state's mandated teacher certification requirements, colleges of education statewide have similarly skewed course frameworks.

Statistics for California's K–12 system as a whole are telling and mirror those cited earlier for the nation as a whole and urban districts in particular.

California denotes school progress in terms of the Academic Performance Index (API), which primarily uses test scores and school demographics to calculate how a school's scores improve (or not) from one year to the next as well as how well a particular school's growth (or lack thereof) compares to other schools with similar demographics. A score of 10 is the highest that a school can receive on either dimension of the API. During the 2000 through 2003 academic years, schools in which 90% or more of the pupils qualified for federally subsidized lunches scored at or below a 2 out of 10 on the API, whereas their affluent counterparts, with less than 10% of the pupils qualifying, had API scores at or above an 8. Not surprisingly, English proficiency levels are an additional correlate of success on the state's standardized tests. Schools with less than 10% English learners (ELs) scored between 6 and 8 on the API during the 2002–2003 period; in schools in which 50% of the pupils were classified as ELs, the API dropped to just above 2, and if the percentage of ELs rose above 80%, then the API dipped below 2.[1] California is already a "majority minority" state: 46% of pupils are Hispanic/ Latino, 32.5% are white, 8.1% are African American, 8.0% are Asian, 3.1% are Filipino/Pacific Islander, 0.8% is Native American, and 1.4% are mixed ethnicity or provided no response. Twenty-five percent, or one in four, of California pupils are ELs (Education Data Partnership, 2007), presenting a remarkable challenge for teachers. Moreover, teachers are likely to have more than one native language represented in their classrooms. Typical teachers have pupils who look nothing like them and share few of their dearly held traditions because of the variety of home cultures and heritages from which the pupils come.

Moreover, the distribution of qualified personnel in the state's public education system reproduces the very inequalities that, at least rhetorically, were eliminated through relative equalization of funding (*Serrano v. Priest*), high standards for all, data-driven instruction, and adequate yearly progress mandates. A correlation study to determine the relationship between teacher quality and numerical outcomes on the state's API found that in 2002–2003, pupils in schools with low API scores were 4.1 times less likely to be taught by a qualified teacher (one with a credential in the elementary grades, one teaching in his or her subject area at the secondary level) than pupils in schools with high API scores.[2] English learners were 2.3 times less likely to be taught by a qualified teacher and low-income pupils were 2.2 times less likely to receive instruction from a qualified teacher.

The persistent test-score gaps associated with social class, language proficiency, and ethnicity also raise serious issues for higher education. California's Education Master Plan was designed to provide opportunities for low-cost, high-quality higher education, which, at the time of its adoption, was unparalleled in other states. Yet, the kinds of test-score gaps produced in elementary and secondary education have serious effects at the next higher level. For example, in 1999, of the first-year students in the California State University system 48% needed remedial coursework in mathematics and 46% needed it in English/language arts (California State University, 2000), with students of color demonstrating a greater need than their white peers. Five years later, after the K–12 curriculum was narrowed to focus on literacy and numeracy standards, 38% of first-year students systemwide still needed remedial math coursework, and 48% still needed it in English. Though there are debates about remediation programs, these statistics nevertheless point out that K–12 teaching and learning challenges have a tangible impact at the university level.

Finally, these data (and firsthand experience) highlight only some of the profound difficulties facing teacher preparation programs and their graduates. Attrition rates for first-time teachers in California have been estimated at between 30% and 50%, with the higher rates occurring in so-called hard-to-staff schools—namely, those in rural areas or those with a high proportion of LI/RCLD pupils. Clearly, our higher education institutions must energetically address the underlying conditions that cry out for better preparation of teachers who are committed to teaching in schools with high proportions of LI/RCLD pupils and who have the necessary skills, knowledge, and pre-service experiences to be effective.

Teacher Preparation for the Urban Context

Teacher education programs nationwide must attend to the dual tasks of recruiting increasing numbers of culturally and linguistically diverse candidates from urban communities *and* preparing candidates from the dominant culture, currently overrepresented in teacher preparation programs and the teaching force, to be effective in diverse urban school settings. Neither task is easy and both require a sophisticated institutional and program response that should, but rarely does, begin before candidates make their way onto college campuses. Although most teacher preparation programs embrace these goals, success has been elusive in both domains.

The recruitment issue has many interrelated facets. Though our campus is fairly diverse, with just 44% of students identifying themselves as white, the pipeline into teaching is narrow and plagued by many of the problems detailed by Goodlad, Soder, and Sirotnik (1990) and Sarason (1993).[3] The long-standing disconnection between undergraduate and credential program faculty underscores the notable absence of dialogue within the campus faculty community about how to approach the preparation of future teachers generally. Thus, there is little agreement about whether preparation for urban environments is a priority, and about how to coherently combine strong subject matter preparation with innovative pedagogical preparation. Unfortunately, students in our undergraduate Liberal Studies major (historically, CSUS's pre-elementary teaching major and the third largest major on campus)[4] are secondary priorities for departments, which focus on majors in their own programs. Recruitment of underrepresented populations into Liberal Studies has not been successful, thus constricting the pool of LI/RCLD students eligible to enter the elementary teacher preparation programs. In addition, many of the culturally and linguistically diverse students on campus are the first in their families to attend a university. They typically opt to enter programs that provide access to higher status and higher paying professions. Moreover, because of the low status of teacher preparation within the university, only limited information about the teaching profession and few opportunities for exploratory field experiences are available; as a result, students often discount teaching as a profession without even having had the occasion to consider it seriously.

Recruitment of candidates to our teacher preparation programs has not historically been necessary, but recent decreases in applicant numbers caused by new entrance tests, increases in fees, and misinformation about a teaching glut now entail recruiting strategies. Recruitment of candidates of color has always received some attention, but, until 2005 when a full-time equity coordinator was hired, the CoE merely released one faculty member from one course to recruit underrepresented students. Not surprisingly, our candidates remain mostly white and female, constituting about 85% of our students and mirroring the national averages. Though a high percentage of our candidates are the first in their families to complete a university degree, evidence from candidate essays collected over several years in the multicultural education course suggests that for most white candidates, these working-class/first-generation roots do not play a strong role in their own identity construction. Rather, they tend to see their pursuit of higher education as part of an inevitable pattern of social ascension, moving up the social class ladder as if it were an escalator that naturally transported people to the next level. We know many of our graduates will go on to teach in urban districts where job vacancies are the highest; without careful preparation, they will begin their careers in settings and with pupils and families that are unfamiliar to them in many ways.

Though they mostly grew up in close proximity to America's "most integrated" city, our white candidates reported limited exposure to people from diverse cultural and language backgrounds and not many opportunities, either in high school or college, to develop a nuanced knowledge base about the state's diverse communities and their histories. The candidates of color in our programs usually have a good sense of their own history and enter our program with a commitment to serve their community; however, they too can exhibit limited cross-cultural knowledge and understanding, having grown up in low-income ethnic communities that are relatively isolated. In addition, all of our candidates tend initially to have narrow conceptions of their future profession. Entrance interviews reveal a definition of teaching rooted almost exclusively in a "love" of children rather than in the intellectual, organizational, political, and moral dimensions of the profession. Occasionally, we have entering candidates who express a desire to change social inequities through their work as teachers, but this is not the norm. Moreover, for many of our candidates, initial preferences for future teaching assignments tend to privilege commuting time over the quality of the working conditions and the kind of pupil and family community that will be present. This preference is echoed in a large national study that found that two-thirds of teachers work within 20 miles of where they went to high school, a trend that disadvantages urban districts (Loeb, Boyd, Lankford, & Wyckoff, 2005). Thus, our challenge is significant, but one that we take on with determination.

Connecting Professional Development Schools and Engaged Pedagogy to Make a Difference in Urban Children's Lives

Because they operate from a premise of shared responsibility and shared resources (material and intellectual), PDSs have greater potential to address the multiple challenges associated with teaching and preparing to teach in LI/RCLD settings. The PDS structure ensures that candidates participate in a program in which university faculty members are involved in field-based projects, thus better integrating theory and practice, and where site-based mentors continually refine their practice through the PDS collaboration. Schools derive advantages from the PDS because of the resources it brings to the school and more specifically to classrooms, benefiting the pupils. With our focus on developing PDSs in LI/RCLD settings, we hoped to reap all of these benefits in addition to helping to recruit LI/RCLD candidates and preparing mainstream candidates for LI/RCLD settings.

Teacher education has a long tradition of field experience. However, delivery models vary, particularly in relation to the amount of time that candidates spend in the field and the kinds of tasks assigned. Before partnering with a teacher education program, host schools and cooperating teachers (also known as mentor or master teachers) weigh the advantages of an infusion of new strategies and an opportunity to shape the next generation of teachers against the disadvantages caused by disruptions in routines and curriculum that can occur when a novice teacher takes over. Even when there is some level of articulation between a school and a teacher preparation program, the resources that both candidates and faculty members have to offer to school programs, pupil learning, and teacher professional development are used in unimaginative and unsystematic ways.

Those involved in school–university partnerships find that the primary benefits to the collaboration emerge in projects in which all stakeholders—pupils, candidates, teachers, and teacher educators—engage in enriched learning experiences that would not have been possible without the combined resources of the partnership (Knight, Wiseman, & Cooner, 2000; Williams, 1998; Wingfield, Nath, Henry, Tyson, & Hutchinson, 2000). Our experience reveals that some key structural pieces make this possible. Equity Network PDSs consolidate a sizable number of candidates at a single school, rather than scatter candidates across many sites; we typically have between eight and eighteen candidates at each PDS. Because the PDS partners had agreed to a long-term commitment, teachers and administrators at the schools could count on the presence of candidates from semester to semester, thereby enabling strategic planning about using this personnel resource to enrich academic programs for pupils.

The presence of such a large group of candidates also necessitated greater involvement by university faculty members at the school, which in turn strengthened working relationships with the teachers. Importantly, the faculty members integrated the academic program and the school community into coursework as tightly as possible. In many cases, this meant moving courses away from the university and onto the school campus, with assignments revolving around school curriculum and events.

Further, PDS in-service teacher education extends beyond matters related to training novices and facilitates CTs' critical reflections on their own classroom instructional activities and relations with pupils. Teachers in the PDS schools generally began the partnership with a desire to assist in teacher preparation, then broadened their commitments as they saw the benefits to their own professional development and to enhanced learning experiences for their pupils. The long-term collaboration enabled these teachers to help design integrated learning experiences for both candidates and K–12 pupils, focused on specific school and classroom needs. PDSs that build capacity for collaboration among teachers, university faculty members, candidates, and sometimes community members, create highly enriched academic experiences and projects that constitute important professional development for the teachers (Fager, 1993; Jett-Simpson, 1992).

These projects afforded similarly important benefits for our candidates and even seemed to increase their interest in a career in LI/RCLD schools, a welcome sign since teacher education programs nationwide have long struggled to achieve this outcome. As in other urban PDS projects, Equity Network candidates participate in intensive and well-structured experiences with LI/RCLD pupils that ensure that they develop relationships in those schools and communities, uncover and then debunk stereotypes, and discover a wealth of pupil interest, knowledge, and experience to tap into as a teacher (Cantor,

2002; Fountain, 1997; Groulx, 2001; Groulx & Thomas, 2000; Menchaca & Battle, 1997). In addition to providing substantial active instructional time with LI/RCLD pupils, our PDS academic projects model an approach to teaching and learning that embodies many principles of engaged pedagogy. They tend to center on pupil interests and/or issues in their community, use interdisciplinary approaches in learning new content, and require pupils to apply new knowledge in innovative and authentic ways. The projects that combine intensive work with pupils with opportunities to apply strategies and practices learned in methods courses energize our candidates about the teaching profession and solidify their commitment to working with LI/RCLD pupils in meaningful and liberating ways. Such projects are possible only because of the long-term commitment of personnel and material resources in order to enrich learning for LI/RCLD pupils, draw from local funds of knowledge held by pupils, their families, and their teachers, deepen professional expertise for our candidates, and build on the resources and expertise of the PDSs K–16 faculty.

What Defines Engaged Pedagogy for Urban Teachers and Pupils?

Clearly there are limits to the kinds of social transformations that can reasonably be expected to be initiated through changes in individual classrooms or even in the school system as a whole. In order to significantly improve urban children's lives, a concerted and coordinated effort across various sectors would be needed. In some countries, social movements galvanize health care providers, social workers, teachers, and parents toward a unified educational agenda, and provide an example of what seems to be a utopian vision that could inform California's urban areas and those of other states (Gandin & Apple, 2004; O'Cadiz, Wong, & Torres, 1998). In the United States, alliances on this scale are still waiting to be forged. Scholars and activists alike have identified the severe limitations of a schools-only approach to transformation in LI/RCLD communities (Anyon, 2005; Berliner, 2005; Lipman, 2004). The promise of enhanced learning experiences for pupils, while certainly desirable and beneficial, will continually be limited by poor health care, limited and unstable employment options for parents, and inadequate and unsafe neighborhood and housing conditions. To truly make urban schools adequate to the challenges they face, a comprehensive and strategic response to social, economic, and educational injustice is required. Key to this will be a coordinated and sustained effort to wrestle political power back into urban areas (Anyon, 2005; Oakes, Rogers, & Lipton, 2006; Shirley, 1997).

Such calls for movements (educational transformation as a part of social transformation) and for school-based projects allied with community development and empowerment can overwhelm interested educators and others who hope for more immediate and tangible results. Projects that ground teachers in direct knowledge of their LI/RCLD pupils and their communities are rarely selected for implementation in most urban schools. Rather, shaped by the quest for immediate increases in standardized test scores and by a reluctance to tackle difficult social issues, schools select packaged programs or workshops that provide superficial, and potentially damaging, responses to the deeply rooted political/economic challenges that face LI/RCLD communities. Such responses (e.g., see Payne, 1996) usually do not demand much of teachers or pupils and require little in the way of structural or material change in classrooms or schools. Structural causes of inequality ("generational" poverty) are portrayed as given and inevitable; teachers learn formulaic ways to think about these causes, but are not challenged to address the role that they, their schools, and educational policies play in perpetuating such inequities. As a consequence, they see only a portion of the picture, and most typically that portion of the picture that perpetuates the image of the unmotivated, uninformed, and uncaring low-income family that sends to school children who are destined for educational failure.

Though the Equity Network efforts have focused primarily on classrooms and schools, we grounded our work in engaged pedagogy principles that assume that broader social issues are necessarily a part of the teaching/learning process and that aim toward broader positive changes for the LI/RCLD pupils and families. Our conception of engaged pedagogy requires a rethinking of central pedagogical questions such as: Who owns and produces knowledge? What knowledge is worth knowing? What is the purpose of learning? And what outcomes define successful learning? In our PDS work, our community of learners—pupils, candidates, teachers, and university faculty members—revisit these questions often, each time uncovering new meanings and confronting persistent contradictions.

The question of "who owns and produces knowledge" has long been discussed by various critical educators (e.g., Apple, 2000; 2001). In asking it, we foreground the ways that schools distinguish "official knowledge" from community knowledge, kids' knowledge, personal knowledge, and other forms of knowledge not generally recognized and rewarded in formal educational settings. Subject matter standards constitute a mandatory official knowledge that pupils are required to learn. Usually, such standards have been developed with little input or review from members of LI/RCLD communities. Moreover, they are, by definition, decontextualized and often far removed from the everyday experiences of LI/RCLD pupils. Thus, at a minimum, teachers working with LI/RCLD pupils need to incorporate strategies and supplemental materials that will connect this standards-based content with pupils' everyday lives. In addition, we validate teachers, candidates, parents, and children as holders and creators of knowledge, both as a way to balance the power of various knowledge holders and as a way to incorporate what learning theorists from Dewey to Vygotsky have argued: real learning must always be scaffolded from the learner's existing knowledge and interests.

The question of "what knowledge is worth knowing" is much more complex than it appears. The Equity Network projects we describe reconstruct the school curriculum by (1) assessing community needs, (2) collecting funds of knowledge, and (3) using community environments as objects of study. These sources of "local" knowledge provide a bridge between experiences familiar to pupils and formal concepts represented by content standards. Integrating local knowledge into the curriculum explicitly values knowledge held by pupils and their families and models for pupils a process of engaging with knowledge and knowledge production that they can apply in the future as adults, citizens, and workers.

As our learning communities dialogue about "what knowledge is worth knowing" we come to focus on important goals other than those reflected in the state content standards. The projects that emerge are directly meaningful to the pupils and community and reach far beyond the standards themselves: assessing community health needs, as in one school's health fair; validating Mexican community knowledge about plants, as in Project CULTURES; preserving natural environments, as in Southport's work in establishing marshlands near the school; and valuing parents' ideas about their children's learning, as in Elkhorn's home visits project. Each of these projects focuses on needs and resources identified in and by specific school populations. An epistemological dialogue with pupils uncovers what they and their communities know while also building new knowledge, and involves pupils in an explicit process of identity construction, a key to our notion of engaged pedagogy. Understanding themselves as knowledge holders and producers regardless of their performance on standardized tests empowers them as persons worthy of respect, as valued community members and citizens.

By foregrounding issues of knowledge in Equity Network practices, a core question and value judgment emerge about the purpose of learning. The No Child Left Behind Act of 2001 substitutes a test score for the ultimate end of learning, and asserts that learning can be measured and rated by quintile, decile, and so on. We have repeatedly challenged these notions, asserting instead that the purpose of learning should relate to creating strong and grounded identities for LI/RCLD children that allow them to act knowledgeably on a vision for themselves and their communities. With engaged pedagogy, the purpose of learning is to enable a more critical understanding of what one knows and has experienced as well as who one is and can be, both individually and in relation to one's community and society at large. With that understanding, engaged pedagogy enables LI/RCLD children to pursue the learning and new knowledge needed to shape their own future and that of their community. What are the outcomes of successful engaged pedagogy? In an urban setting, where learning is often reduced to rote reception and repetition of standard curricula, pupil engagement is one important measure of success. We deployed a variety of proven strategies in this regard, including: (1) cooperative learning in cross-age groups, (2) modeling of skills by adults working closely with small groups of pupils, and especially (3) meaningful projects with "real world" applications. Equity Network projects position pupils as active learners, constructing their own and others' learning while absorbing challenging new material that is necessary for testing requirements. We worked hard to ensure that our pupils do not face a bleak either/or choice of drill and kill test prep or fun activities without an important learning focus. Another measure of success is pupil achievement in the subject areas and in language development, a constant, cross-curricular goal for urban pupils, many of whom are English learners. We documented the realization of such achievement in a number of our projects, such as in science and math learning embedded in activities connected to health and ecology. A third measure of success is community involvement in teaching/learning, also achieved in various Network projects that involve parents and other community members as experts and partners in their children's educations. Such efforts not only strengthen pupil learning but also build positive home–school connections.

Organization of Section One

The three chapters in this section profile our efforts to make a difference in the lives of urban children, using approaches that focus heavily on the classroom but also reach into the community to effect change there. In chapter one, "Floating Boats and Solar Ovens," we chronicle the science-based projects at Golden State Middle School through which candidates and EL pupils used tools from math, science, and technology to address an environmental issue affecting the community. Chapter two, "Science for Social Responsibility," recounts the experiences of the Bowling Green PDS in anchoring its science program to health issues faced by the pupils' families and to social action to address them. Chapter three, "Education of the Community, by the Community and for the Community," profiles the Language Academy of Sacramento, beginning with its politically contentious efforts to become a charter school and concluding with the implications and outcomes of a dual-language immersion curriculum focused on community development themes and created by teachers, parents, and university faculty members.

Notes

1. Futernick, 2003.
2. Futernick, 2003.
3. There will be further discussion of these issues in section three.
4. Unlike many other states, California does not offer an undergraduate education major. Until 2000, all teacher certification programs were post-baccalaureate programs. Since 2000, a small proportion of programs offer a 4.5 year program where the B.A. is earned simultaneously with teaching certification.

Chapter One

Floating Boats and Solar Ovens

Involving Candidates in Science, Mathematics, and Technology Learning Communities

Lorie Hammond, Julita G. Lambating, Michael Beus, Paul Winckel, Jane F. Camm, and Larry Ferlazzo

What I finally decided, after three or four years of reading and studying and trying to figure this thing out, was that the way to do something was to start doing it and learn from it. That's when I first understood that you don't have to look for a model, you don't get the answers from a book. You look for a process through which you can learn.

—Horton & Freire, 1990, p. 40

In Middle Ground, an urban professional development school centered in Golden State Middle School and several feeder elementary schools in West Sacramento, we developed an integrated approach to achieving the PDS goals through the creation of inquiry oriented cross-age learning communities. These learning communities constituted a "process through which you can learn." The middle school pupils learned standards-based subject matter, academic language, and social skills; the adults involved discovered ways to teach and learn together.

Over a five-year period, Middle Ground PDS candidates were involved in several learning communities per year, in various subject areas. This chapter presents snapshots of several mathematics and science learning communities that demonstrate the variety of forms possible in these projects, along with a more in-depth case study of one science and technology learning community. As will become clear, strongly enhanced learning opportunities for the middle school pupils provided equity opportunities not otherwise available.

The Setting

Golden State Middle School (GSMS) is an urban school serving all of the 7th and 8th grade pupils in West Sacramento. Its 1000 pupils range from academically advanced pupils enrolled in GATE (Gifted and Talented Education) courses to English language learners and academically struggling pupils, from upper-middle-class pupils living in a new upscale development on the city's edge to the majority who are low-income and/or transient pupils living in motels, trailers, and apartments. The student body is about 44% Caucasian, including a large number of Slavic immigrants; 35% Hispanic; 11% Southeast Asian; 4% African American; 2% Filipino or Pacific Islander; and 3% Native American. Forty percent of its pupils are English learners (ELs), and a majority are eligible for federal lunch subsidies. In many ways, the GSMS student body is a microcosm of the state.

Pupils who attend GSMS are academically tracked into programs such as GATE, AVID (a college preparatory program for above average pupils from underprivileged circumstances), "regular" classes, self-contained classes for "at-risk" pupils, special education classes, and several levels of English as a Second Language (ESL). Levels I and II ELs (beginners and early intermediates) are in self-contained classrooms, while Levels III–V (intermediate and advanced) are integrated into sheltered content area classes, such as science and social studies. Levels I and II pupils do not receive a laboratory science course in 7th or 8th grade, but receive science along with other subjects in a multiple subject ESL classroom. Although these pupils gain advantages by being in self-contained classrooms with teachers who integrate various subjects to make them meaningful to ELs, we considered their lack of laboratory science to be an equity issue. In order to remedy this and give candidates the opportunity to learn how to teach science to ELs, we focused on two classes (one 7th and one 8th grade) of Level II ELs. The collaborating teachers (co-authors Winckel and Beus) participated in planning, overseeing learning community activities, and reflecting with candidates after class. Pairs or trios of candidates worked with small groups of pupils to conduct hands-on science labs, creating a learning opportunity not otherwise available. Other mathematics and science learning communities also provided such experiences. Generally, GSMS math pupils are in large classrooms where they cannot receive individual attention and that preclude hands-on activities. Likewise, 4th grade pupils in the Westfield living laboratory garden project experienced hands-on, small group science lessons that could not have been presented in a whole class setting. The learning community activities became highlight experiences of the school year.

The Equity Network's Middle Ground PDS annually prepared fifteen to twenty candidates to work in grades 4–8.[1] Middle Ground occupies a classroom at GSMS where candidates receive all their methods classes and participate in coordinated field experiences. Candidates also student teach at GSMS one of two semesters of their teacher preparation, spending the other semester in a grade 4–6 classroom in one of several feeder schools (including Westfield, our garden site) serving the same diverse population of pupils. The staff at GSMS and associated sites welcome candidates as members of their community, and appreciate the many contributions they make to their classrooms and to general programs at the school, such as after-school tutoring, student clubs, athletics, and music programs. Hence, the learning communities occur in a context familiar to both the candidates and the pupils.

Science Education and Equity Issues

In recent years, researchers in the science education community (Barton & Osborne, 2001; Lee & Fradd, 1998; Rodriguez, 1998) have realized that "science education for all," as mandated by national standards, is in reality "science education for the privileged" (Kyle, 2001, xi). Urban LI/RCLD pupils often receive few opportunities for quality science learning. In 2001, the science education community broadly critiqued traditional science education and described new reforms for urban science education programs that would be more relevant and meaningful for LI/RCLD pupils (Barton & Osborne, 2001; Lynch, 2001). Several themes are prominent in these critiques and are evident in our situation. The first and most obvious is access. The district where Middle Ground PDS is located went from being a recognized leader in science education for ELs in the early 1990s to eliminating science in favor of a curriculum emphasizing only language arts and mathematics taught through scripted, standardized curriculum packages.[2] This generation of pupils is receiving little or no science instruction during their elementary years. In addition, GSMS eliminated once required technology classes in order to implement two periods of language arts. This is of particular concern for ELs and other LI/RCLD pupils who are less likely to have computers at home and thus experience the "digital divide" both at home and school.

The Middle Ground PDS science methods classes focused on intensive, small group, hands-on experiences. Some are intermittent, as is the case with special math events, presented once a week for three weeks, and special garden days, presented twice a semester. In the primary case we describe, however, the enrichment is a stimulating 10-week integrated science and technology unit with 7th and 8th grade ELs that also creates intensive mentoring relationships through an adult:pupil ratio of approximately 1:4.

A second critique expressed by science education researchers concerns the nature of the science provided for LI/RCLD pupils. "Project 2061," the national standards written by the American Association for the Advancement of Science, recommended access to science in a "one size fits all" manner that is not appropriate for many female and LI/RCLD pupils. Rather, an education for these children "involves rethinking foundational assumptions about the nature of the disciplines, the purposes of education, and our roles as teachers. It does not mean remaking children into our own images. It involves remaking schooling and science in their often multiple images" (Barton & Osborne, 2001, p. 13). This quotation sums up the purpose of our PDS methods courses. We engaged pre-service and in-service teachers in rethinking such foundational assumptions about science education as: Who engages in producing science knowledge? Whom does science knowledge serve? How can historically marginalized communities become engaged in and served by science?

Barton and Osborne (2001) compare three kinds of science education: traditional, progressive, and critical. Traditional science education is exemplified by standards-centered, transmission-oriented pedagogies, and is based on a worldview in which knowledge is seen as an objective representation of how the world works. Pupils access this knowledge by memorizing concepts and demonstrating their mastery on tests. Progressive science education centers around inquiry activities designed to help pupils gain understanding of science concepts through discovery. Conceptual understanding rather than rote memorization is the goal, although knowledge is still viewed as objective and separate from cultural context. While this approach is central to good science teaching, it may not by itself fit the needs of LI/RCLD pupils, especially ELs. For example, inquiry activities are often language intensive and must be specially designed to be accessible to ELs. Likewise, some researchers suggest that inquiry alone may not be enough to motivate pupils from nonacademic backgrounds (Barton & Osborne, 2001; Hammond, 2001). These pupils need demonstrations that science is relevant to their lives, and can help them to solve problems their communities face.

Critical science education addresses these concerns and defines scientific knowledge as created by and contextualized in the human community. Science concepts then become important for solving problems better in everyday life, such as by cleaning up a nearby river, improving community nutrition through a garden project, or holding a health fair to screen for common diseases. A major goal of critical science education is to enable pupils to become knowledgeable citizens who participate in decision-making about how science can be used to promote environmental and social justice. It should be noted, however, that a critical approach to science education does not serve pupils well unless it provides a strong intellectual basis in traditional science and academic language. Inquiry activities modeled by progressive science education need to be incorporated within problem-solving activities. For example, pupils who grow healthful foods in the school garden need standards-based lessons about plants. Similarly, pupils attempting to improve habitat along a neglected urban river need to learn about the plants native to their area before they can successfully propagate them.

The activities described in this chapter were intentionally designed to demonstrate a critical model of science education to pre-service and in-service teachers with the following elements included:

1. **Small learning communities that promote engaged, democratic learning.** One or two candidates and a small group of middle school pupils work together over time in a cross-age learning community to devise and solve a series of problems. Small learning groups encourage candidates not only to become aware of pupils' cognitive and linguistic needs, but also to learn about their lives and interests as cultural beings. They also equalize roles between teacher and learner, in that everyone is a knowledge producer, solving problems together.

2. **The problems addressed emerge from and are grounded in the culture and the environment of the school.** The connection between experiences in daily life and science forms the basis for the curriculum, which is then linked to an understanding of standards, rather than the other way around. In some cases, as in our garden project, necessary activities such as growing food are made possible through science activities. In other cases, such as the river experiments, the emphasis is on understanding how science concepts manifest themselves in the daily life of our community. We use the term learning places[3] to refer to a localized process of curriculum development based on needs, resources, and environmental and cultural opportunities.

3. **Links are made between local science, world issues, and human values.** As an example of such linkage, pupils are able to find a socially responsible solution to the problem of creating heat for cooking through a solar oven activity, and are then asked to reflect on the environmental implications of using conventional energy sources.

4. **Activities center around hands-on inquiry experiences that involve pupils in discovering mathematics and science concepts; these activities are modified to meet the needs of ELs and LI/RCLD pupils.** Lessons center around activities that engage groups of pupils directly in discovery. However, academic language is taught explicitly to pupils through vocabulary development, guiding lab sheets, and instruction in scientific writing. In addition, instruction surrounding the lesson is "sheltered" through the use of visuals, realia, primary

language use, and total physical response, so that ELs can understand the material presented.

5. **All participants, including pupils, teachers, and professors, reflect together before and after lessons about what worked and what did not work in their learning communities.** These oral and written reflections influence future lessons, in a cycle of planning, action, and reflection. They focus not only on science content and process, but also on the attitudes that EL and LI/RCLD pupils develop toward science and math.

The following snapshots describe two different settings in which learning communities were successful in our PDS. The first demonstrates a series of math lessons that candidates prepared and presented using the lesson study model. The second is part of Project CULTURES at a West Sacramento elementary school populated by ELs and diverse, transient pupils. It illustrates how a PDS can foster services for LI/RCLD pupils through complex partnerships that involve but go beyond teacher education. The university provided both people-power, in the form of candidates who created learning events, and expertise, in the form of teacher educators and visiting scientists. It also provided support for teacher leaders to write grants and carry out special projects.[4]

Snapshot I (as told by Julita Lambating, CSUS mathematics methods professor): One of our candidates commented during the debriefing session we had after her first teaching experience with a small group of kids, "I am amazed that students actually know a lot more than we expected." The candidates were engaged in a series of three teaching events as part of the field experience for their PDS mathematics methods class. This is the third year (2004) we have done this activity as part of establishing a learning community. The candidates were divided into groups of three and worked as a team with a small group of pupils.

In every teaching event, one candidate taught the lesson, another was the observer, and the third was the teaching assistant. The classroom teacher determined that her pupils most needed a lesson on geometry, so that was the lesson content area. The particular class was chosen because the pupils were doing poorly in math. The challenge the candidates faced was how to get the pupils engaged and interested so that learning could occur. They assumed that these pupils knew very little math and were not motivated to learn.

The instructional objectives were the same for all teams, but each team had to develop its own three-week lesson sequence. Afterwards, each team conducted a collaborative reflection and then shared what they learned with the whole group. Then, the members rotated roles (teacher, observer, teaching assistant) and began the process anew.

Candidates devised creative ways to make math challenging. One team took their small group of five pupils outside in order to teach them the definition of a polygon, the names of the different types of polygons, and other related terms such as diagonals, perimeter, and area. Using the pupils as posts with string wound around their waists, they formed polygons by slight movements and shifting. Thus, they could form and discuss different types of polygons and other related concepts. The pupils were highly engaged with the activity, and were so proud of what they learned that they asked if they could show it to their teacher. It was quite a sight to see this group trying to move together as one shape, connected by a string, so they could show their polygons to their teacher.

Two groups conducted lessons inside the classroom. One group asked pupils to draw something they like and then identify the polygons embedded in their figures, thus empowering pupils with choices about their learning. They were also able to relate a potentially abstract notion, polygons, to their own life experience. While some drew simple figures and others drew more complicated ones, all seemed to find the activity to be relevant and meaningful. Another group used tessellations and balls for teaching. Two of the teams took their pupils to another room where one group learned polygons by using paper quilting, similar to a cultural tradition for some pupils in the school, and the other group identified objects around them and in illustrations from books they found in the room.

The 7th graders our candidates were teaching were characterized as difficult and underachieving, and could be considered potential drop-outs. One candidate commented, "The pupils really seemed to enjoy working in small groups. Pupils who do not usually participate were participating in the activity. These kids are sharp. Their mental skills are amazing, but some of them are failing in math. It's nice to learn about your pupils from some of their previous teachers but it is important to keep an open mind." Clearly, this activity challenged the candidate's assumptions and demonstrated a greater learning capacity than expected among the pupils. Disrupting such assumptions is the first step in creating awareness about equity. Creative teaching can change the labels applied to the "low track" math pupils with whom we worked.

Letting candidates work with a small group of pupils gives them an opportunity to see themselves as teachers who have the ability to turn around pupils who are failing in "normal" circumstances. The creative small group activities provided a firsthand experience of how a well-designed math lesson can get pupils interested in learning. In addition, the activities gave the pupils an opportunity to use their imagination and their previous knowledge to learn something. It gave them settings for demonstrating abilities that would otherwise go unnoticed in a rigidly structured classroom.

These teaching–learning activities are part of the early field experiences embedded in the Middle Ground PDS mathematics methods class. An inquiry method of teaching is emphasized and we consult with teachers to plan lessons that address topics relevant to their classrooms. This co-planning makes the experience particularly meaningful for the middle school pupils involved, and this was confirmed by feedback the pupils provided to their teachers. The candidates also were required to write reflections on the following prompts after completing the lesson: What is the composition of the group? What are the steps taken to know the pupils and their prior knowledge? How are the lessons introduced? What are the strategies used to promote active and meaningful learning? What are the strategies used to accommodate possible difficulties for ELs? How is learning monitored while the lesson is going on? How is learning assessed in relation to the instructional objectives? What is it that you have learned about your own development of becoming an effective teacher?

The resulting narratives affirmed the value of these learning community teaching experiences. For example, Larry wrote:

> I tried to determine, through another formal assessment, if the [performance] differences were because the pupils were unable to understand math vocabulary, or because they did not understand the equations and formulas themselves. It finally appeared that the problem was primarily one of language, not mathematical ability. In order to incorporate the context of students' lives into my lessons, I tried to formulate word problems using what I know of their lives—talking about Russian and Mexican food, culture, and history.

Another candidate, Jennifer, wrote:

> I have realized how much creativity and trial and error play into the teaching process. . . . Since I am relearning some of these concepts before I teach them, I must break them down into simple pieces so I can understand them first. I think this helps me see the lesson from a student's perspective and present the concepts as new to students in a way they will understand.

Overall, our PDS university-school partnership in the mathematics methods classes has enhanced the lives of LI/RCLD pupils by giving them positive experiences with math. It enhanced the learning of candidates regarding effective ways to teach math while it transformed their ideas about the capabilities of "at-risk" pupils. Candidates have come to understand that pupils who appear apathetic when presented with standard school assignments can become engaged when given attention, interesting challenges, proper language scaffolding, and chances to interact.

Snapshot II (Vignette): In Alice Peralta's science laboratory, thirty 4th graders use hand lenses to examine the corn and bean seeds that they are dissecting with toothpicks, observing the structure of monocots and dicots. These pupils, a majority of whom are Spanish speakers from Mexico, are learning California 4th grade science standards in the context of plants familiar to their families. Outside, in the school community garden, these pupils and those from two other 4th grade classrooms have been tending a milpa, a garden in which the "three sisters"—corn, beans, and squash—are planted in circles typical of Native American and Mexican traditional agriculture. Michael Plotkin, an ethnobotanist and doctoral student at UC Davis, explains how these crops are complementary: how beans provide nitrogen for the corn, which in turn supports the climbing beans, while the squash covers the ground to retard weeds. The following week, parents will come to a meeting in which they will demonstrate the cooking of corn tortillas and beans, and share recipes with teachers and children. Their traditional knowledge will be recorded in notebooks, which, in a later writing project, pupils will form into community accounts and recipes.

That same week, all the pupils will experience a special science day in the garden led by candidates from the PDS science methods class. These candidates work in pairs to create small group hands-on lessons that teach grade level science, language, and arts standards. Pupils rotate in groups of eight, spending 20 minutes with each pair of candidates. The pupils learn about predators in the garden, make compost in a bottle, examine leaf structures with hand lenses, make a corn-cob doll of natural materials, create musical instruments from gourds, and more. Candidates simultaneously learn to devise lessons that use garden materials and to do outdoor environmental science with EL and LI/RCLD pupils.

Case Study: Project CULTURES

Through Project CULTURES, the 4th grade science standards, which focus on plants, are contextualized through ethnobotany, the study of how people use plants in cultural contexts. Several kinds of activities are interwoven in this project, just as Mexican traditions, which represent the background of 60% of the student body, are interwoven with the other cultures represented in this diverse, urban school.

Project CULTURES involves many players, including Network PDS teacher educators, candidates, and teachers, and also graduate students from UC Davis who share their science expertise. The lead teachers were trained by the California Science Project and participated in SPREE. Fourth grade teachers receive training in both ethnobotany and literacy through science, and collaborate with university partners to invent classroom activities that fit local school assessment priorities. Like other complex Network PDS partnerships, CULTURES fits the specific community it serves, and evolves as the needs of that community emerge. While it might not be directly replicable, we believe that the elements it combines could be used to create appropriate adaptations in other settings.

Element #1, Laboratory Science
Project CULTURES occurs at an urban school that, like many similar schools, has focused on literacy and math for the past five years and omitted systematic experiences in science, social studies, and the arts. The recent reestablishment of standardized tests in science at the 5th grade level has caused this school to examine its intermediate curriculum for opportunities to teach science. The principal created a mathematics and science specialist position and hired Alice Peralta, a California Science Project teacher leader.

As a first step in bringing science back into the intermediate curriculum, Peralta, assisted by teacher colleagues and university and county science partners,[5] established Project CULTURES through a Toyota Tapestry grant. This provided support for a variety of activities, including a series of teacher work and in-service days in which 4th grade teachers, the science specialist, the school's language development specialist, and university partners collaborated to create a program that meets science standards while supporting district language development requirements. A PDS science methods professor doubles as a provider of in-service professional development and as an evaluator for this action-research project.

All 4th grade pupils at the school participate in one to two hours of science laboratory activities per week, taught by Peralta, that focus on state science standards and are taught through inquiry experiments, such as the dissection of corn and bean seeds. The small amount of time afforded to pupils for science lab is not sufficient for developing the academic language needed to be successful in science, especially given that ELs are the majority of the school's pupils. This is why the second element of Project CULTURES, language development in the regular classroom, is so important.

Element #2, English Language Development Through Science
California schools with large numbers of ELs are required to spend a designated time each day on English language development (ELD). This time must be used to address specific language tasks, but is not always linked to subject areas. Our premise is that English can be most effectively learned in the context of meaningful subject area activities. In Project CULTURES, language development activities are linked to the experiences pupils have in

the science laboratory. Some activities, such as developing vocabulary and reading background materials, precede science laboratory inquiries in order to make them more comprehensible to ELs. Other activities, such as writing lab reports, follow laboratory experiences and promote pupils' ability to pass required writing proficiency exams and their skills at reflecting on science.

Like most California teachers, our 4th grade teacher team reports that there is not enough time in the school day to cover everything that they are required to teach. In this situation, developing academic language through science must integrate with other required parts of the school day. Combining the preparation for the writing proficiency test with writing in science, and using the time provided by the ELD period, has made it possible to build academic language development into the science program. At another school, our science project has used the inquiry part of a reading program, Open Court, in a similar fashion. If we are to integrate science and academic language development into our schools, we must negotiate with teachers to find existing settings in which they might fit. Science can become the subject material around which language is developed, and about which reading and writing occur. PDS schools provide ideal sites for experimenting with the integration of science with other subjects, since professors, teachers, and candidates can closely collaborate within classrooms.

Element #3, Ethnobotany and Family Literacy
The mother of Alicia Mendez, the language development specialist at the school, is a *curandera*, an expert on Mexican herbal remedies. Mendez herself did not realize how much her mother knew until we interviewed her for our ethnobotany project, and her own school experience had never valued her mother's knowledge. Yet Mendez recognizes that language development is made easier when children are able to connect their home language and the things their parents teach them with the language and science they learn at school.

In addition to scientific literacy, Project CULTURES has the goal of developing family literacy, so Mendez, Peralta, and our teachers are experimenting with several ways of involving family cultural knowledge about plants in the school science curriculum. A simple way is to assign children homework tasks in which they interview family members about their experiences with farming, and how to grow, use, and cook plants. Another strategy is to bring herbs to a parent meeting and ask parents to write about how they use them, then share information with each other. This activity is particularly powerful when several cultural and language groups are present. Parents are amazed that many cultures use the same herbs, and are always interested in how the uses vary. The candidates also participate in family nights, and sometimes prepare lessons for parents on how to work with their children in science or other subjects. They thus provide a community service while learning how to work with LI/RCLD parents. Parent workshops have also been given by CSUS professors, as well as UC Davis graduate students working with the Public Interest Research office, a partner in our PDS efforts.

Data gathered from families, either as homework or through parent meetings, can be used as material for writing books at school. In producing these books, children and parents practice their literacy skills. In sharing them, children are able to celebrate their heritage knowledge in the context of school literacy.

Element #4, Creating a Cultural School Community Garden
Westfield School is proud of its large community garden, which was established through the PDS partnership and a United States Department of Agriculture FIELD grant that focused on food security. The garden serves both the school and its community: family garden plots allow families to raise and harvest their own food; classroom garden plots are used for educational purposes; a park-like area is used for school and family gatherings; and some plots are used by Project CULTURES and other special activities. Several special plots are grown to enhance the ethnobotany curriculum. They include a milpa, a salsa garden, and an international herb garden. These plots are used as a basis for the school science days prepared by candidates. The family garden, like the family literacy project, provides a place where immigrant families can share their knowledge with the school community. Parents and grandparents help to plant the gardens and demonstrate the harvest and preparation of food. Families also maintain the gardens in the summer when teachers and pupils are not at school. Many immigrant families are uncomfortable assisting in the classroom because they do not speak English or are unfamiliar with school skills, but they are happy to contribute to the garden. Through their input, the garden becomes a reflection of the community as well as the school. For example, one garden reflects the Mexican cultural majority at the school, whereas another reflects its community of Southeast Asian families.

For pupils involved in Project CULTURES, the garden provides a real-world manifestation of the science learned in the laboratory. Pupils experience how plants grow and are able to harvest and enjoy the results of good horticulture. Child nutrition is a major challenge in the low-income communities of the Network PDSs, and many pupils eat "fast food" as a substantial part of their diet. Many of these pupils are in transition from Mexico or another country of origin to the United States, and they and their parents need support and instruction, such as that provided through Project CULTURES, in the health advantages of maintaining their traditional diet in the face of media-promoted foods of limited nutritional value.

Project CULTURES models the five principles of "critical" science education that research has shown to be advantageous for LI/RCLD pupils (Barton & Osborne, 2001; Lee & Fradd, 1998; Rodriguez, 1998).

1. **Small learning communities** of five to eight children during garden science events are made possible by the concentration of candidates in their PDS science methods classes. In addition, small learning communities involving parents and candidates occur during family literacy nights. In both cases, all parties become both learners and teachers as they solve problems together.

2. **Local and culturally appropriate themes:** CULTURES is grounded in features specific to the school since the ethnobotany theme, centered around a milpa and other Mexican gardens, responds to the active Mexican community that makes up 60% of the school's population and has an historic interest in traditional gardens and food.

3. **Links to real-world issues:** Ethnobotany explores how people grow and use food, so links to community nutrition are already being made. Other links, to heritage, history, and social studies (e.g., the Native Americans and Early California framework) are easy to make.

4. **Linking science and language development:** Pupils have hands-on, inquiry experiences in their science lab along with language development activities in their ESL classroom that support the science.

5. **Reflection:** Candidates reflect on the effectiveness of the lessons in their science methods class, and teachers and professors reflect on pupils' written work as well as assess the overall effectiveness of the program for achieving the science and language objectives.

CULTURES is a complex partnership that created successful science learning communities. It illustrates how a PDS fosters the ongoing relationships that are the foundation of the work, which involves various university departments, numerous candidates, and teachers, pupils, and families at a neighborhood school.

Case Study: Floating Boats and Solar Ovens

At another Network PDS, the science methods class developed a 10-week learning community involving eighteen candidates and sixty-five 7th and 8th grade EL pupils. Our science methods class was held twice a week at the school site. Thursdays were planning days, on which candidates worked with the professor to design and modify two 10-week science units (one unit for the 7th grade and the other for the 8th grade). Half of the candidates worked on and taught each unit. Every Friday afternoon, each candidate worked with the same group of three or four pupils for one and a half hours. This group became their learning community. Together, they would conduct an experiment and fill out a lab report.

In between the Science Friday sessions, the candidate regularly assigned to the classroom would conduct introductory and follow-up lessons that provided continuity with the rest of the week's curriculum. Much attention was given to the pupils' EL needs. For example, the candidate might teach the particular vocabulary required to participate in the science activity. Attention was also given to background concepts pupils might need before conducting experiments. For example, before we experimented with buoyancy, the candidate and teacher assisted pupils in computing the density of water.

Each semester, the focus of the science unit is determined in collaboration with the middle school teachers involved so the units enhance rather than distract from ongoing curricula. For example, one semester, a teacher wanted to do a unit on sound in preparation for a community folk festival that would feature guitar-makers from the local Mexican community. In the fall of 2003, several themes in the 8th grade physical science standards—velocity, buoyancy, and the scientific method—were chosen as a focus because the teacher felt they were not subjects he presented strongly. The candidates and professor worked to situate these standards in the local environment, focusing on the river behind the school as a place where velocity and buoyancy could be explored through the construction and testing of little boats. Everyone agreed that this would be engaging since pupils like to visit the river, but that it would also be challenging since the river is swift and the principal expressed concern about safety issues. The professor was attracted to this theme because pupils in urban settings rarely utilize neighborhood resources as a classroom, partly because of a general fear of unpredictable issues that may arise. Middle Ground PDS borders on a riparian environment that offers rich opportunities for science, yet people fear this environment both because of the river itself and because it is a place where illegal activities occur. Yet teaching middle school pupils to use this environment safely is important, since they venture into it in the course of their daily lives.

In addition to covering science standards, our unit needed to integrate technology and language development. The main technology project was teaching pupils to write lab reports on a computer, and to use the computer program EXCEL to graph data comparing the velocity of various objects floating down the river. An approach to language and academic writing development through science was generated based on the work of Merino and Hammond (2001, 2002). Pupils and candidates began with an ice-breaker science activity on paper airplanes, in which they practiced working in their learning groups, conducting an experiment, and writing a simple lab report. They then launched into a series of lessons involving computing the velocity of the river at various points in the current by catapulting various objects into the river and using the formula $v = d/t$ (velocity = distance divided by time). This introduced how to use a formula to solve problems, a notion that was expanded in their later work with density and buoyancy. EXCEL spreadsheets were created to graph the velocity with which various objects moved through the current. Next, pupils conducted experiments with buoyancy in tubs of water, deriving principles they would apply to the making of small boats.

The goal of creating a boat that was both buoyant and fast had motivated pupils, and we promised a competition: the "First Annual GSMS Regatta." However, an environmental dilemma was posed. Since we might not be able to retrieve all of our boats from the river, we agreed that we could not in good conscience put materials into the river that would either pollute the environment or cause a hazard to passing boats. Pupils decided that we needed to make miniature boats out of natural materials, which occurred in the riparian area and might fall in the river anyway. This involved collecting vines, sticks, bamboo, and other materials near the river, and fashioning these creatively into boats. Connections were made to the 8th grade history curriculum that included study of native peoples who engaged in boat-building. The highlight of the fall activity was the regatta. Flags marked 10-meter intervals along the river, and groups of pupils were stationed at intervals to serve as judges as our little boats bobbed along the quarter-mile course. Since the river is dangerous, a candidate launched the boats from his own speedboat, thus enabling them to start from the same point in the center of the river.

The unit ended with the building and testing of solar ovens. This activity once again tied physical science to the environment through the energy crisis then current in California. Alternative energy sources were discussed, as well as the reasons why they are not seriously pursued. Finally, candidates led pupils in a vocabulary review activity involving the creation and playing of a jeopardy game using key scientific terms.

Candidates set three academic objectives for their middle school learning communities.

1. To engage EL pupils in science by using hands-on experiences in an outdoor environment complemented by small group problem solving and technology use. This objective was assessed through oral and written reflections by both candidates and pupils, as well as by commentary from the ESL teachers and the professor.

2. To familiarize pupils with the scientific method, as tested in their increased ability to write a coherent lab report. Pupils were mentored

through the process of writing a lab report several times. First, they did a paper airplanes lesson and, with mentoring, wrote a lab report as a pre-test. Then, they practiced writing a lab report on their boats on a river, integrating EXCEL, on the computer. Finally, pupils were required to write a lab report independently, in response to a solar oven building challenge. This served as a post-assessment.

3. To use experiences and discussion to develop a conceptual understanding of key physical science concepts related to velocity and buoyancy as reflected in pupils' ability to define key scientific vocabulary. Pupils were introduced to key vocabulary both academically and through field demonstrations. Finally, they were tested on the vocabulary they learned over the 10-week period. The testing situation involved a Jeopardy game, which pupils invented with the help of candidates.

The professor and the two ESL teachers, together, mentored the candidates through the planning, teaching, and evaluation process of creating an integrated unit on physical science.[6]

What Did Pupils Learn?
Pupils produced three kinds of products that were assessed and that we discuss here. They were lab reports, done both by hand and on computers; vocabulary tests, given at the end of the unit in preparation for a Jeopardy game; and reflective essays, assigned by their classroom teacher.

SAMPLE PUPIL ASSESSMENT, LAB REPORTS. Pupils produced three lab reports, one for each activity (paper airplanes, boats, and solar ovens). These lab reports were structured to illustrate the scientific method. They began with a hypothesis, reported on data collected, and connected the hypothesis with a conclusion. These lab reports were also used to structure pupils' investigations, and to illustrate various kinds of lab report forms as pedagogical tools for candidates to consider. Two lab reports, on paper airplanes and solar ovens, were done individually at the beginning and end of the unit. While these reports can be used to trace the thinking of individual pupils, their original assessment intent was not entirely successful due to time management problems (the solar oven lesson ran too long and pupils did not have time to complete a good lab report). However, individual lab reports did show a lot about pupils' thinking, and illustrated that pupils' English skills and understanding of scientific problem solving were not necessarily correlated. The grammar and spelling errors typical of ELs did not hinder pupils' display of good scientific thinking. This leads one to question the elimination of laboratory science in the middle school EL program on the grounds that they need to learn English first. Omitting science seems particularly inappropriate since it is a subject that involves concrete experiences that can aid pupils in learning English. Even when pupils had very limited English, as in the following example, they were able to express scientific thinking: "I learn that you needed weight to move the air plain. It chanch [changed] wen I puted paper kips [clips] and I went more father [further]." It is also important to note that fluency in English did not correspond to pupils' levels of understanding in science. Some pupils understood a great deal of science even if their English was very limited. This was possible because the experiments were so hands-on, providing nonlinguistic modalities for understanding concepts.

Not surprisingly, several candidates described their pupils as displaying understanding of concepts through discussion, but not in their written lab reports. For example, one candidate comments:

> After reviewing the boys' lab reports and spending a couple of hours with them, I believe that they have achieved a decent understanding of the concepts of gravity, air resistance, lift and thrust. However, if I had made this determination based only on their lab reports, I would not have come to the same conclusion. Student A's writing is very sloppy. His sentences are poorly constructed and only one was an actual sentence. (He made a better plane.) Student B on the other hand used carefully constructed sentences that had verb tense problems, but did contain complete thoughts. . . . I was surprised that none of the boys used any of their new vocabulary words in the lab reports. The ideas were there, but they avoided taking the chance with a new word. Their science in finding new ways to adjust thrust and design to overcome gravity and optimize lift was very insightful. . . . Although the boys are able to explain what they are doing, they could not write about it effectively. Student A was the one whose comprehension seemed to be the least. I wonder if that isn't a result of his English development being somewhat less than Student B and Student C.

This experience helped candidates grasp that standard ways of measuring pupil understanding, such as reading the lab reports, may not suffice as fair assessments of ELs' learning. This led them to examine how they could better mentor their pupils in how to write a lab report.

After discussing our first experiment and lab report, the candidates decided to do the next set of lab reports with their pupils, working in groups and using computers. Their goal was to model for pupils what a lab report can be like. They also decided to teach pupils to use EXCEL graphs to emphasize the visual nature of the data. The assignment centered on learning to use the formula $d = vt$ (distance = velocity $\times$ time) to compute velocity in various settings, including the velocity of people walking and running, of a ball being thrown, and of various objects thrown into the river current. Each group gathered data of their choice, then created a lab report in Microsoft Word, enhanced by EXCEL graphs. Candidates were impressed with how the lab report process was enhanced by technology. One candidate comments:

> This was possibly my favorite lesson so far, which surprises me, given that I would usually much prefer the river to a computer. I think the reason that this lesson was so rewarding is that writing a lab report and creating the graphs and charts really brought our experience at the river to fruition. . . . There are several benefits to working on the computer. First, the pupils enjoyed typing and consequently they wanted to write and say more. . . . Second, once the pupil had typed a sentence, the group was able to easily go back and edit/improve. Third, we were able to take advantage of the "copy and paste" functions available. . . . Rather than retype (an) entire sentence we simply "copied and pasted" and then changed "walked" to "rolled a ball." . . . Another benefit to writing the procedure was the emphasis on past-tense verbs. First the pupils wrote "walk" and then we talked about "ed" endings and the pupils edited "walk" to "walked." . . . This "ed" ending presented itself numerous times. . . . Working with EXCEL was also very beneficial. . . . They were amazed that we were able to input the data we had collected into EXCEL, and easily create graphs that represented the data. The graphs were wonderful visual representations of the results of our experiment. Most people find graphs helpful in analyzing data, but EL (pupils) especially benefit from visual aides. . . . They were very proud of their finished lab report, and this experience provided them with vital tools that they will need later in their education.

This reflection demonstrates the importance of asking pupils to write in science. Our learning community lab reports are different from short-answer worksheets in that they require pupils to think through what they learned and how to present it. The graphs they produced could be arranged in various ways, only some of which illustrated significant things about the exercise. Another candidate commented: "It was obvious to them that some charts were meaningless and that other charts had the conclusions almost jump out at you." Pupils were challenged to create and choose meaningful ways to present their data, a process new to most of them. Most school assignments involve worksheets in which the problem of how to express data is prestructured; while this may help pupils to organize their thoughts, it robs them of the possibility of solving problems in their own way.

Writing group lab reports demonstrates the power of the learning communities model. In the previous comments, we can see that the candidate learned many things about her pupils' reactions to technology, and also about how to develop language in EL pupils. Her discussion of past-tense verbs ending in "ed" took advantage of a natural learning opportunity. Perhaps even more important, the exercise gave middle school EL pupils a chance to receive intensive mentoring, not only in science but also in writing and technology. It would be very difficult for a classroom teacher to do either the science or the writing exercise without the help of candidates working with small groups of pupils. The PDS enabled EL middle school pupils to create a lab report and participate in a level of academic writing that they could not produce on their own.

These lab reports raised interesting pedagogical questions, particularly in terms of how much adult intervention should be given in producing them. Vygotsky (as cited in Moll, 1990) suggests that pupils learn best when in a Zone of Proximal Development in which a more experienced person mentors novices and expands their level of inquiry; in accord with this, modeling can be a useful way of teaching. In contrast, most inquiry approaches to science education generally favor the questioning of pupils in open-ended ways. Thus, we wondered just how much the candidates should influence pupils' responses on their lab reports. Is it "cheating" to work with pupils in writing the reports, and more authentic to let them write their own responses, then analyze these responses to judge what pupils need to learn next? These questions were left open in our work, to be discussed as part of our own process of inquiry about teaching and learning.

Assessing Pupil Vocabulary Development
Since key terms in science correspond to important concepts learned, the candidates decided to test pupils on their definitions of a list of key terms covered in the unit. These terms included both content words, such as "reflection" or "buoyancy," and terms about the scientific method, such as "hypothesis." In order to make vocabulary testing more motivating, the candidates decided to play a game of Jeopardy centering around pupil-written question cards, each of which defined a key term. For example, a pupil might write "A rock does this in water," and the Jeopardy answer would be "What is sinking?" Each pupil had to pick at least five key terms and define them by writing a Jeopardy question. These questions were then analyzed to see how accurately pupils could define the terms.

In general, pupils seemed to have the strongest mastery of terms related to the scientific method—namely, hypothesis, experiment, and conclusion. No pupil got these answers wrong, and many pupils chose to define these terms. This is almost certainly because the terms appeared repeatedly on lab report forms, and represented processes repeated on each Science Friday. Candidates were confident that the pupils had learned to participate in a simple inquiry, making a hypothesis, testing results, and comparing these results to their hypothesis to draw a conclusion. Physical science lends itself better to this kind of inquiry than some other types of science, so pupils had a lot of practice with simple experiments made possible in this unit of study by the PDS structure.

Pupil mastery of more specific terms related to experiments on only one or two days, such as the vocabulary about solar ovens, was less complete. However, in general, the EL pupils learned a lot of scientific vocabulary, mastering the same standards-based vocabulary as their English-speaking peers. This reinforced the notion that EL pupils can benefit from laboratory science, since ELs can learn academic terms at the same time that they are learning common vocabulary. In fact, science also reinforces common words, like "distance" and "time," which are more easily learned in context.

It should be noted that the pupil definitions that we counted as correct did not always reflect an in-depth understanding of the concepts. This raises an important point about the kind of experiments we created. While applied experiments, such as designing boats or solar ovens, teach functional definitions of academic vocabulary, they do not always emphasize the scientific concepts behind these definitions. For example, pupils learned that "reflection" occurs when light bounces off of a substance. They also learned that aluminum foil, white paper, and other shiny surfaces are reflective. However, the experiment emphasized the practical aspect of reflection in the design of an effective solar oven. It did not emphasize physical principles such as radiation and convection at a molecular level. One solution to this problem would be to pair applied experiments, which tend to be motivational to EL pupils, with more traditional laboratory experiments, which center on the understanding of basic scientific principles. This is a challenge that reform science education does not always face (and we too fell short). If EL and other diverse pupils must compete with more privileged peers, who take basic rather than applied laboratory science courses, they will eventually have to learn in-depth conceptual understandings of science principles as well as their application to daily life.

Pupil Attitudes Toward Science
The science learning community pupils experienced several kinds of academic writing through their science lessons: writing lab reports; writing definitions; taking field notes (and drawing pictures to illustrate them); writing a narrative; writing and creating charts and graphs on the computer; and answering questions. Their teacher also asked them to write essays (one to two pages each) reflecting on their Science Friday experiences. One set of essays responded to digital photos of various experiments, and another responded

to four questions: (1) What did you learn about science? (2) Did you enjoy doing science outside by the river? (3) Were you afraid or uncomfortable doing science by the river? and, (4) How did you and your group behave in your learning community?

Before we worked in learning communities to engage ELs in science, many candidates were nervous about whether they could successfully involve Level II ELs in 8th grade standards-based science. Yet in their essays, twenty-five pupils responded that they liked Science Fridays, while only four were ambivalent and three disliked the activities. Most responses were highly enthusiastic:

> We didn't have any problems with behavior because we were so excited. And the candidate was too. He acted like an elementary kid.
>
> I think on Friday in the science project it was so funny because I didn't know there was a river there. And I thought it was illegal to climb the little mountain [the levee behind the school] without the permission of the police. We learned lot about velocity how to measure speed. . . . Me and my group were behaving good. Our student teacher is not mean, he is a good person. He is like a friend to me. That's why we were behaving good.
>
> Last Friday when we went to the river, I was so excited because I like so much the river.
>
> I like to lurn science a lote. . . . It was fun to go by the river with a group. We all did some stuff like walking, rolling the ball, and throwing the sticks in the water. I wasn't scared that much but I was a little, because I thought that I might do something wrong. But I didn't. I was good at it. We even sing a song on the way to the river.

One of the strengths of Science Fridays was the integration of activities, including science, writing, technology, and sometimes even music and art. This integration, coupled with small groups and going into the river environment, created highly motivational activities. Their teacher reported that the pupils looked forward to these activities, and associated them positively with science. Several pupils began saying that they wanted careers in science. The opportunity to work in small groups doing meaningful, hands-on work is hard to provide in the context of a crowded middle school, and is one of the enrichments enabled by the PDS.

What Did the Candidates Learn?

Candidates learned most of the skills required in their science methods classes through preparing for, participating in, and reflecting on Science Fridays.

While the 8th grade project has been the subject of this chapter, a similar 7th grade project based on life science standards related to evolution occurred simultaneously. These standards were localized through a study of how the local environment evolved since the last Ice Age, and pupils produced a giant diorama on this theme. One of the main things being modeled to candidates was the learning community process itself, which can be applied to many subjects and situations. The candidates experienced a "process through which you can learn" that was centered in the localizing of standardized curriculum, in collaborative planning and reflection, and above all in experiencing cross-age learning communities in which everyone contributes knowledge and solves problems. Some people have questioned this situation as not realistic, in that typically teachers never get to do sustained work with small groups, but our purpose was to construct authentic teaching and learning free of the overwhelming behavior management tasks that exist when working with a 1:30 ratio. Through the PDS, the candidates could focus on how the kids learn, how their language develops, what their skills are, and what motivates them. Then candidates can extrapolate their experience to other situations. These days, schools are overly focused on the transmission of knowledge. Too often, novice teachers do not experience children as knowledge creators, capable of solving open-ended problems. But if candidates can learn this in the PDS, they may find more ways to create such learning environments in other contexts.

Central to our "process through which you can learn" was the notion of inquiry. This means both inquiry for kids, solving problems for themselves, and inquiry for adults, evaluating and reevaluating their teaching, never being too certain that a final answer has been reached. The spirit of our class was captured by a candidate who, a year later, wrote a paper about teaching as community organizing (Ferlazzo & McGarvey, 2005). This is how Larry Ferlazzo tells the story:

> We were doing a unit on density and buoyancy, and I was having pupils explore with various items, some of which floated in water, some of which didn't float, to help them discover for themselves these physical principles. I was having the pupils build boats out of tin foil and compare them to wadded up tin foil that sank. An experienced teacher took me aside in the teacher's lounge and said, "Larry, you're wasting time. Just tell them that the density of water is one." . . . Sometimes we get to be "action junkies," we've got to get the action to come out well, and we shortchange the reflection. Or we don't take time to create a "lesson plan" that will help people take ownership of the idea for themselves. . . . It's working inductively, from the specific to the general, rather than deductively, from the general

to the specific. You are guiding the experience, for certain, you give the students a "data set" to work with; for example, I picked the items they were experimenting with in the water. But then, within that data set, you get the students to explore and come to their own understandings of the ideas, rather than lecturing them about the general case that somebody else figured out. It's about "enactment" and "reenactment." (Ferlazzo & McGarvey, 2005, pp. 2–3)

Learning communities can work in many situations, as can an inquiry approach to education. Combined, they create a powerful pedagogy for a PDS setting. In our case study, these approaches were applied to community-based science and math education. They are by no means limited to science, and we used them with other subjects in the Middle Ground PDS. For most of the pupils in urban schools, education is the only way to improve their chances for a better life. Yet many of these pupils do not relate well to school, and drop-out rates are much higher for them than for middle class pupils. Something needs to be done so that LI/RCLD pupils find school to be a place they want to be while they acquire the knowledge and skills they need to succeed. Promoting a better life for these pupils starts with getting them engaged in the learning process. What better place to start than with mathematics and science? Both subject areas are still considered "gatekeepers" since they have high rates of failure and are foundational for many other subjects. Providing pupils with meaningful experiences is a central purpose in our mathematics and science learning communities.

Project CULTURES illustrates how PDS learning communities have worked in challenging school settings. Our PDS partnership provided a springboard from which further complex partnerships became easier to negotiate, and led to the grants that enabled CULTURES to extend between two universities, a county office of education, and the school and parent community. Such partnerships assist in building the social capital so needed in LI/RCLD schools. Our middle school learning communities demonstrated that ELs who typically do not receive laboratory science are capable of being successful in science and, furthermore, that their language and technology skills can be enhanced in the process of learning science. Too often, ELs and pupils with special needs are denied the authentic kinds of educational experiences that motivate advanced pupils. Gifted pupils often receive inquiry experiences, and certainly receive laboratory science at the middle school level. How can we motivate LI/RCLD pupils if we do not provide them with exciting educational opportunities? And how can we consider education equitable when pupils receive very different opportunities?

The Equity Network PDSs provide enrichment opportunities for pupils through a deeply engaged approach to teacher education, in which candidates learn to teach subject areas such as science, math, and social studies by working directly with pupils. This model integrates all four goals of a PDS: candidate education, improved programs for pupils, professional development for teachers, and inquiry.

Above all, in the Equity Network PDSs, the candidates not only serve the school community as it is, but help to make it what it could be. In the case of mathematics and science education, a critical approach relevant to LI/RCLD urban pupils provides a desirable model that could only be demonstrated through creating unique learning communities. By designing lessons based on the community resources, and presenting them through authentic inquiry activities, urban pupils became engaged with science. Only through planning, implementing, and reflecting on these lessons did candidates experience an education transformative of their own prior assumptions about pedagogy and about their pupils, so that they could create "a process through which you can learn," rather than one that reinforces failure.

LI/RCLD urban schools often experience overcrowding and lack of both human and material resources. A PDS can provide creative people-power that builds on the natural strengths of a community, as it does in the family literacy and garden experiences. In order to maximize its positive effects on a school community, a PDS must be directed toward the needs of K–12 pupils, as well as those of university students. This requires collaboration on the part of teachers, parents, and professors, united in a commitment to create a rich and exciting learning community. Based on our experiences, we suggest that if teacher education devotes itself to learning to work in diverse school and community-based settings, where candidates become learners along with professors, teachers, parents, and of course K–12 pupils, the pursuit of equity will be forwarded in significant ways.

Notes

1. Regrettably, the enforcement of NCLB's Highly Qualified Teacher mandates forced our innovative middle school PDS to make changes too great to sustain itself. Implementing HQT in California resulted in the virtual elimination of the middle school credential. Though some partnership work with co-authors of this chapter still occurs, and the PDS work with the feeder elementary schools has been maintained, we still lament yet another negative outcome of NCLB for LI/RCLD communities.

2. The district and UC Davis jointly received and implemented a 12-year, multimillion dollar federal grant award for the Bilingual Integrated Curriculum Project, a Title VII Exemplary Bilingual Education Project that involved high-quality, bilingual education-focused science curriculum.

3. The term "learning places" was coined by Joyce Gutstein, and defined by a "think tank" of science educators from UC Davis, Yolo County Office of Educa-

tion, and CSUS, engaged in defining a localized and culturally relevant approach to science education appropriate to students in the Central Valley.

4. One such project was CULTURES, which was created collectively by teachers at Westfield and faculty partners from CSUS, UC Davis, and Yolo County Office of Education. It was chosen from submissions across the nation as one of fifteen projects sponsored by Toyota.

5. In addition to the Toyota Foundation, partners in CULTURES include CSUS faculty members in Teacher Education and Bilingual Multicultural Education departments, the Equity Network, Joyce Gutstein and graduate students from the Center for Public Service Research at UC Davis, and Deb Bruns, science coordinator at the Yolo County Office of Education.

6. This unit was presented as a model of teaching language through science at the 2004 California Association for Bilingual Education conference.

Chapter Two

Science for Social Responsibility

Claudya A. Lum, Elizabeth M. Aguirre, Ricardo Martinez,
Mercedes Campa-Rodriguez, and Rita Ultreras

Dedicated to the Memory of Dr. Hugo Chacón

This chapter tells the story of "SEDBED,"[1] a school–university collaboration that brought together the teachers in the Spanish-English Developmental Bilingual Education Department (SEDBED) at Bowling Green Charter Complex with candidates and instructors in the university's Bilingual/Multicultural Education Department (BMED). The initial vision was for candidates, teachers, and teacher educators to develop a social justice-oriented science curriculum that would engage pupils in high-quality science education, candidates and teachers in "best practices" science teaching, university faculty members in authentic integration of theory and practice, and community members in supporting the pupils, their school, and their own community. We begin with some comments on the recent history of science education and the current "state of affairs" in our schools. We next describe the key elements and milestones in our collaboration. We conclude with an assessment of our PDS work, informed by personal reflections from key teacher leaders and an analysis of pupil and candidate data. We hope that our SEDBED experience will inspire others who strive toward a constructivist, social justice science curriculum that can unite a broad community around pupil learning and success.

Recent Trends in Science Education

Various science education reform efforts have paved the way for new models and methods for teaching and learning science since the 1950s. While some of the more current research on cognitive misconceptions and inquiry-based learning has commanded teacher interest in professional development workshops and conferences, and within teacher credentialing programs, significant issues remain. First, studies across the nation continue to show LI/RCLD pupils scoring lower on science standardized tests as compared to white and affluent pupils. Second, a gap continues to exist between what teachers learn about good science teaching and what they implement in their classroom. Finally, the connection of pupil achievement in science, as measured on standardized tests, to teacher knowledge and instructional methods is also poorly understood.

Some initiatives are encouraging. For example, groundbreaking work on cognitive misconceptions in the 1980s created a new way for science learning to be examined, via pupils' prior and/or background knowledge (Driver, Guesne, & Tiberghien, 1985; Novak, 1987; Osborne & Freyberg, 1985). This approach focused pupils on their own learning as they grappled with what was believed to be common misconceptions of foundational science concepts. Researchers thought that facilitating pupils' struggle through their misconceptions would eventually enable them to replace the misconceptions with more accurate understandings of the concept (Posner, Hewson, & Gertzog, 1982). Specific hands-on/minds-on experiments were designed to transform cognitive misconceptions into scientifically accepted knowledge.

However, this approach to learning was difficult for teachers to implement successfully. There were many barriers: higher classroom enrollment, insufficient amounts of time required for pupils to work through individual misconceptions, difficulties in designing experiments that would lead to the revealing of misconceptions, insufficient depth of teacher knowledge necessary for understanding the science misconceptions themselves (especially for K–6 teachers for whom science is not their subject specialty), lack of lab resources, and the extensive training required for teachers to become skilled at facilitating and altering pupil misconceptions (Cochran-Smith & Lytle, 1993; Evans, 1996; Kozol, 1991). This model required teachers to develop lessons that sparked pupil interest and engaged them in carefully researched and crafted learning activities that teachers facilitated instead of giving out factual information. But cognitive misconceptions research usually harnessed science learning around a fairly restricted and noninterdisciplinary set of scientific questions, which often reduced the relevancy of the science concept or topic for pupils, especially LI/RCLD pupils (Barba, 1995). Based on these and other findings related to pupil motivation and interest in learning science, research turned toward an inquiry-based curriculum and teaching practice to help make science more meaningful and socially relevant to the pupils. Constructivist inquiry-based teaching and learning methods presuppose that knowledge construction happens in a meaningful, social, and culturally relevant way (Brooks & Brooks, 1993; Tobin & Tippins, 1993). This insight about learning encouraged another set of changes in the way that new science materials were developed and introduced and then studied by pupils. The constructivist teaching approach was fraught with difficulties as well. The same struggles involved in the development and implementation of a cognitive misconceptions teaching practice were also experienced in the development of an inquiry-based teaching practice (i.e., issues of time, resources, teacher training, crowded classrooms, etc.) Moreover, with the constructivist model, teachers would have to take into account the social-cultural relevancy of science topics for pupils in their planning and implementation, and allow pupil interest, culture, and background to guide the progression of the curriculum year to year. This often prevented teachers from utilizing time-honored standardized worksheets and preparing their favorite science lectures months in advance.

More recently, a push for multicultural science education prompted an even more demanding set of recommendations for how the teaching of science was to be approached. A critique of Eurocentric perspectives in science education led to advocacy for antiracist educational practices, raising questions about the assumptions in science instruction, about who benefits from the content and approaches, and about who has access to the science materials (Barba, 1995). Multicultural science education challenged the assumption that "one size fits all" as was implicit in both the misconceptions and constructivist teaching paradigms (Lynch, 2001). In addition, although these paradigms facilitated learning models that were more hands-on and inquiry-based, the models failed to address the issue of pupil access to the scientific discourse required to participate in both types of methodologies. Particularly, English language learners' level of academic discourse may prevent them from full participation in these paradigms, especially if the teachers and/or the curriculum do not provide such pupils with scaffolding support and mediation strategies (Gibbons, 2003). This is a major issue in California since one in four pupils is an English language learner. Furthermore, researchers now believe that teachers in diverse, urban schools also need to address the "space" that individual pupils need to have for learning and that must be created at the classroom level in order for effective learning to take place for all pupils (Calabrese-Barton, 2003).

Clearly, each of these teaching and learning paradigms contributes to our understanding of best practices for teaching science to pupils, including LI/RCLD pupils, and exemplifies huge leaps in the development of a more hands-on/minds-on, meaningful, relevant, pupil-centered, antiracist curriculum and instruction in science. However, many barriers continue to present obstacles: the complexities of state, district, and local policies and politics; inadequate resources; low teacher buy-in; high stakes testing; underprepared teachers; and various classroom limitations. Science is still not accessible to all pupils, especially those in LI/RCLD settings. Currently, non-inquiry-based, teacher-centered teaching practices dominate the way pupils acquire science knowledge in K–16 classrooms; this is especially true for pupils in LI/RCLD communities.

The pressures of standardized testing and the language arts and math specific content of these tests have actually eliminated science from the elementary curriculum in many LI/RCLD schools; in our region, science was left out for almost five years. Schools where standardized test scores are relatively high—mostly schools where majority culture pupils predominate—have been more likely to keep science as part of the core curriculum. With the introduction of 5th grade science content on the state test in 2004, science has slowly returned to LI/RCLD classrooms, but the pedagogical gains made since the 1980s seem to have dissipated as traditional, top-down, transmissionist forms of science pedagogy prevail. Schools that had been forced to narrow their curricula to just language arts and mathematics are now struggling to teach science in a way that will help their pupils pass the state standards science tests. History tells us that such a motivator is unlikely to entice teachers to use creative pedagogy and content; instead, choices will be made that favor expedience and efficiency in meeting testing demands, which will only exacerbate the inequities that plague education for LI/RCLD pupils. Not only will they still have limited access to science instruction, but the mode of instruction will serve to further alienate many of them from the content learning that is a key to higher education and a professional future.

Where We Started: A Personal Story by Ricardo Martinez, 4th Grade SEDBED Teacher

Once upon a time . . . "No," I tell the students, "your reports on César Chávez are not a fairy tale. César Chávez was a real person, a leader of the people—a leader for a cause. His sacrifices and courage were not make-believe!" Over 10 years ago when I first started teaching full time I always encountered some difficulty convincing my students that the life of Chávez was no make-believe story. My name is Ricardo O. Martinez and I am a 4th grade teacher at Bowling Green Charter Elementary School in South Sacramento. Being a 4th grade teacher is perfect for me because I enjoy California History, a focus of the 4th grade Social Studies Content Standards. It has always been a goal of mine to expose my students to the sociopolitical climate our state has had from its tribal natives to its present-day Hollywood governor.

Our school charter calls for us to create a social action plan that involves our students in helping their neighborhood community. In the past, I used to have students pick up garbage along the busy street next to our school.

We used to read and analyze *Our Wasteful Society* and discuss what could be done to improve it. This was all important information, but there was something missing. The students were not very excited about the project. As a result, something that started out as exciting for me became a disappointing requirement that my students and I had to complete for my school.

Luckily, thanks to a group of colleagues, I was able to be a part of a model that was going to allow my students to contribute to a positive community service project, a community health fair that was sure to have an impact on them and their families. I tell the students, "We can save lives, we can change lives." Every year I get curious looks from the students, but it beats the looks I used to get when I would announce we were going to pick up garbage. Our central anchor for the project was going to be César Chávez. "The boxer?" many students would ask. "No, not the boxer, but the leader of the farm workers in California," I would respond. Once again I had that excitement in me; not only would I work with a group of supportive teachers but, thanks to a grant, we had the funds to make this a project we could all be proud of, one that I know Chávez also would be proud of.

I was born in Patterson, California—the apricot capitol. My parents worked for a dominant company in the grape and wine industry. As with many other jobs in this region, working conditions in the wineries were abusive and low paying. My dad, being a true Mexican political rebel, joined the United Farm Workers led by César Chávez in the hope that conditions in the company would change. When my mom became aware of the sacrifices everyone would have to endure with a possible "HUELGA" or strike looming, she was having no part in that. My dad was willing to strike, but he had no chance to change my mother's mind. She wasn't going to have my father stop putting food on the table or lose the house we were renting for the strike.

I never asked my mother why she was not willing to strike with the others. I did not have to, because as a young boy I quickly learned what she had gone through as a hard-working woman. She lost two children to very difficult pregnancies and barely survived my birth; it took a toll on her emotionally. As a child I would complain about why I didn't have any brothers or sisters and all I remember was my mother with tears in her eyes saying, "No puedo tener mas hijos, mi corazón." (I can't have any more children, my love.) The next working season, instead of marching on strikes, my father worked for another company irrigating fields and my mother did other jobs. They moved on, but in a way they did not. They kept their UFW cards. I have them with me as a reminder of my childhood and the difficult times my parents went through. I remind my students with a heavy heart. "Whether you joined the cause or not, the farm worker's life was nothing like a fairy tale. Nothing like a fairy tale."

Where We've Gone: Elizabeth Aguirre, Science Coordinator at Bowling Green Charter School

Until the implementation of the PDS, Bowling Green Elementary Charter School could have been a case study of the kind of traditional science education we described earlier. For this school and its 860 students, the majority of whom are Latino and over 48% of whom are bilingual Spanish/English speaking, priorities were driven by strict state testing requirements. Though Bowling Green is a charter school that makes many of its curriculum decisions free from district mandates, the push to raise test scores threatened to eliminate core subjects like science. Taking this path would have surely reinforced structural inequalities that already were shaping our students for lives without science, for academic and career choices that did not require science knowledge. A 1999 survey of the students indicated that they had neutral to somewhat positive attitudes toward science and science careers, but the majority remained unconvinced that science would or could be a future career for them. This survey data energized the site administrator and key teaching staff to put high-quality science instruction at the heart of the school's curriculum, particularly for the SEDBED program students and teachers.

Our first steps focused on what outcomes we wanted our students to achieve. Initially the discussion was merely about meeting the California Content Standards, but as discussions continued, we wanted to know what we could do to help our students be successful beyond the 6th grade. We began by examining the reasons why many Latino students were not successful in school. We identified a few factors and were determined to do something about them. We found we were all teaching to the standards, but we weren't ensuring that students could apply their knowledge in novel situations. We also discovered our students had no goals beyond what was familiar to them. A college education was the goal of only two out of each classroom of thirty students. We also admitted we were not preparing our students in technology. Although we had the technology, few of us had the training to properly use it in our teaching. Examining the courses our students failed most in high school, we learned that science was a great weakness, not only for our students, but for our teachers as well. And, finally, we wanted to ensure that our students learned how to effect change, that they learned about their heritage, and that they understood the power they can have within their community to make changes for the better. After examining all of our goals, it was clear we wanted not only to teach students, but to help prepare them for life. If we could offer students the tools they needed to overcome obstacles, perhaps more of our students could then succeed. We decided to address the challenges by beginning with science from a social/political perspective.

In addition to identifying key content, conceptual, and skill components of our science curriculum, we also needed to thoroughly think through the social action component of the project. When the charter was first developed almost 15 years earlier, it was well understood that in order for the school to emerge from being designated as one of the worst and most problematic schools in the entire district, it would have to develop stronger ties to the community. The community did not view the school in a positive manner. The site administrator who spearheaded the charter process made it clear that teachers had to put a greater emphasis on academics with 'no excuses,' but they could do this by putting the same effort into creating a social action project to benefit the community in some way. In the beginning, this project was not easy. Teachers would generate a great idea, but the students were uninterested and their efforts were lackluster. However, we understood the value that a community project done correctly could bring to the overall school environment, so we persisted toward our goal. We believed that social justice-oriented curriculum, positive relationships with the community, and quality teaching can all occur interconnectedly. This belief guided our initial PDS efforts, and the idea of linking the curriculum to social action is now firmly embedded in our work.

As we considered how to begin the process of developing a social justice science curriculum, we drew from history lessons that were meaningful for most of the teachers and for the community as well: the life and accomplishments of César Chávez. Emulating his example, students began learning about various challenges in their own community, and quickly discovered that diabetes was severely affecting many of their families. In nearly 90% of the Latino families within the SEDBED, one or more family members were diagnosed with diabetes. Diabetes was clearly having an impact on the community at an alarming rate. In an attempt to break the cycle, students decided to learn more about the disease.

The teachers supported the idea of addressing diabetes, but they were also aware of the need for training. None of the teachers had the necessary content knowledge. Also, we didn't know how to relate diabetes to the California Content Standards. However, SEDBED teachers were involved in technology training through the Preparing Tomorrow's Teachers for Technology grant, and they realized the César Chávez social service unit could be connected with the diabetes science unit using the National Science Frameworks. The California Standards could be addressed through literacy, math, and social studies. Addressing the need for science training, two teachers attended the Society for the Advancement of Chicanos and Native Americans in Science conference and acquired information about diabetes, which they later shared with the other SEDBED teachers.[2]

At this same time (1999), science education professor Dr. Hugo Chacón sought out the SEDBED teachers to help jumpstart a PDS partnership to address the challenges facing the school as well as to improve teacher preparation in his program. Dr. Chacón had a passion for a multicultural, social reconstructionist, hands-on and inquiry-based science curriculum and was committed to supporting students in the bilingual program to learn science in a more effective manner. He was also committed to developing high-quality elementary science teachers who knew how to teach science in a socially relevant way.

We began to construct the building blocks of our partnership for science for social responsibility. For SEDBED students, this involved an articulated curriculum that, though ever-evolving, follows specialized units at each grade level, all developed by the PDS educators. Kindergarten and 1st grade focus on fitness, the 2nd grade addresses dental hygiene, and the 3rd grade emphasizes nutrition. The 4th grade focus was the two types of diabetes and diabetes prevention. Students extended their learning by interviewing members of the community affected by diabetes and then doing research and conducting inquiry-based science lessons. As a final product, 4th graders produced a brochure that could be disseminated to the community. Fifth graders focused on heart disease awareness, and were also engaged in inquiry-based lessons; they conducted research on the heart and heart disease and developed a PowerPoint presentation as their final project. The 6th graders focused on the human brain, and particularly the effects of drugs. Students in the 6th grade demonstrated their learning by writing and producing a play that they then video recorded and edited into a final, polished piece.

We developed a model that allowed both candidates and SEDBED teachers to deepen science content knowledge and enhance science pedagogy. During the semester-long elementary science methods class, candidates observed multicultural, inquiry-based practices in each of the SEDBED teachers' classrooms as well as practiced teaching multicultural, inquiry-based science lessons. Because social justice issues, multiculturalism, and strong ties to the community were at the center of Bowling Green's charter, this PDS collaboration was a natural fit. SEDBED teachers and candidates utilized a variety of inquiry-based social justice science lessons, implemented best practices in science inquiry, and provided a core curriculum to SEDBED students that included science. These experiences facilitated professional development opportunities and growth for pre-service and in-service teachers alike. This high-quality preparation for the PDS candidates demonstrated that effective science teaching can be grounded in a multicultural, inquiry-based, and socially and culturally relevant paradigm.

The elementary science methods class met once a week for 15 weeks, and was divided up into three five-week increments. During the first five-week segment, Dr. Chacón modeled multicultural, inquiry-based science; this allowed the candidates to experience this approach from the perspective of being a student as well as a teacher. Often, partner teachers also observed instruction and were thus exposed to the underlying theories. For the next segment, groups of four to five candidates developed a grade-specific, five-week, standards-based unit around a local community issue through the backwards design model (Wiggins & McTighe, 2005). Candidates were placed into classrooms based on the credential they would be receiving (i.e., either bilingual or standard).

Each week the candidates also observed and participated in delivering "best practices" and developmentally appropriate science lessons that were carefully constructed by SEDBED teachers, with input from Dr. Chacón. On occasion, Dr. Chacón would also facilitate a lesson. During the final five weeks, candidates developed and implemented their units collaboratively, with one group member in charge of the lesson each week. During this time, Dr. Chacón would visit each classroom and observe the candidates, and during the methods class time the groups would debrief each lesson in light of various issues related to teaching multicultural, constructivist lessons. Each semester the methods course became a way for candidates, SEDBED teachers and Dr. Chacón to work together to learn about, develop, implement, reflect on, and revise multicultural, inquiry-based science lessons.

As characterizes PDS work, the science methods class and the social justice science curriculum developed together. After the first year of our collaboration, the basic content structure of both programs was set. With the units completed, all that was needed was an organizational piece to link the units and provide a forum for students and candidates to engage in social action in their community. Because of the unit focus on health and service learning, the ideal forum was a health fair.

The health fair began and continues to be a collaboration among students, candidates, teachers, community members, university professors, and other outside agencies. During the health fair, PDS candidate and community member volunteers screen for blood pressure, diabetes, and cholesterol. Sixth grade students get hands-on experience by assisting volunteers at each of the stations. A doctor supervises all screening and consults with individuals screened in order to determine their medical needs, if any. Individuals from the community arrive to be screened and if necessary are referred to a clinic. They learn about heart disease from the ongoing PowerPoint presentations or about diabetes from the brochures being distributed by the 4th grade students. Individuals can also stay and enjoy the drug awareness play presented by the 6th grade students or they can listen and watch primary grade students singing and dancing to tunes about health and nutrition. Outside activities include a tour of an ambulance, nutritious snacks, nutrition games, and physical fitness activities. As years have passed, the health fair has become more elaborate and gathered broader support, such as from the wonderful doctors and professionals from the Rosales Medical group, and Mexican American Alcoholics Prevention, who volunteer their time. SEDBED PDS educators and students serve from 300 to 400 people annually at the health fair.

The health fair plays a crucial role in helping reach SEDBED's ultimate goal: preparing students to be socially active citizens. The health fair makes the curriculum meaningful; students know they will be using what they learn about health to help their community. The health fair and all that accompanies it are just part of our commitment to social justice, which intersects the curriculum across all of our learning activities. We do not start the day without discussing or reading about issues that affect our community. If we are not talking about the violence that is occurring around the neighborhood, then we are reading about national issues such as immigration. Although the district recognizes our progress on test scores (from the bottom to the upper middle of district schools), these symbolic gestures pale in comparison to the feedback we get from the community health fair when our students bring the community together for a good cause and to share in their education. Our messages to the students have been the same since the beginning: "Be the change you wish to see in the world," as Mahatma Gandhi astutely counseled; follow the example of César Chávez's life, emulating both his personal values and his lifetime struggle to improve working conditions for farm workers;[3] remember that no matter how successful you are in school and in life, there are city communities like this one that need your help and your support to make them better places for all. Sadly, Dr. Chacón passed away in the fall of 2005. It was a tremendous loss for all those who knew him, though he left an impressive legacy that will affect students and teachers for generations to come. Now we also say to students, follow the example of Dr. Chacón.

Thinking about Results: Rita Ultreras, Sixth Grade Teacher

Our efforts in the SEDBED/Bowling Green PDS always emphasized assessment and reflection. Before discussing data that we formally collected (e.g., student surveys or a small-scale comparative study), it is important to mention teachers' perceptions of the work that are less quantifiable. The teachers have no doubt that these science units build student knowledge about health and community service. Students learn about dental hygiene, nutrition, diabetes, heart disease, functions of the brain, as well as drug awareness. They also learn about taking responsibility in regard to their individual well-being and their community as a whole. The health fair plays a big part in the community surrounding the school. The science curriculum prepares the students to be active participants in this process. They also have opportunities to demonstrate their knowledge in a variety of authentic and performance-based ways.

In the past, we had struggled to interest students and wanted to break any stereotypes they had by connecting science to issues that they were aware of and that concerned them. This process has completely changed the way the students feel about science. Recently, a 4th grade student expressed to Ms. Aguirre that she had an interest in finding a cure for autism. The 10-year-old student has a brother who has been diagnosed with autism. She had always expressed an interest in becoming a teacher, like her mother, but has recently shown an interest in becoming a scientist. Her mother asked her what had caused her to change her mind. She said, "I always wanted to be a scientist and try to find a cure for autism, but I didn't think I was smart enough." Her mother asked, "Do you think you are smart enough now?" She responded, "Yeah, I found out science is not as hard as I thought it would be and it's fun." Her mother was surprised to learn her daughter did not think she was smart enough, even though she has always been given the encouragement and the confidence to try things. Exposure to science has now given this 10-year-old girl the confidence she needed to strive for a career she perhaps would have never considered. My own experience echoes this story: "Maestra, this is so cool. I can see the right and left hemispheres on this brain." Those are the words I look forward to hearing when my classroom is conducting a science inquiry. I still remember that the first year teaching science was not an easy one for me. That is why those words connecting the student to the knowledge they are receiving means so much. I have gone from hearing "Maestra, do we have to do science?" to now hearing "Maestra, when are we having science?" Students have gotten over the fear they had of science. Since they are exposed to it at a much earlier age now (kindergarten), they expect to have science as part of their curriculum.

These touching anecdotes complement data about student and candidate learning that reveals the powerful ways in which a robust PDS partnership can positively affect all participants. In 2003, 4th graders in SEDBED were given a survey measuring their attitudes toward a career in science as well as their attitudes toward science in general. Three years later, those students, now 6th graders, took the same survey (see Table 2). While the percentage of students who reported that they enjoyed doing science was initially high (88%), by 6th grade it was even higher (95%). Interest is certainly a key factor in engagement, but so is self-confidence and knowledge. Students spent considerable time researching the body, how it works, and how it can be compromised; this grounded research yielded an impressive increase in students' sense of competence and knowledge: 95% (vs. 53%) of the students report they are comfortable explaining diabetes; 100% (vs. 41%) report they are comfortable offering preventive solutions to diabetes; and 100% (vs. 53%) report they are comfortable presenting science information to adults.

Table 2. Survey Results from Bowling Green

Questions on Survey	2003	2006
I can see myself as a scientist when I become a grown up.	12%	24%
I can see myself as a medical doctor helping people with diabetes or heart disease.	33%	65%
I can see myself finding a cure for a medical illness such as cancer.	41%	57%
I can see myself as a science teacher when I become a grown up.	35%	49%
I have enjoyed doing science when we have done investigations.	59%	86%
I can explain what diabetes is to another person.	29%	95%
I can offer two solutions on how to prevent diabetes.	12%	100%
I feel confident in taking part in a community health fair.	88%	86%
I feel confident presenting science information to grown ups.	12%	81%
I can compare the life and work of César Chávez with our community health fair.	71%	95%

We noted earlier that one of the primary motivators for our PDS work was that we wanted our students to have serious goals beyond elementary school. We feel encouraged by what several surveys have revealed. First, the number of students interested in college has increased very substantially according to surveys conducted in 1999 and 2004. From about two of every thirty wanting to attend college, we went to about twenty-eight out of every thirty students intending to go to college. We believe that this increase can be attributed to the PDS collaboration in science, field trips to the university, community guest speakers, and also students' increased confidence about their competence as learners. Further, more students became interested in science careers: 12% (2003) to over 24% (2006). It is not unreasonable to attribute this increase to our strong science curriculum coupled with many presentations by professionals working in science careers. In addition, we should consider the power of relevance and social justice since students were learning about and acting on illnesses that affect their families and community. The survey showed increases in the numbers of students wanting to address the community health challenges and also wanting to become science teachers. Perhaps this interest in science teaching can be traced to the opportunity to meet candidates who serve as positive role models; we hope to see some of these students in the BMED teacher preparation program in the future.

While student enthusiasm for learning is infectious and gives teachers enormous motivation, concrete data on student knowledge and skills are essential to proper and thorough instructional planning. In addition, while our partnership efforts were satisfying for all involved, they did add layers of complexity to our work; it was important to determine if all of it made any concrete difference in terms of student learning. The SEDBED teachers tackled this issue with vigor and rigor. Two groups of students were selected from the school: group 1 was from the SEDBED 6th grade class and group 2 was from a 6th grade class in another department at the school (and non-bilingual). A performance task was developed to compare the two groups' knowledge and skill. Group 1 students participated in the PDS science collaboration and had three years of inquiry-based science. Group 2 students had a science experience that was more lecture-based. Each class was given the same set of scripted directions, much like the California Standards Test. Students were asked to read about a health problem, rickets, and use the data provided to try to figure out what was causing the disease. In order to solve the problem students had to rely on the scientific process. Students were encouraged to problem solve in groups of four to five, though each group had to work independently. Each group was given a worksheet with a series of questions and asked to record and explain their findings. In our evaluation of the results, we examined both the content and the process using a rubric.

The results demonstrate that students exposed to inquiry-based science were better able to problem solve than the students in a traditional setting. SEDBED students were able to work independently, problem solve, and use the data to support their findings. All of the SEDBED groups were able to determine at least one cause for rickets and substantiate their claim with at least one data element, if not more. Of the non-SEDBED groups, one was able to identify a cause and use at least one data element to support its conclusion. The other three groups did not succeed in identifying a cause for rickets, although two described symptoms and one attempted to use the charts but was unable to connect the data appropriately. SEDBED students clearly demonstrated the benefits of inquiry-based science: they were skilled in problem solving and were systematic in their data analysis. At the same time, we gained "eye-opening" data about a need to provide students with more independent problem solving experiences. Although the data reflect better results for SEDBED students, it also signals to us that there is still work to be done to improve the instructional experiences of our students.

How Do the Candidates View their Experiences in Teaching Science?

While we are delighted at the impact that this work has had on students, it is also important to understand how the PDS affects future teachers, as their enhanced preparation for these LI/RCLD settings is one of our main goals. In addition, because this model is distinct from other higher education experiences candidates have had—class is conducted at a school, teachers are co-instructors, candidates engage in authentic tasks that demand their active learning, and so on—it is important to understand how they experience this innovative model.

Liz Aguirre, a program graduate and PDS teacher leader, reflects on her observation of the candidates.

For five years I sat quietly in the corner of my classroom observing Dr. Hugo Chacón teach a science methods course. He always opened the class with a story about his family. It was his way of getting his students to feel comfortable in his class. He shared his personal experiences humorously and related them back to his interest in science. He often referred to how his father was not a "school-educated man" but knew so much about life and science because he was a handyman. Hugo would explain how he was fascinated by everything his father did and how that fascination grew to an interest in science. Hugo was passionate about science and how everything about it related to life itself. I watched as he led his students to experience science. Hugo was a firm believer that he couldn't only lecture to his students about inquiry science, but he also had to make them experience it. As a teacher, I would listen to Dr. Chacón every Thursday morning and envy the rich experience his students were receiving because although I had a great science professor who taught me many great science lessons, I never had someone explain how the theory and the lessons were related. Even many years into my teaching experience, I didn't understand inquiry science well. As a candidate I didn't get to experience such passion for science. I didn't get to observe others teach science related to a social objective. I didn't have the opportunity to try my lessons with students, and I certainly didn't get to experience teaching science to English learners.

Candidate feedback and reflections about the Bowling Green PDS reveal that they are grateful for the opportunity to teach science and obtain extra classroom experience through the collaboration. The majority consider science to be a weak area in their own education and indicate that sometimes this leads to a great deal of anxiety and a special challenge when it comes to presenting the science lessons. However, the overall support they obtain from the classroom teacher, their fellow group partners, and, most important, their university professor, leads to an overwhelmingly positive experience.

The majority of candidates also noted that teaching inquiry-based science was completely new for them and presented special challenges, particularly in relation to the role of facilitator rather than authority who directs students throughout the entire lesson. Candidates have had to learn to be comfortable with questions that they cannot answer and with students arriving at incorrect answers the first time during the inquiry process. Some candidates also worried that inquiry science seemed to take up a lot of time and resources; eventually, most came to understand the importance of allowing students ample time for the learning process, and allowing validity to the quest for the answers or methods to get the answers. Ultimately, candidates were able to see that the students were taking ownership of their learning through the inquiry process.

The PDS experience also introduced candidates to charter schools where they could observe alternative forms of governance and organization. Some expressed a desire to work in a school that does not follow a top-down model and a highly scripted curriculum. Candidates noticed the power and impact of teachers working together to develop and create change in a school community through science. They also acknowledged the importance of developing collaborative leadership and the value it brings to a whole community in an event like the health fair. Many were even inspired to hope to re-create some of the features of Bowling Green at their own future school site.

The SEDBED Teachers and Professional Development: Mercedes Campa, 5th Grade SEDBED Teacher

We have tried to ascertain the effects of our PDS work on the SEDBED teachers. In addition to the intensive collaboration that has now spanned six years, SEDBED teachers have participated in various types of professional development made possible through the PDS partnership. One such opportunity involved attending the conferences of the Society for Advancement of Chicanos and Native Americans in Science (SACNAS). SACNAS offers K–12 workshops on inquiry-based methodology, strategies for teaching science to English learners, and motivational strategies to encourage LI/RCLD students to pursue careers in science, mathematics, engineering, and technology. The conference also introduced us to science mentors, many of whom continue relationships with SEDBED teachers to this day.

The myriad of professional development efforts have helped SEDBED teachers improve in many ways, not only in terms of the department's science program but also in their individual development as science teachers. At times, it has been a struggle to come up with lessons or to improve/modify existing lessons to make them better and understandable to the students. But through teaching and feedback from other colleagues, candidates, and the students, our efforts have resulted in the high-quality science program we have today. One of our colleagues, Rita Ultreras, offers this reflection:

> The science program in place at SEDBED has not only helped the students, but the teachers as well. Some members of SEDBED have been involved in Lesson Study, and in the near future all members will have participated in this powerful professional development experience. In today's current trends, curriculum has become scripted. Teachers are allowed little flexibility. Assessment and standards now drive curriculum. Our science curriculum is challenging the status quo of the current standards-based movement.

Conclusion

> If I had to describe the way Dr. Hugo Chacón taught his science methods class, it would be a circle. He would mention theory, but most of his time was on experiences. His candidates observed experienced teachers for about five weeks. Then, using the Guided Inquiry Method, they developed a unit of study related to making a change to a "real-world" problem. Candidates had the opportunity to revise lessons every week by debriefing and self-reflecting. Once all the lessons had been taught, Hugo would ask the candidates to reflect on the theory and determine the best method for teaching science, and for helping EL students. In order to answer his questions, they had to really understand the theory and how it related to the experiences they'd had in class. As a teacher, I benefited as well from Hugo's teaching. It has made me reflect more and analyze how my students learn. I have been able to adapt more of my teaching to make it more meaningful for my students. I know working with Hugo has forever impacted all of the teachers in the Spanish English Bilingual Education Department at Bowling Green Charter School. Though Hugo is no longer with us, his influence, his teaching, and his passion will forever be with us. (Liz Aguirre)

This reflection highlights the importance of praxis in PDS work—through the circle that Dr. Chacón's instruction followed to the rigorous and iterative process that this extraordinary group of educators has pursued where innovation, assessment, reflection, and refinement occur in all aspects of their work, even when life's tragedies threaten to cloud their vision. The Bowling Green PDS is strong and has many important structures solidly in place. Dr. Chacón trained a new assistant professor, Dr. Claudya Lum, to take over the science methods class, and she has continued its social justice objectives and kept Dr. Chacón's passion for teaching science alive. The PDS partnership has brought positive and eager learning to the classrooms. The candidates learn how to teach science with small group hands-on lessons/activities, and the teachers have had multiple and ongoing opportunities to improve their own science instruction. The university instructors have confronted the challenges of integrating LI/RCLD student learning with teaching candidates effective methods.

In a time of high-stakes testing when science has been put on the back burner for many LI/RCLD schools, the Bowling Green-SEDBEDS PDS has improved science teaching and science learning. The final question to ask is: "Who is really responsible for preparing the next generation of teachers for social justice, and what does this need to look like with regards to collaboration, professional development, and curriculum and instruction?" The answer to this question at Bowling Green seems to lie in the collaboration among the candidates, the teachers, and the university faculty, specifically in the way that pedagogy, practice, and research are tied together in the continual development and redevelopment of the science SEDBED program. Pupils and candidates for years to come will benefit from the innovations, teaching, and passion of this great instructional team of university and school educators.

Notes

1. California State University Sacramento Professor Dr. Hugo Chacón led the formation of SEDBED. His tragic death from pancreatic cancer not only left the university, school, and community bereft, but left behind his spouse and six young children. We honor his legacy in our work and in this chapter, which had to be written without him.

2. In fact, the SEDBEDs teachers have been very proactive in pursuing professional development. In addition to the PT3 work and involvement with SACNAS, they have made presentations at the National Association for Bilingual Education Conference and they have participated in science professional development offerings at Sacramento State including Science Projects Related to Educational Equity (SPREE), lesson study, and Science in the River City short courses.

3. In addition to his many other attributes, Dr. Chacón was able to successfully secure several grants. One of them was a GO-SERVE grant from the state of California that he used to develop and promote curriculum related to the celebration of César Chávez' work and contributions (his birthday is a state holiday for public schools). These resources as well as those from the Title II TQE grant supported some of this work.

Chapter Three

Education of the Community, by the Community, and for the Community

The Language Academy of Sacramento

Susan Baker, Eduardo de León, Pam Phelps, Mario Martín, and Cynthia Suarez

Educational research documents the disconnect between schools and the low-income, racially, culturally and linguistically diverse (LI/RCLD) communities they serve (Ladson-Billings, 2001; Tatum, 2000; Valdés, 1996). Teachers come from largely homogeneous backgrounds compared to those of their pupils, and are not likely to have had deep experiences with people from racial, cultural, social class, and linguistic communities different from their own (Bell, Washington, Weinstein, & Love, 2003; Sleeter, 2001). Thus, most educators of LI/RCLD pupils lack firsthand knowledge about their pupils' communities, and how community definitions of social justice regarding adequate health care, employment, child care, public transportation, and so on, have important implications for schooling (Delpit, 1988). Tangling the roots of these disconnects are unspoken assumptions that can contribute to widening the test-score gap between pupils privileged by class and race and LI/RCLD pupils, who are systematically disadvantaged. When teachers teach with unchecked assumptions about LI/RCLD communities, they cannot fully identify and respond to the pupils' pedagogical and curricular needs, or develop the necessary school policies and program structures (Warren, 2005). This chapter discusses efforts that addressed such concerns.

We focus on (1) the inception of a neighborhood school: the Language Academy of Sacramento (LAS), and (2) a Community Study conducted by LAS in partnership with the Bilingual/Multicultural Education Department (BMED) of California State University at Sacramento. LAS is a K–8 dual language immersion program within which neighborhood pupils can become bilingual and biliterate, learn state-mandated content, and become advocates for social justice. The Community Study has four main goals: first, to provide an arena in which school people can surface and reflect on their own assumptions about the community; second, to learn about the community from a diverse group of community members through democratic dialogue and research methods; third, to create an interactive process in which local definitions of "social justice" were communicated to school people, thus facilitating the creation of curriculum and school policies that address local challenges and therefore forward a locally defined social justice agenda; and, fourth, to aid school people and community members in identifying community resources to support the previously stated goals.

Understanding the emic perspective of what constitutes social justice is foundational to schooling's role in a participatory democracy. Our study sheds light on how schools can become a space for democratic dialogue that then leads to culturally responsive school practices, pedagogy, curriculum, instructional methods, and program structures and policies that embody the locally defined social justice agenda (Bartolomé, 1994).

Language Academy of Sacramento: Historical Background

LAS opened as an independent K–8 charter school in September 2004. Despite early opposition and concern, many progressive educators now warily accept some charter schools. On the surface, there is little that is remarkable about LAS, but a closer look reveals its significance. To get to LAS, one must drive through Sacramento's largest marginalized community, Oak Park. In the early 1900s, streetcars and trolleys made this area, once covered in orchards, an attractive suburb for downtown Sacramento. Remnants of this up-scale past are still visible—classic California bungalows with wide porches overlook grassy lawns, elegant but neglected commercial buildings with ornate facades cluster in an historic business district, and expansive boulevards betoken an imagined grandeur. But navigating through the narrow residential streets, one sees the devastation of poverty—cars in disrepair, houses decaying on their foundations, liquor stores on too many corners, and young adults milling about, drinking beverages concealed in paper bags. A recent crime study revealed that four of ten crime hotspots in Sacramento were in this very neighborhood.

Looking even closer reveals a more nuanced picture—neatly manicured homes are more numerous than those in disrepair; children stroll casually with adults, chattering away in a range of languages; houses of worship, though less prevalent than liquor stores, offer a wide variety of fellowship activities for a similarly wide variety of congregations; and schools mark their presence with marquees announcing numerous events.

It is significant that LAS is located in this community that is character-ized as marginalized by all conventional measures. Much of the attendance area for LAS is unincorporated county land that the city ignores and the county neglects. LAS presents a counternarrative to the xenophobic backlash against immigrant families.[1] Its low-income, immigrant parents resist rather than resign themselves to the dominant ideologies that force their children to give up important parts of their heritage to be successful "Americans." LAS's existence in this Oak Park neighborhood gives testimony to the commitments that this community has to the education of its children and to the partnership among families, teachers, and university faculty members that makes these commitments a reality.

The school's history illustrates both the community commitment to education and the strength of the partnership. Though LAS is only three years old, its Spanish/English dual immersion program had existed at Fruitridge Elementary School for 12 years prior. LAS now occupies a set of portable buildings on the north side of the campus. The genesis of the dual immersion program can be found in the dream of one bilingual teacher, who in 1991 wanted to provide a quality bilingual program to Spanish-speaking pupils in the school, about one-third of the student body at that time. Joined by two additional bilingual colleagues, and with the support of the principal and BMED faculty members, the program developed into a reality. Although the district provided little in the way of material, professional, or moral support, the teachers persevered and, now a team of six, conducted research into models that would be most appropriate. After examining programs in California, Arizona, New Mexico, and Texas, the team concluded that a 90/10 two-way immersion model would offer pupils the richest education. This model promotes the minority language as much as possible among both language groups on the assumption that this is the language that needs the most support; 90/10 refers to the amount of time spent in each language. Kindergarten and 1st grade use 90% Spanish instruction with more English instruction added at each grade level. In 5th grade and each subsequent grade, the day is balanced with 50% instruction in each language.

Two-way programs include a balance of language majority and language minority pupils in the classroom while incorporating instructional strategies that promote cross-cultural cooperation and learning. Two-way immersion programs share the following goals: attainment of challenging, age-appropriate academic skills and knowledge; advanced levels of functional proficiency in English along with an additional language; and understanding and apprecia-tion of cross-cultural differences (Cloud, Genesee, & Hamayan, 2000).

Having identified their preferred model, the teachers began to build a deeper sense of community with pupils' families. Monthly parent meetings were held that fostered a family-like structure and resulted in an everlast-ing connection among families and teachers. These meetings provided opportunities to develop relationships with parents, to educate them about the principles of the program, to share details of classroom activities and projects, and to provide support across members for a range of challenges and issues. Moreover, these meetings also reinforced everyone's commitment to bilingualism, biliteracy, and biculturalism—a task constantly complicated by nativist campaigns to declare English the state's official language, accelerate pupils' English learning at the expense of their own native language, and otherwise denigrate the heritage language of the families. Such strong and personal ties would later prove to be critically important.

The Charter

In the late 1990s, a series of events made the operation of the dual immersion program at Fruitridge Elementary increasingly complicated. The passage of California's Proposition 227 in June 1998[2] created one of the first critical battles for the program's survival, and the No Child Left Behind Act (NCLB) of 2001 added to an atmosphere hostile to native language instruction. High-stakes tests in English were the only ones deemed valid under NCLB; Spanish-language exams testing the same content knowledge were not acceptable for tracking pupil progress. Moreover, the Sacramento City Unified School District responded to NCLB and the state's own accountability and standards program by adopting highly scripted curricula and accelerated pacing schedules. Though these measures applied mostly to English-only programs, it was clear that the district had seized upon these tools as *the* way to improve test scores; what "worked" for native English speakers would surely be pushed onto bilingual programs if their pupils' test performances lagged. In fact, scripted curriculum did emerge as one critical issue in the program's fight to survive post-1998. In 2000, the publishers of *Open Court* debuted a Spanish-language curriculum, *Foro Abierto*. This, the district announced, would soon be *the* curriculum for Fruitridge's dual immersion program. Moreover, the district pressured the program to drastically modify its model to one using less Spanish and more English. The community's desire for its children to be biliterate and bilingual, and the teachers' ability to deliver a program designed to help pupils attain this, did not seem important. Accelerated proficiency in English and improved test scores in English were all that mattered.

These combined pressures and other looming challenges forced the teachers to consider options that years earlier would have been off-limits. New progressive charter schools spurred the interest of program teachers and parents, who began visiting nearby schools and looking into the possibility of chartering the program. In fall 2002, parents, teachers, and BMED faculty members organized to protect the program by creating an independent charter school. The community remained committed to its goals, and simply wanted to continue implementing its model without constant external distractions and unrelated mandates.

The typical teacher preparation program does not prepare teachers to create school plans, curriculum guidelines, three-year budgets, and legal compliance documents. Similarly, a mother who lovingly raises her children and competently manages her household does not necessarily have ready expertise needed to design a facilities plan or create a bell schedule. And finally, university professors have lots of ideas that work out neatly in theory, but they may be short on the skills needed to strategically budget Title I funds or design a prep schedule. Though these profiles do not fully represent the skill set of stakeholders who pursued the LAS charter, the fact was that meeting the procedural, curricular, and legal demands of the charter process, not to mention navigating the political landmines of pursuing an independent charter, forced the entire community—of families, teachers, and BMED faculty members—to upgrade their skills and knowledge, quickly and intensively.

This grassroots team researched pedagogical practices, charter law, and existing charter schools. Weekends and evenings were fully occupied as they banded together to pursue their educational dream. They interviewed bilingual program experts and carefully examined the results of different bilingual education models. They reviewed curriculum. They considered facilities plans. They learned about ADA and how school budgets are constructed. They educated themselves and each other about the school they hoped to create, and with each step (and sometimes also with missteps) they consolidated their commitment to their vision and each other.

A critical decision in this process related to the nature of the charter—dependent or independent. A dependent charter included the channeling of funds and kept the teachers within the bargaining unit, but also kept the charter under the district's purview. An independent charter would allow autonomy from the district and direct handling of funding, but would remove teachers from the teachers' association. The teachers also had qualms about divesting from an association that represented a source of power and solidarity, and wondered about the implications of an independent charter for the salary schedule. Ultimately, the team decided to pursue an independent charter. Though this created significant risks, the team was confident it could weather them successfully.

As the charter document went through the various stages of review and approval, this grassroots team was tested again and again. Misinformation, lack of information, and ever-changing parameters from the district were complications that produced frustration but also posed opportunities to strengthen the community's efforts. Expert negotiating by some of the members and hard work and attention to detail by others helped the team maneuver around roadblocks. After months of tireless effort, anguish, and strategizing, the team members were finally ready to submit their charter application. Families and the community came out en masse, each person wearing a blue T-shirt with the LAS logo on it, to testify at a series of school board meetings. In fact, buses were chartered to transport families to these meetings. BMED professors, bilingual and monolingual, and other community experts lined up for their three minutes of public comment time. In February 2004, the school board unanimously approved the charter. Though the victory celebration was sweet, it was brief—school would open in six short months and there was work to do. In July, the State Board of Education granted the Language Academy of Sacramento charter #6, making it an official independent charter school. In August 2004, LAS opened to 241 pupils in grades K–6.

This victory was the result of an organized, disciplined, and hard-working grassroots group that was energized by each other and by a clear educational and political vision of how schooling could be for the children in Oak Park. Though the most significant outcome of this effort was the opening of LAS, other important objectives were also reached: members of an inner-city community stood up against the power structure in favor of a progressive educational vision that included language rights for their children. All stakeholders gained immeasurable new knowledge and skills that have since proved critical in the operation of the school. And a unified group of people from various sectors (school, community, university) successfully forged and achieved a common goal.

The Community Study Group

As anyone who has participated in this kind of mobilization effort knows, there is a difference in the specific skills required when advocating for a project versus those required for actually putting that project into action. Translating a vision or a set of objectives into day-to-day practices taps different kinds of knowledge and competencies. As the LAS staff began to organize its curriculum and get used to being self-directing rather than responding to top-down mandates, it was imperative that processes and structures be developed to enable the full implementation of LAS's academic vision. The partnership with the university proved especially helpful. Several BMED faculty members served in various support capacities, and two served on the Governing Board of Directors. Two additional faculty members acted as consultants and assisted with professional development for curriculum development, assessment, and English language development. These working relationships laid a foundation for a larger curriculum development project, the Community Study, that was initiated in fall 2005 and continues to this day. It represents our joint efforts to put the charter vision of community-based education into practice.

The Community Study Group (CSG) consisted of four LAS teachers, two BMED faculty members, and five to seven candidates, depending on the semester. The CSG was a fairly diverse group, ethnically and in terms of community association (some CSG members lived in the LAS community, others did not). The CSG hoped to implement Freirean-based educational practices, and drew some of their ideas from Workers' Party educational reforms in Brazil (Freire, 1993; O'Cadiz, Wong, & Torres, 1998). Key in this effort was the commitment of the CSG to better understand the community and the issues that it faced by surfacing and carefully analyzing the "talk" of the community and what its own members identified as important community issues. In designing its project, the CSG strove to work in concert *with* community members, as opposed to *on* them. Ultimately, the CSG hoped that its efforts would both identify key issues that could be used to organize teaching and learning at the school and strengthen the relationship between the school and the community.

After some research, we elected to use a set of tools that we adapted from the Catholic Relief Services' Participatory Research Appraisal (PRA)/Rapid Research Appraisal (RRA). These tools were created for international relief workers and were designed to structure relief work in a participatory framework to address genuine community needs and result in a gradual transfer of responsibility from the relief workers to the community members. The design principles of the PRA/RRA are congruent with the social justice missions of both LAS and BMED, in that the PRA/RRA is based on "respect for human dignity—affirming the right of people to participate in all decisions that affect her or his life and the life of the community," and "subsidiary—outside interventions are necessary when (and only when) the demands of the common good cannot be met at the lowest level" (Freudenberger, 1999, p. 17). Given our shared goals of education for social justice, creating a rigorous academic curriculum designed to understand and address community issues, and forging closer school-community relationships, the PRA/RRA presented a compelling mechanism for forwarding our mutual agenda.

In spring 2005, the CSG began its work in earnest. We identified the following five focus areas for study about the local community: education, economy, family and social structures, geography, and history. After identifying the focus areas for study, the team then selected several tools deemed appropriate for collecting information on these focus areas. The first tool we used was participatory mapping. Much like Paulo Freire's notion of "codification" (Freire, 1973), the participatory mapping process asked community members to create a visual image of significant instances and places in their daily lives. Our intent was an open-ended process that would shed light on local definitions of "community." We sent home notices with the pupils asking for community members to come after school to participate in the mapping activity. We asked a group of English-speaking and one of Spanish-speaking community members to create maps of the community, using large whiteboards and dry erase pens; they were to include whatever they felt was part of the community. CSG members observed and took notes. Afterwards, CSG members asked such open-ended questions as: What are your favorite places? Least favorite places? What services are missing from the community? If you could change anything about X, how would you change it? What additional services would you like? We also asked them to mark zones that were considered unsafe.

This process was extraordinarily revealing. The Spanish-speaking "mappers," which included both men and women, deliberated for about one minute then dove right in to drawing their map. At first, a man drew; then a woman completed the map. People talked simultaneously, each adding a new store, restaurant, or service. Often, there would be a pause in the conversation, then one person would suggest, "what about ——?" and the others would approve, "Oh yes!" Their view was from the perspective of a walker. Their map was full of all kinds of details. But what was most compelling was the wealth of resources that "their community" had. They appreciated how accessible everything was—from banks, to health centers, to grocery stores. They felt that the crisscross of bus routes and the closeness of freeway on-ramps was a plus. They lamented some of the crime and security issues, adding that not only was police response to their calls inadequate, but that officers often imperiled their streets as they raced through their neighborhoods to address other calls. They wanted a movie theater in the neighborhood, but, other than that, felt they had all they needed. They put LAS at the center of their map.

The English-speaking "mappers" took an altogether different approach. This smaller, racially mixed group of men and women likely had more formal education than the Spanish-speaking group, and more of its members were professionals rather than laborers, something more common in the Spanish-speaking group. Nine minutes into the process, they were still deliberating on how to organize the map and not a single mark had yet been made. Ultimately, they drew a very orderly map. The community was bounded by certain streets, buildings, and parks; side streets were placed in proper scale. In fact, scale was actually part of the initial conversation, and the map's perspective appeared to be based on driving, not walking. They identified far fewer commercial and other services within the community, locating these instead outside the community and in more upscale venues (the local malls, e.g.). However, they did identify almost every school in the neighborhood, including alternative schools. Like the Spanish-speaking group, this group also commented on crime and they concurred with the idea that more cultural outlets—movie theaters, performance venues—would enhance community resources.

While we cannot say with certainty what made these group dynamics so distinct, a few possibilities have surfaced. The Spanish-speaking group members more likely knew each other and had contact with each other prior to the meeting. They were, in many ways, a more homogeneous group than the English-speaking group. The English-speaking group tended to have deeper roots in the community; though many of the Spanish speakers had lived in the neighborhood for eight years or more, most of the English-speaking group members were the second generation in their family to be in this neighborhood. Thus, they had significant memories of the area during a more prosperous past; they were more likely to lament the neighborhood's decline because they had known it during safer and more stable times. Reference points probably also made a difference for the Spanish-speaking group, which might have compared the relative accessibility of a wide range of retail and services to the inaccessibility of such things in their hometowns in Mexico.

Whatever the root causes of these differences, the manner in which the mapping activity played out left a strong impression with the CSG members. Moreover, the Spanish-speaking group's portrayal of the neighborhood as one that was crammed full of places to go and things to do shed light on some of the CSG members' own deficit views about the community. For some of us, the Spanish-speaking mappers described a neighborhood that we could barely reconcile with our own impressions. It forced serious reflection and we were encouraged to look at the neighborhood with eyes that were informed by community members' perspectives.

The community map was the first step in uncovering community issues, building working relationships with community members, and helping us identify neighborhood locations that played central roles (a place for paying bills, a place for looking for jobs). This informed our construction of a survey that queried respondents about social structures and organizational ties, and that was sent home to the families of pupils in CSG team members' classrooms. The survey results suggested that few family members belonged to any type of formal organization, other than church. This forced us to reflect on the assumptions built into the survey from our unwitting, educated, and middle-class values and biases. We also wondered if our relationships with the community were still tentative enough that people were reluctant to share private information. With the survey results yielding less information than we hoped, we decided to conduct semistructured interviews to elicit additional information about the community and prevalent issues.

Semistructured Interviews

We conducted three waves of semistructured interviews. The first wave focused on residents of the community who had lived there for 25 years or more so as to gather some of the history of the community and better contextualize more current information. Interview questions included: What changes have you seen in the community over time? Why do you think those changes have happened? What do you see as the strengths of the community? This first wave of interviews generated compelling information. Many respondents spoke sentimentally of the beauty that they remembered in the neighborhood of their childhood. The sense of community and unity stuck out in their minds. Similarly, others shared recollections of block parties and taking their children trick-or-treating. And it always filled team members with awe to imagine the older person before them as a young, fresh-faced 2nd or 3rd grader sitting in one of the classrooms of our school, knowing that while so much had changed in the community, the school, its structures, and many of its physical features still remained relatively constant.

We also reflected on the respondents' commonsense explanations for why the neighborhood had changed, particularly in relation to what caused its decline into a high poverty and high crime area. These older residents, most of whom owned their homes, suggested that the renters were the source of such problems as crime and lack of interest in the community. Although this is an area mostly of small single-family homes—there are neither large rental complexes nor public housing units—there is indeed a significant problem with absentee landlords and slumlords who are unresponsive to the needs of their tenants and negligent in maintaining their rental properties. This is evidenced as well by the number of boarded-up houses in the area.

We were intrigued by the singling out of the "renters" by the older residents. While it was somewhat tricky to identify "renters" to interview, we did so with the help of family members active at the school and the pupils themselves who lived in rental housing. They, like the older residents, also observed an increase in crime, streets littered with garbage, and a lack of cohesiveness among neighbors. In fact, the renters claimed that the garbage was being dumped by people outside of the community.

Our third wave of interviews included residents who were representative of the ethnic, racial, and cultural diversity in the community. Our first and second wave of interviews was done mostly with Latino residents. Thus, the CSG decided to conduct a third wave of semistructured interviews, focusing deliberately on African American and Asian residents. Yet again, these respondents mentioned lack of cleanliness on the streets and crime as major issues.

Focus Group

At the point of concluding our three waves of interviews, we had amassed impressive amounts of information about the community. We transcribed much of this onto charts to display information about some of our initial categories (social structures, economy, etc.). We called a meeting of the original community mappers and, with them, analyzed the information. Our objective was to identify community strengths, challenges, and hopes and dreams and to prioritize these into focal points for curriculum development. This was an exciting point in our process and we all approached this meeting with a good deal of anticipation. As we reviewed the charts, we recalled the various voices that had spoken to us.

For example, all three waves of interviewees agreed that the ethnic diversity and variety of cultures were strengths. They also felt that the new schools in the community were a strength. The older residents and the renters expressed a sense of unity among their neighbors, though for the older residents, this existed "despite the many new renters." The African American and Asian American residents valued the size of residential plots (larger than average because of county land use regulations). Hearing from community members themselves about what was special and important to them about their community was a valuable process for the CSG members. It was encouraging and refreshing to note that many community members viewed their diversity as a strength. This was certainly something that the teachers could capitalize on in developing their curriculum. It gave validation to the teacher educators on the CSG who taught courses on multicultural education to their candidates. The sense of unity was a strong foundation from which future efforts could build; in the midst of tremendous diversity, people felt connected to one another.

Though encouraged by these strengths, the list of challenges identified by community members was daunting. All interviewees lamented the neighborhood's deterioration. They named crime, slow police response to crime, illegal dumping, and traffic as increasing problems. They also felt that low-flying police helicopters and high-speed squad cars—which often traversed the neighborhood en route to other locations—had an adverse impact on their quality of life. Wave I (the elders) and Wave II (the renters) interviewees voiced particular concern about the illegal activities and associated dangers in the parks. Wave II felt that the influx of African American and Asian American gangs was a challenge. These various issues are apparent to anyone who spends time in the community and all impact LAS pupils and teachers. It was not clear to us exactly how to build a standards-based curriculum around these issues.

The many hopes and dreams that interview participants eloquently articulated provided a direction. All three waves wanted more opportunities for youth to be successful. Wave I wanted neighborhood meetings or work-shops to address parenting issues, how to be a neighbor, and how to address foul language. Wave II wanted training for people coming out of jail and workshops to bring Child Protective Services and parents together. Wave III wished for a recreation center. All three waves thought a movie theater would enhance the community.

When we began the CSG, we had unformed ideas about where it might take us, though we knew that we wanted a school curriculum that enabled pupils to delve deeply into building a skill and knowledge base to understand and address community issues. We also wanted all aspects of the process to include community participants and to be driven by their interests and concerns. We reviewed what we had collected and learned with some participants of the mapping activity, and then used a priority-setting process to identify the most pressing and important issues for our first round of curriculum development. These included the explicit teaching of advocacy steps, historical studies of the surrounding neighborhood, and also having LAS pupils engage in the CSG process themselves (i.e., identify strengths and obstacles, identify an issue, and choose a project to address it).

As we concluded this portion of the Community Study, several teachers shared the powerful insights they gained. Mario Martín explained:

> After the study, I have a better anthropological, structural, and historical understanding of the community. The people in the com-munity allowed me to gain a deeper insight into the deep corners and crevices of the neighborhood. Some of the older residents shared historical information I was not aware of while other interviewees also shared a glimpse of their daily lives. Structurally, I learned that the rules and regulations, as well as the penalties, are vague due to the ever-confusing county and city lines, and this results in complaints and increased levels of distrust regarding the enforcement of the law. Inconsistencies within the different levels of government have allowed for this neighborhood of African, Asian, and Latino-American people in the United States of America to be neglected.

Another CSG member, Pam Phelps, recounted similar insights:

> This community study not only focused on the disconnect between the school people and the community, but brought to light a discon-nect between the school's community and the community at large [Sacramento]. I learned of the rich community structure that once existed and was supported by Sacramento social service groups. Now, it is an often ignored neighborhood within the county. This awareness

has not only connected me to the challenges facing my pupils, but inspired me to support my pupils in becoming change agents.

Community members also gained deep insights. CSG parent members Rosalba Medina and Rafaela Martínez appreciated the substantive connections between teachers and parents that the process enabled, going beyond the pro forma discussions of pupils' academic progress into the daily routines, struggles, and successes that the different parties experienced. Mrs. Martinez asserted, "*no podemos ignorar los sentimientos plasmados en letras*/we can no longer ignore the feelings because they have been written in black and white." And Mrs. Medina added, "The study gave teachers ideas that can be applied immediately. Maybe they will not solve the problem, but the seed has been planted." The parents also learned more about the community, and about their neighbors. CSG gatherings allowed for interaction among African American and Latino families beyond what was typical, so families discovered common experiences, values, hopes, and dreams that gave reality to what Mrs. Martínez called "waking the spirit of the community."

Though parents were always welcomed to help with reading and math, the elevation of community issues to the level of the daily curriculum heightened the status of the parents as experts on their own lived experiences in this community. With teachers now understanding their pupils' lives more intimately, more opportunities also emerge for them to better support the pupils' learning. Ultimately, the community members saw these deepened relationships—among people and between the community and classroom inquiry and knowledge—as promising greater unity and power, which gave them a sense of hope that positive changes could be made in the community.

Third grade teacher Cynthia Suarez concurs:

Being part of this study has been a very humbling experience for me. Because I live in the same neighborhood and share a background similar to many of our community members, I had made assumptions about what our community was like. I wrongly assumed that the community members viewed themselves as lacking resources and felt isolated. Although this is certainly a part of their experience, they are also a community full of hopes and dreams for themselves, their families, their children and their school. As a teacher, it is important for me to learn what these hopes and dreams are in order to better serve our children. I see the community study as an ongoing process in which parents, teachers and students have a forum to communicate with each other and work to improve our neighborhood community in general, and our school community in particular.

As with other Network PDS projects, the community study project was a path made by walking (Horton & Freire, 1990). Having identified key concerns, the teachers then took on the task of making instructional changes at LAS. While different content areas would lend themselves to studying the history, contemporary forms, and ramifications of various community issues, an overarching pedagogical frame was also needed to orient teachers' work. Ultimately, the teachers selected a systematic approach to developing pupils' advocacy skills, with the confidence that this process would add rigor to their academic program while simultaneously energizing pupils to become advocates for their community.

As the CSG teachers developed their curriculum around community issues and advocacy skills, they focused on several key elements. Each CSG classroom explicitly teaches advocacy steps, including: identify the problem, obtain information, consider other perspectives, speak with others, make a plan, and take action. In addition, teachers threaded a wide range of social science tools in their instruction of how to operationalize the advocacy steps: tracing community histories through archival artifacts; using historical photos to document important community events; conducting oral history interviews; and writing field notes.[3]

Examples of this new instructional focus and innovative curriculum development can be seen at all grade levels. As Cynthia Suarez recounts:

> With younger students it can be difficult to try to incorporate such abstract ideas as advocacy into the daily curriculum. The CSG decided it would be important for our younger students to at least be introduced to the concept of effective advocacy, as this would be a fundamental tool in the process of affecting change in one's community. We started small by introducing several of the advocacy steps into an ongoing language arts and science unit on the tropical rainforest. The students were already excited about ecology and the conservation of the world's environments and were very knowledgeable about the rainforest. They had read many books in which characters advocated for conservation and for a cleaner, better world. After reading these stories, students were asked to create a short dialogue in which a chosen character would use the steps of the advocacy process to address the character that was causing the damage to their environment. Students role-played their dialogues with each other and, after debriefing, it was clear to me that many of them had a general idea of what it entails to advocate for one's beliefs. One of our students wrote: "Hello, my name is Omar. There is a big problem in the Lacandona rainforest. This is what is happening: they are cutting the trees to make money. Because

they are cutting the trees there's going to be deforestation. You can help me by writing a letter to the president." It is our hope, in keeping with our charter mission, that our students will gain a better understanding of effective advocacy in years to come as they gain a deeper understanding of what it means to become a socially conscious community member.

Eduardo de León, middle school teacher, describes his pupils' work:

In the first year, 6th and 7th grade students generated their own community mapping activity. Areas of concern included unlit parks and parking lots, trash, drug dealers, and the need for more security. One group of students wrote, "Clear the area and make it neighbor-friendly." 7th grade students also researched and presented written reports on community services available to combat areas that they identified as problems.

During the present year, social studies classes are forums where advocacy is addressed. Whether the focus is ancient culture, medieval times, or U.S. history, pupils are able to analyze how advocacy steps influenced changes, or, in cases where these steps are not evidenced, pupils can analyze how they might have changed history. Relating these historical events to present-day examples of advocacy will not only bring more clarity to the work that they are doing, but it will also provide a historical context from which to base their analysis.

Speech and debate pupils are participating in two projects: (1) a transect walk of the community and (2) selecting community interest projects to research, speak, and debate about. For example, one pupil is investigating illegal dumping in the area while another is looking at crime statistics. Pupils will then have significant information that can be presented to other LAS grade levels, or in community forums such as the LAS Parent Association or County of Sacramento Board of Supervisors meetings.

It is in keeping with the CSG goals and the LAS mission that pupils learn how to become participating members of their communities. Building knowledge related to this process and providing opportunities in local and state government settings is a goal of the CSG, and one that enhances the outcomes delineated for LAS pupils. Mr. de León reflects:

Students are now identifying problems that *they* see in the community, researching resources that *they* find in the neighboring areas, and planning to share *their* findings with the local community. The sense of empowerment that such an authentic research project brings to the lives of our students is truly a work inspired by the community members that expressed to the CSG the strengths, challenges, hopes and dreams that *they* have developed as members of a rich community.

Finally, the CSG has helped to align and operationalize concepts and ideas that are pivotal and emblematic in the LAS charter. For example, the LAS charter petition makes numerous mentions of community involvement, including references to service learning focused on the school's attendance area, yet, until the CSG, there had not been a community-based mechanism for making such references a concrete reality. Similarly, prior to engaging in the CSG, the LAS professional development plan focused largely on standards alignment, assessments, and instructional strategies, but seemed potentially at cross purposes with other charter elements that promised authentic community participation in key aspects of school operations. Though all LAS staff wanted as many aspects of school operations as possible to be tightly linked with the community, it was not until the implementation of the CSG that a viable tool for making such linkages was identified. These linkages are also emerging in the realms of governance and budgeting. Knowing what we now know about the community's challenges and its hopes and dreams, such information can be incorporated into the overall framework of choices and priorities set by the school.

The experience of BMED faculty members in the CSG has been especially fruitful. Both faculty members have taken insights and tasks from the CSG and incorporated them into courses in our PDS teacher preparation program. For example, the interactive tools from the RRA/PRA have been modified for use in both a literacy methods course and a multicultural foundations course. Moreover, our experience with the CSG provides concrete examples that we share with our candidates, who often wonder about how exactly the compelling ideas of multicultural education for social justice can actually be put into place in the classroom. Beyond student teaching experiences at LAS, candidates benefit from step-by-step descriptions—provided by faculty members and LAS teachers—of the CSG: listening to the "talk" of the community, uncovering one's own assumptions, using new insights to look afresh at the community, and finally building curriculum around important community issues.

We are too early in our work with the CSG and the construction of a community-based, social justice curriculum to discuss outcomes or results. However, this much we are sure about: we have developed a rigorous curriculum for LAS pupils that not only helps us to see how we can better enhance their lives, but supports them as they develop the knowledge and skills needed to improve their own lives and those of others in their community.

Notes

1. This backlash reached its zenith with the passage of California Proposition 227 in 1998.

2. Proposition 227 effectively outlawed native language instruction in California by only allowing families to "waive" their students into a bilingual program, if available.

3. In this instance, a budding new partnership with the urban geography and public history programs at Sacramento State have introduced all CSG members to engaging new tools that make this work more authentic and exciting for teachers and students alike.

Section Two

The Power of Connections

Re-creating Teacher and Teacher Educator Roles

Pia Lindquist Wong and Ronald David Glass

Brief Background

There are some key features of our teacher preparation program that are worth noting as we delve into our description and analysis of the ways in which the PDS model connected urban teachers more meaningfully to several realms of teacher education and development. First, as mentioned earlier, most credential programs in California (including those discussed here) are 5th-year post-baccalaureate programs. Second, in our college, three departments offer a basic elementary credential and two offer a basic secondary credential. Third, two of the main credentialing departments cohort candidates into teacher preparation "Centers." (The third department is Special Education, which offers a combined elementary and special education credential to a relatively small number of candidates who are not cohorted.)

Center Coordinators manage the cohort(s) of candidates and perform such tasks as finding adequate field placements, facilitating articulation among faculty (who typically have regular assignments to particular Centers), communicating policies and procedures to cooperating teachers (CTs), university supervisors, and faculty liaisons (described below), and keeping track of myriad assessments related to candidate progress through the program. Each of the Centers has evolved an identity and philosophy over time. Although all candidates in the same department take the same courses, the sequencing is different depending on the Center that the candidate is in, and the structure of Centers also varies. Some Centers use the familiar model where candidates are placed in CT classrooms and supervised by university supervisors. Other Centers use a model in which candidates are placed with CTs who are the primary mentor and evaluator; these CTs receive training and support for their work from faculty liaisons.

Until the PDS work was initiated, Center Coordinators (especially in the Teacher Education Department) were typically nontenure track faculty. This was not a position that was widely desired by tenured/tenure-track faculty (rightly or wrongly). Moreover, supervision was also typically done by nontenure track faculty, many of whom as part-time or retired teachers brought a wealth of skill and expertise to the job but, by the very nature of their part-time status, were not fully integrated into department or program functions. Clearly, many of the critiques of teacher education programs (Goodlad, 1994; Murrell, 2001; Sarason, 1993) were relevant to our program, as detailed further in the chapters in this section.

Rethinking Teacher and Teacher Educator Roles

Though we know "two heads together are better than one," the prosaic narrative of educational change still too often depends on the heroic and often charismatic efforts of a single and singular leader. When this is not the narrative line, we often find an ironic reversal in which change is seen as dependent almost not at all on particular people but rather as based in strategic technical solutions to educational problems (Simmons, 2006). The Equity Network does not subscribe to either narrative, but rather has discovered that both people and structures must be understood as embedded in wider contexts and systems that shape their behavior and their possibilities.

While charismatic heroic leaders exist, they are rare and the longitudinal effects of their efforts often fade once the leader has moved on to new projects. Even though we rejected the myth that putting resources into finding the *right* person is a more effective strategy than building professional capacity across the multiple actors in a school community, we also learned that leadership does count and that PDS structures can be vulnerable to changes in leadership not only at the school but in larger affiliated structures such as the district or university. We discovered that we had to think both in terms of establishing leadership skills across the Network, and in terms of solidifying structures and relationships that enable multiple actors to perform their own roles to full capacity and provide coordinated leadership. This section will tell the stories of change that took place when the connections between people and places, between people and institutional structures, and between people and people were brought into the foreground in order to support the transformation of professional roles in teacher education. These transformations enabled all of the key people in schools to better realize the Network aims of a more meaningful education for the pupils, more authentic modes of instruction and pupil assessment for teachers, a more grounded preparation for candidates, and a more engaged practice for university faculty members.

Traditional Thinking about Leadership

Research on leadership in schools has only recently broadened its sights beyond the notion of *the* "educational leader" (Bridges, 1982) and has become more critical of education's wholesale adoption of industrial modes of management organization. Despite the inherently decentralized practice of decision-making in schools, where teachers necessarily make hundreds of independent professional decisions each day and have always recognized a professional "accountability" for pupils' learning, local school systems operate in largely centralized ways. These hierarchical and bureaucratic organizational forms seek only limited, if any, participation from stakeholders, consolidating most decisions and policy actions in the authority of purported "leaders" at higher levels of the organizational structure. Moreover, many of the decisions that would be best and most efficiently made by local actors (i.e., classroom teachers making decisions about how to teach content to their particular mix of pupils) were typically determined at the district level or even higher, and those of less importance to local actors (e.g., school uniforms, or how to spend small amounts of money to supplement the curriculum) were decentralized to local sites.

This undemocratic tradition of school governance, policymaking, and program development and implementation has widened the gap between those who make educational policy and those who enact it, and it has not served LI/RCLD pupils well. Moreover, despite few structures that allow practitioners to provide comprehensive or regular inputs, policymakers do not feel limited by this lack of participation from those actually implementing the policies. Rather, they presumptively enact policies that reach into practices throughout the system and across a wide range of issues, mandating specific instructional strategies and curricular content, identifying particular limited aspects of pupil learning to be assessed, and selecting topics for teachers' professional development. Not surprisingly, the values and outcomes associated with the policy development process often favor the needs of the bureaucracy and powerful political interests outside the schools, rather than the needs and interests of other key actors, especially pupils, parents, and teachers. The bureaucratic need for control, efficiency, and adherence to often unrealistic timelines (not to mention the accrual of political capital for elected officials) appears to wield more influence on policy development than field-based perspectives, university research, or community/stakeholder input.

Finally, hierarchical organizational forms make teachers marginal participants in the ongoing political debates about how teaching and learning should be organized and what its outcomes should be, despite the fact that they are most actively involved in professional practice and innovation.

These organizational tendencies are ideologically predictable given the history of schooling, the demographics of the teaching profession, and the sociopolitical context of LI/RCLD communities. In the nineteenth century, several generations of influential men reconstructed public schooling into the "one best system" that depended on undemocratic and hierarchical organizational models borrowed from the industrial revolution, the army, and the railroads (Tyack, 1974). Mirroring gendered structures in other sectors, women were the workers (teachers) and men were the managers (principals) (Tyack & Hansot, 1982). While fewer people would agree with the naturalistic explanations of this gender order for schooling, we all have inherited its effects and its continuing prevalence. Nationally, women comprise 84% of the total K–12 teaching force, and are even more concentrated in elementary schools. Nevertheless, women comprise only 44% of school administrators (www. nces.ed.gov). In urban districts, only 23% of superintendents are women and 39% of school board members nationwide are women. We continue to find a similar imbalance in the racial composition of school leadership: 56% of urban school superintendents, 84% of school administrators, and 85% of the school board members nationwide are white (Hess, 2002). Thus, the construction of school leadership concentrates power in the hands of those who already hold ideologically inflected social, economic, and political power. Not surprisingly, efforts to reshape the organizational form of school leadership to make it more collaborative and democratic have not been broadly successful.

In the early 1980s, various strategies to redefine school organizational forms and leadership structures through innovations such as site-based management (also a corporate implant) and comprehensive school reform projects emerged. These strategies sought to engage and empower key stakeholders more effectively and to create educational organizations that were more responsive to pupil needs and community involvement (see such projects as the Accelerated Schools Project and the Comer School Development Project). Research revealed that these less hierarchical forms of leadership distributed expertise and decision-making authority across multiple actors, who exercised leadership in their particular locus of work (Camburn, Rowan, & Taylor, 2003; Spillane, 2003). However, these changes were more often achieved at the individual school level rather than at the system level. Moreover, these new leadership forms often remained stymied by the unequal social relations that seep from the larger social context into schools (Carnoy & Levin, 1985) and by the persistent hierarchical structure of policymaking and separation of policymakers from practitioners. In addition, these attempts at democratizing school reform were cut short by new emphases in the 1990s and onward on test-based accountability systems. Ranking, efficiency, control, and timeliness once again trumped participation, inclusion, and equity.

New Thinking About Systems

As the Equity Network members struggled to implement a more collaborative, democratic, and decentralized decision-making and leadership structure in its PDSs, we discovered that the historically sedimented organizational forms within and between K–12 schools, school districts, colleges of education, and universities presented serious obstacles to realizing the Network's vision. Our preparation as educational researchers, schoolteachers and administrators, and teacher educators provided little insight into how to approach these obstacles, and little guidance about how to establish these new structures within the body of the old institutions. Nonetheless, we were committed to the goals and believed that an honest and open approach to experimentation could uncover pathways toward them as we made our way, even if we couldn't clearly see the way forward at the outset. We soon learned to think outside the box of our particular organizational form and institutional structure and to reimagine our work in relationship to the interconnected systems in which it was embedded.

The Equity Network had to develop flexible, resilient, strong, and dynamic connections across many boundaries to link institutions and groups (or even subgroups) that previously had tenuous, random, or no interactions at all. To make these new connections, all the partners in the Network had to stretch their prior self-understanding as professionals and acquire new knowledge, skills, and dispositions. At the same time, our organizations had to adapt to the new demands of our professional activities so that they could be undertaken responsibly and with appropriate accountability. Since we could not fully articulate what these emergent connections and leadership forms would look like, nor could we fully predict how they should best be assessed, we had to launch ourselves into the transformation effort with more enthusiasm and goodwill than assurance. Our early efforts were tentative, but gained strength as we found out what was needed from the institutional partners and our colleagues. As researchers have demonstrated, there is an inherent unpredictability in systemic transformation efforts (Fullan, 1993) and the multiple layers of action and meaning require that mechanisms be established to facilitate communication and provide flexibility as the necessary organizational frameworks emerge from practice. Only as the broad outline of the Network's structure began to come into view could we look more critically to theory to help us enhance its durability and effectiveness.

Open systems such as schools, universities, and communities present a number of difficult challenges to any practical effort to reconstruct their leadership dynamics and organizational modalities. They also present a challenge to any effort to theorize the systems themselves since their boundaries resist clear demarcation, their often multiple (and even conflicting) purposes defy standard definition, and their interactions (among the component parts, between the component parts and the whole, and with other systems) cannot always be specified or measured (Bailey, 1994). Even within the framework of one set of relatively straightforward features of systems—their inputs, throughputs, outputs, and purposes (Hansen, 1994)—we can see that the Equity Network approach to organizing PDS work radically shifted and expanded the meaning of these features. As a result, the schools and universities experienced fundamental changes and their already open systems encompassed even more connections. These shifts and expansions exposed important tensions and contradictions in our work in the K–16 sector, and forced us to adopt more strategic approaches to systems change that built on local success and the insights achieved through the critical praxis of bringing the PDSs into existence.

The typical way that the inputs, throughputs, and outputs of schools are regarded by policymakers and administrators in this era of standards and testing reduces the reality of the highly complex and contextualized processes of the educational system to the management, instruction, and assessment of the children in order to "produce" competent pupils or learners as defined by test scores (euphemistically known as "achievement"). Prior to establishing the Equity Network, a teacher in the PDS schools typically viewed these system elements as transactions involving only herself, her pupils, her instructional materials, and, sometimes, the pupils' parents, with occasional reference to other colleagues and site administrators. A university faculty member in the college of education typically only paid attention to the preparation of teachers—a kind of "pre-input" stage—but thought fleetingly about the rest of the stages. For example, the teachers, pupils, and administrators in schools, as well as their associated parents and communities, may have barely been considered as system elements in the preparation of teachers. Thus, a central challenge for the Equity Network was to enable the key actors to take on the view of the others involved in the system (and connected systems). An additional challenge for all PDS actors was to embrace parents and communities as important actors in the system. And, finally, we all worked to understand the impacts of other, often remote, systems on our own immediate system (such as the systems that produce scripted curriculum materials and standardized tests, or the systems that establish standards for the teaching profession).

To achieve these deep and broad connections, the Equity Network induced changes in the purposes of the systems that it brought into relationship through the PDSs. K–12 teachers and administrators came to see the preparation of new teachers and deeper connections to parents and the community as among their purposes and as critical to the success of their instruction and the achievement of their pupils. On the university side of this new relationship, teacher educators came to see that the daily cycle of teaching and learning in K–12 classrooms and the social and cultural realities of pupils' lives outside of school had to be deeply integrated into their university courses. The purpose of their university teaching began to encompass improvements in schools and LI/RCLD communities. Furthermore, the PDSs changed the way that subsystems within the university related, fostering substantive collaborations between teacher educators and subject matter faculty in the arts and sciences, and leading the promotion and tenure committees at both college and campus levels to see the critical value that collaborative work with schools, community colleges, and communities added to the university.

The implementation and coordination of all these changes in the systems, spurred by the Equity Network PDSs, were rarely smooth, but when the connections became reliable and stable without losing their flexibility and responsiveness to emergent situations, all of the collaborating institutions were strengthened. Sometimes, simply navigating the offset academic calendars of schools, districts, and the university was a noteworthy achievement if this could be done without some flare-up of anger or mistrust. We discovered that merely identifying and naming key interacting cycles within the systems helped to establish more trust among the actors in the PDS since they could reinterpret what had previously felt like personal problems as the structural binds they actually were. Better and more comprehensive understanding of these complex systems resulted in some measure of predictability and routine, both strengthening the patterns that facilitated effective work and mitigating patterns that made the collaborative work problematic. By bringing separate institutional cycles into closer alignment, we were each in a position to effect greater gains in relation to our primary goal of helping improve learning for LI/RCLD pupils. Even though this alignment required sacrifices on the part of all PDS actors, ultimately benefits to pupils, enhancements for candidates, and the recognition of these innovations from non-PDS faculty mitigated these sacrifices.

It was not easy to find a balance in the dynamic and sometimes chaotic processes of creating the new institutional structure for PDSs at twelve sites in five districts coupled with the collaborating university, teachers associations, and community groups. It could seem at times as if the PDSs would fly apart from the effort to connect with and bring into harmony all of the competing demands of the associated systems and people within them. There were even moments of longing for the old static patterns of organizing our work, which memory had converted to the comfort of familiar routines that seemed to offer relief from the stresses of building a new way of working. As we tried to understand the needs and perspectives of our Network partners, we were challenged to give up old assumptions about who they were and how their institutions operated. Similarly, we were forced to develop new modes of communication that could convey our views and open channels to hear more voices. Over time, we achieved a kind of dynamic equilibrium with reliable structures that enabled our multiple institutions to be attuned to each other. What kept things from either imploding or exploding at any given time was the solid commitment of the K–12 teachers and administrators, university faculty members, and other Network members to the overarching purpose of our work, to improve teaching and learning in LI/RCLD communities. This aim was deeply felt as both a moral and political commitment, and it was the bond that made all the new connections hold together through all the stresses and strains of establishing the PDSs.

Rethinking Leadership and the Systems that Structure the Learning of LI/RCLD Pupils and their Teachers

The Equity Network has sought to interrupt top-down forms of educational leadership and the lack of coherence in the K–16 system through the introduction of opportunities to reach consensus on a range of important issues so that our independent actions can be more synergistic. We also have created new governance practices where power, knowledge, and leadership are distributed more democratically and broadly. Our experience highlights urban schools as increasingly complex organizations that contain layers of relationships negotiated across institutional boundaries, between institutions and communities, all within multiple diversities: economic, ethnic, social, religious, linguistic, and cultural. Tensions between the interests and demands of the dominant culture and the interests and needs of the communities of color and low-income families, palpable in urban schools, exacerbate the inherent disconnect between policymakers and policy implementers (e.g., teachers). Tensions across organizations within the educational sector stymie genuine collaboration in the service of common and basic goals. These disconnections can have grave consequences for LI/RCLD pupils. Thus, in order for urban schools to address the challenge of providing high-quality education to all of their pupils, they must develop heightened capacity to work effectively and collaboratively across institutions on key teaching and learning issues. This requires a level of organizational efficiency and coordination that can only exist if expertise, competence, knowledge, skills, and resources are distributed across the organization and strategically focused rather than haphazardly utilized. Conventional modes of K–16 systems centralize and isolate important expertise and knowledge resources in one person, position, or unit; these semiautonomous elements pursue apparently competing objectives, thus fracturing attempts to coalesce resources and initiatives. Moreover, all stakeholders must have regular and systematic opportunities to continue to refine and deepen their knowledge and expertise, particularly if they are working in dynamic LI/RCLD communities.

The imperative for connecting university faculty to school reform and teachers and administrators to greater roles in teacher preparation is not simply idealistic thinking. Because our different institutions are systemically connected (even if these connections are not made explicit or deliberately enacted) deficient preparation of future urban teachers reverberates throughout the K–16 structure. Districts must distribute more resources to shore up new teachers. Until recently this has been done through stopgap measures, which can work for some teachers, but do not constitute a strategic plan. As a result, the overall quality of the teaching force is weaker than it needs to be for LI/RCLD pupils, with immediate repercussions for those pupils and their life opportunities, and long-term accumulating effects on the broader society and economy. Effects emerge at the university as high school graduates enter their freshman year with insufficient skills, thus causing the university to funnel resources into remedial education, which in turn diverts university resources and increases pupil costs to attend college. Urban school–university partnerships, like the Equity Network, can interrupt these patterns and trends, starting with better preparation of new teachers, continuing with more focused and effective professional development for existing teachers, and reaching out through the classroom into the community to improve life outcomes for LI/RCLD pupils and their families.

While the tradition in education is to tinker with the system without making fundamental changes to the grammar of schooling (Tyack & Cuban, 1995), we have tried to take a wider and more strategic view to see beyond the boundaries of the particular subsystem in which our own work had been situated so that the interconnections could be visible and thereby focused on to make change. Our work interrupts decades of practice that has separated researchers from practitioners and created divides between teacher educators at the university and the CTs in public school settings. The benefits of our approach are many. University-housed teacher preparation programs gain invaluable and contemporary knowledge of best practices in the field, as well as current ways of defining educational challenges. Such applied knowledge is essential as educators grapple with the implications of various learning and teaching theories. The collaboration among educators bears fruit through carefully scrutinized practice, bringing with it possibilities for increased effectiveness. Increased accessibility to theory and conceptual frameworks can also assist K–12 educators as they endeavor, with their university partners, to address persistent educational challenges (second language acquisition, learning disabilities that produce late readers and mathematical misunderstandings, behavioral problems, health issues, and a variety of other special needs among children) that contribute to inequities and disparities in pupil learning.

Much of the literature on school reform has identified new forms of leadership as crucial to successful efforts to invigorate learning and connect schools and LI/RCLD communities more effectively. Leadership has traditionally been defined in terms of a set of organizational functions that are performed by someone in charge—school and building management, budget oversight, personnel management, and external relations (Camburn, Rowan, & Taylor, 2003). Stein and Nelson (2003) expand this vision of a leadership knowledge base to include "leadership content knowledge." Drawing parallels with Shulman's construct of pedagogical content knowledge (1986), they argue that rather than helping administrators master various ways of improving technical knowledge, more effort should be expended in helping administrators learn key leadership content knowledge including: pedagogical content knowledge (subject matter, how pupils learn it, and effective subject-matter specific strategies—though not as in-depth as teachers), information about teachers-as-learners, and effective strategies for organizing teacher learning (Stein & Nelson, 2003). Though Stein and Nelson deepen our understanding of the knowledge base needed for effective leadership, they still focus on the administrator as the one who acquires this knowledge base, thereby promoting high-quality, but still hierarchical, leadership in schools. Other research (Camburn, Rowan, & Taylor, 2003; Goldstein, 2003) provides additional insights about how such deepened conceptions of leadership might be exercised if the power and authority were distributed across school actors. Various studies (Hart, 1987 & 1995, as cited in Goldstein, 2003) suggest that as teachers develop skills for exercising leadership at their sites, the quality of teaching and professionalism improves. Our PDS experience confirms this—PDS teachers engaged in new actions (evaluating peers, mentoring candidates, collaborating with university professors), all of which rendered important applications to their own practice.

While concept-building around alternative notions of leadership is important, our experiences in the Equity Network have led us to a vision of operation and governance that focuses less on "leadership" and more on empowerment, on enabling stakeholders to engage the institution and the learning process more effectively by creating opportunities for them to make more connections. After six years of collaboration on the four main goals of the Equity Network, we have found that leadership in school and university reform is not about being in front or on top, but that leadership comes from being engaged and connected across roles and boundaries. This promotes greater innovation, more flexibility, and broader participation.

In order to orient the formation of the PDSs at the nexus of multiple institutions, we situated the components in relation to the larger system of PreK–16 education rather than in relation to the institutions in their apparent separateness. A central task was to identify the natural or nascent connections as well as potential connections that might occur as a result of institutional, role, and attitudinal shifts. In our work, PDS stakeholders have been required to incorporate new domains for action as a means to make better progress toward our primary goals. Many new leadership roles have proven to be harmless at first, and then ultimately useless (Little, 1990), and we wanted to be sure that PDS leaders were grounded in meaningful work supported by processes and structures that allowed them to cross domains, thereby gaining new information, new perspectives, new knowledge, and new power. For example, in order for candidates to be better prepared to teach in LI/RCLD settings, they have had to move out from their classrooms into the life of the school as a whole and the community beyond. University faculty members have had to view the learning of LI/RCLD pupils as an important goal in their own professional domains, and then reform the teacher preparation program as a result. In order for LI/RCLD pupil achievement to improve, teachers in these settings must work to refine their practice and then transmit these "bettered" practices to future generations of urban teachers and current teacher educators. As stakeholders begin to act in new but related domains, they uncover fresh avenues for understanding their own professional practice, deepening their professional knowledge base, and improving their effectiveness. In effect, they begin to know better what they already know.

Members of the Equity Network have worked to institutionalize processes and structures—from the formal to the informal—to sustain these increased connections—across roles, across disciplines, and across domains of action. New knowledge, understanding, skills, and dispositions have emerged from this increasing connectedness, allowing us to move beyond old solutions and on to innovative efforts that address recurrent challenges.

New Connections for Teachers

The teachers at our PDSs have quickly increased their realm of responsibility in the preparation of new teachers. For decades, their role has been to host candidates and little more. With the implementation of the PDS, most participating teachers have added candidate supervision and evaluation to their areas of expertise. As they engage in this responsibility, they both deepen their existing knowledge and generate new knowledge, often co-constructed with their mentees and university faculty. In addition to the role of candidate evaluator and mentor, many of our PDS teachers took part in intensive reaccreditation efforts at the university and participated in discussions about tailoring aspects of the teacher preparation program to best meet the needs of pupils, classrooms, and schools in urban settings. Moreover, some of the PDS teachers conducted action research and still others mentored fellow PDS teachers in aspects of candidate supervision and evaluation. These are some of the significant instances of PDS K–12 classroom teachers crossing into the domain of teacher educator—in the field and at the program level—and, consequently, generating new and better knowledge about their teaching practice as well as significant innovations for the teacher preparation program.

These efforts and their impact on the teachers involved are discussed in "Connecting Teacher Educators Across Roles, Domains, and Knowledge Bases." This chapter, by William T. Owens Jr., combines interview data with vignettes that demonstrate classroom teachers' actions in new domains as well as the innovations and knowledge generated by these new connections.

Connecting Candidates to the Real World of the Classroom Teacher

Creating opportunities for candidates to deepen and broaden their understanding of the urban, LI/RCLD context is central to our mission in operating the Equity Network PDSs. Our candidates are no different demographically from teachers in the nation and state as a whole—over 80% are white, female, and monolingual, they have had few experiences in the types of urban settings where they will complete their student teaching, and they come to these schools with misinformation and preconceptions that work to the disadvantage of the LI/RCLD pupils they will be teaching. It is essential that their student teaching experiences support them in developing skills and habits needed to understand, appreciate, and build on the complex context that surrounds the school—but most factors will militate against this without active intervention and a strong foundation. Thus, the educators in the Equity Network have created activities, experiences, and projects that push candidates to connect with pupils, across classrooms, throughout schools, and beyond the schoolhouse into the community. As they make these connections, they reformulate their understandings of poverty, diversity, teaching, learning, achievement, and the role of schooling in our democratic society. Chapter five, by Malvetti and Wells-Artman, paints a compelling picture of candidates as they journey through the humbling experience of learning to teach in schools where the conditions are challenging and the pupils and their families seem so unfamiliar. This chapter documents the candidates' experiences, the role of the PDS in supporting their development, and the ways in which the challenge to make connections has reaped professional, practical, intellectual, and psychological benefits.

Connecting University Faculty Members to Each Other and to Schools

Our PDS effort has been fortunate to have a core group of faculty members who have led the way from our college/campus to urban schools. As they pioneered this new territory, they were animated by a belief in schools as vehicles of social change and the university as a central partner to schools in that process. Their work focused squarely on the classroom and on supporting teachers and candidates in order to enhance learning for the LI/RCLD pupils in those classrooms, through an integration of the multifaceted expertise present in the school–university partnership. As faculty members became more connected to pupils, teachers, classrooms, and schools, they began to seek out connections with others at the university, coming to see their own institution as a place full of resources for their K–12 partners. Similar to the experience of K–12 teachers in the PDSs, these connections to schools and to other university colleagues resulted in innovations that broadened and deepened the knowledge base of the faculty members. Moreover, because we tried to be systematic in the implementation of new projects and to plan for their regular assessment, we developed an emerging knowledge base that validated PDS concepts. This in turn strengthened faculty members' efforts to advocate for changes in the existing university programs and policies.

In chapter six, Noel and Sessoms capture the highs and lows of the faculty members' experience, detailing instances where increased connections were incredibly fruitful and reflecting on efforts to cross domains and make connections that were ultimately unsuccessful. Their chapter uses vignettes and data collected through faculty surveys that describe the ideologies and orientations that faculty used to transform their roles and activities as well as the strategies used to effect important changes in programs and policies at the department and college level. These data also provide insights into knowledge bases and skill sets developed by faculty to assume these transformed roles.

Our efforts to reconstruct the roles of teacher and teacher educator by maximizing the connections between these domains expanded leadership capacity and also democratized leadership roles in our PDSs. These efforts emerged out of an ethical and political commitment, supported by empirical studies (Ball & Cohen, 1990; Elmore & McLaughlin, 1988) to create and enact programs and policies that enable practitioners to be the primary shapers of their professional practice. This is important not only because it democratizes schools but because infusing local knowledge of classroom and school realities into the policymaking process will surely improve it and make it more responsive to the needs of LI/RCLD pupils. It is vital to use the power that comes from this kind of connectedness among educators across the K–16 spectrum in the service of high-quality education for LI/RCLD pupils. These connections must be attended to consistently so that they become increasingly stronger and more intense; without such attention and persistence, the powerful forces that pull apart the sectors in the schooling system will overrun the nascent efforts to integrate them more fully.

Some scholars voice skepticism about democratic and distributed forms of leadership, as well as other new forms of leadership (Jansen, 2005), because they distrust that the system can indeed achieve equitable reform. Others view the system as inherently standardizing, such that over time, for various reasons, responsiveness to local concerns and a wide range of stakeholders will give way to more bureaucratic and ideological demands for conformity (Meyer & Rowan, 1977; Rowan & Miskel, 1999). Such skepticism cannot be ignored because the forces it sees as ultimately dominant cannot be wished away and must be consciously and strategically countered. However, we argue that the real question is less about who leads and who follows or what increment of change can be correlated with which amount of force, than about what happens when educators competent in one domain begin to act and assert their knowledge in new and interrelated domains. Many of the new domains of action for our PDS stakeholders have always been appropriate arenas for their action, given their professional expertise, but were historically off-limits. The connections made through the PDS work not only generated more strongly warranted knowledge and effective innovations, as the chapters in this section detail, but shifted power and authority in ways that acknowledged and privileged the expertise, understanding, and skills generated at the local level for the purposes of benefiting local communities. This local knowledge also became instrumental in improving the more distant, but interconnected, realms of research and policy.

Chapter Four

Connecting Teacher Educators Across Roles, Domains, and Knowledge Bases

William T. Owens Jr.

Whether consulting the research (e.g., Haycock, 1998) or reflecting on one's own personal experience, it is clear that a good teacher is an invaluable asset—to pupils, to colleagues, to schools, and to communities. What is still a topic of considerable debate is exactly how to best cultivate the "good" teacher. Nonetheless, there is a growing body of research related to teacher development, from pre-service to continual renewal for in-service teachers. Some of this research focuses on issues of central concern to our urban PDS effort—why do teachers persist in teaching amid the often relentless challenges and resource shortages ever present in urban public schools? What factors do they draw on for support? What are key factors that shape teacher development throughout a teacher's career?

Insights and findings from this research indicate that the structures most favored by PDSs—those that promote innovation, inquiry, and collaboration—are exactly the ones needed to create positive professional cultures in urban schools (Borthwick, Stirling, Nauman, & Cook, 2003; Dresner & Worley, 2006). Such cultures provide teachers with opportunities to hone their collective and individual talents, mentor future generations of teachers, and engage in projects that stretch their teaching and leadership capacities (Carroll, 2006; Erickson, Brandes, Mitchell, & Mitchell, 2005; Kindall-Smith, 2004; Oplatka, 2006; Snow-Gerono, 2005). The teacher leadership opportunities linked to PDS work include such natural domains for teacher leadership as: (a) deepening instructional expertise (including pedagogy and curriculum development); (b) deepening effectiveness as a mentor (including knowledge of pedagogy for adult learners); and (c) participating in governance bodies at the school and other sites (e.g., their unions) (Cooner & Tochterman, 2004; Darling-Hammond, Bullmaster, & Cobb, 1995; Gehrke, 1991; Gonzales & Lambert, 2001; Lecos,

119

Cassella, Evans, Leahy, Liess, & Lucas, 2000). The core structural features of PDS work—inquiry into practice, collaboration with university faculty, and mentoring candidates—authentically engage teachers in activities noted earlier. In the examples shared throughout this chapter, we will see teachers organizing and participating in PDS activities that provide rich opportunities for teachers to reflect, objectively analyze their practice, conduct action research, formalize tried and true practice into the professional knowledge base, and deliberate over important policies with impacts on their everyday lives. Equity Network teachers make connections at the programmatic level and to the university, to the California Standards for the Teaching Profession and the Teaching Performance Expectations, to governance structures for the teacher education programs, and to the professional knowledge base. Through these connections, PDS teachers come to know better what they already know.

Making Connections at the Programmatic Level and with the University

The Equity Network provided a mechanism to move existing conversations with schools and districts into a new level of intensity and provide sharper focus on specific issues. Though a collegial relationship between schools and the university existed prior to the creation of the Equity Network, the general feeling, at the levels of individuals, administration, and programs, was one of "us versus them." A typical critique from a classroom teacher was that university faculty were too theoretical or idealistic. University faculty members often complained that schools and districts wanted "training" rather than professional education or preparation. The Equity Network connected these groups around concrete projects that drew on their areas of expertise and compelled them to better understand the institutional and policy demands faced in each setting and to work together to create viable solutions, thus diminishing that "us versus them" dynamic. These improved connections led the Network members to expand discussions beyond an exclusive focus on candidates and what the school and CTs should be doing for the candidate to two new goals: integrating more input from school folks into teacher preparation program decisions and reorienting the focus of university actors (faculty members and candidates) to pupil learning at the sites.

Though all faculty members had had conversations in the past with teachers who proposed ideas for program improvement or change, typically only ad hoc adjustments resulted. The PDS conversations brimmed with enthusiasm because CTs were particularly energized by the invitation to propose changes to the teacher preparation programs. The new focus on pupil learning was an enticing challenge for faculty members and candidates and required difficult but ultimately rewarding changes in university curriculum and related practices.

Creating opportunities to connect CTs and their knowledge and expertise to the PDS teacher preparation programs resulted in several collaborative innovations that have since been incorporated across all our teacher preparation programs. The Middle Ground PDS (described in chapter one) used a sophisticated model of integrated planning and teaching that connected CTs firmly to the teacher preparation program. In this case, the middle school teachers and the PDS faculty members used advanced planning to identify the key themes and skills for the 7th/8th grade curriculum and then built the methods courses for all subject areas around these themes and skills. In particular, this PDS created project-based learning opportunities in which pupils experienced enhanced learning and candidates strengthened their instructional strategies. In Middle Ground, classroom teachers helped to determine the teacher preparation curriculum and were an essential part of delivering it—whether as a co-instructor, or through modeling particular practices and mentoring candidates as they implemented a new activity, project, or strategy.

Bowling Green PDS (featured in chapter two) used a similar structure. Teachers and the university instructor collaborated closely to identify content and pupil learning objectives. These then became the foundation for instructional units, key concepts, theoretical frameworks, and instructional strategies to be taught to the candidates. Ultimately, the university instructors and teachers created integrated curricula for the teacher preparation program and for the intermediate grades' science program. This model proved so successful that in 2006–2007, while the primary university instructor was on leave, the methods course was actually taught by a team of teachers from the school.

The mathematics methods course for the San Juan PDS offers a variation on this model. The methods instructor worked closely with the math specialist at one site. They targeted one particular grade level, used its foundational content standards, and then created a lab setting in which the university instructor explained the theoretical underpinnings of the math standards and the math specialist demonstrated various strategies for teaching and assessing the content. After each session, the candidates tutored each of the pupils in a particular grade, putting into practice the theory and strategies that they had recently learned. This model yielded important results for this school, designated for program improvement by the state and federal governments. The first year of its implementation resulted in math score gains of 18%.

In the San Juan PDS, Content Cluster Teams provide a structured opportunity for teachers to connect to the university program. In 2004, reaccreditation efforts related to new state program standards resulted in all methods courses in the teacher preparation program incorporating a field-work component. Content Cluster Teams included a methods instructor and representatives from each of the PDSs to work out the curricular and logistical components of these field experiences. These teams were charged with matching these new field experiences to department guidelines and to the PDS goals, most especially the goal of improving pupil learning. Ultimately, these field experiences simultaneously enriched pupil learning and enhanced field experiences for candidates.

In other Network PDSs, the new enthusiasm for collaboration became focused on a single event. A clear example of this is Curriculum Mornings at Bidwell PDS (described in chapter five). This day-long academic event brought the school community and a cohort of candidates and their instructors together to plan an interactive and academically rigorous day of learning. Structures to facilitate planning, communication, and logistics for this day involved the administrators, teachers, faculty, and candidates of this PDS. This event became the focal point for one of the methods courses in the program. Eventually, these structures enabled small groups of PDS teachers, faculty, and candidates to launch additional initiatives together, including newspaper clubs, afternoon book clubs, and a science club; activities to support these initiatives were also folded into teacher preparation coursework.

Although CTs enthusiastically participated in coursework deliberations, their highest priority was rethinking student teaching; they had many critical reflections to share about this key element of our program. Across Network PDSs similar conclusions were reached about the length of the student teaching experience (too short in the past) and its substance (not focused enough on the realities of Title I schools). Several partners noted a fundamental flaw in the university's policy at the time that placed candidates in Title I schools for only one semester of the three-semester program. One district took the position that candidates should be placed in Title I schools for most or all of their student teaching assignments so they would be more realistic about the challenges that awaited them and more able to cope with the challenges successfully. The hope was that this would significantly reduce the high attrition rate of 30–50% in the first five years of the career (Henke, Chen, & Geis, 2000; Ingersoll, 2004). These deliberations led to a requirement that candidates spend a more extended time at the PDS either in formal student teaching placements or doing service learning projects integrated into methods coursework (or a combination of both). The nature of the candidates' experience changed as well, and they were exposed to frequent guest lectures, orientations, and trainings by PDS teachers. These reflections from a PDS teacher underscore the benefits of these changes:

Honestly I don't know if you could ever prepare a candidate in a year and a half enough to really get the full, full meaning of what it means to work in a Title I school. I go home after 11 years of this still wondering how I can be walking at the end of the day. And so I can't even imagine how to articulate that to somebody in a year and a half. But, to compare what we do now with the traditional model, I think this is way, far and above a better program because they're immersed in it; they're understanding Title I culture; they're understanding poverty; they're understanding that there are lots of differences between themselves and Title I children but lots of similarities too. I think it creates less of an "us vs. them" mentality, and they start to see the kids as just kids. And our kids can learn.

Despite rhetoric at the university level about the importance of practitioners' experience and expertise, the effort to connect classroom teachers to the university has been more difficult than expected. A particularly vexing obstacle has been the established routines of university coursework. No one argues with the benefit of a practitioner's perspective on fundamental teaching and learning issues—and this is one way in which connecting practicing teachers to the teacher preparation program enhances the experience of all stakeholders. However, these enrichments still tend to come in traditional forms—an engaging lecture with more real-world examples, samples of pupil work integrated into an instructional activity, and so on. The next step in making these connections more authentic will be to find structures and mechanisms for these K–12-based instructors to bring candidates into their classrooms as they model the theory-practice connections, with real children, in real time.

Other challenges related to policies that were not within our purview. Our efforts to establish PDSs coincided with systemwide efforts to reduce the proportion of part-time faculty instructors and with an intensive effort by existing part-time instructors to protect workload entitlements. Thus, just as we were advocating for part-time positions for our PDS partners, the system was pushing to limit new part-time hires and grant temporary contracts only to those existing part-time faculty.

When we found ways around these restrictions, other obstacles appeared. Lack of organizational coordination on basic issues can create complex problems. For example, attendance calendars differ from one partner district to the next; the university calendar is not in synch with any of them. The university is unable to provide seemingly simple supports such as library privileges or parking passes for off-campus instructors who need to be on campus one day per week. College program meetings occur during the classroom teacher's instructional day and efforts to move them either off-campus to the school site or to late afternoon times frequently meet with resistance. Moreover, while we have done a credible job of supporting the classroom teacher as primary evaluator of our candidates, we could be more systematic in our support for PDS teachers who teach university courses by, for example, providing some focused and relevant in-service training. Something that holds little mystery for veteran university faculty members, such as writing a syllabus, is totally unfamiliar to classroom teachers, and mentorship on such tasks would be a big help. Teaching elementary children and teaching adults may have some similarities, but there are vast differences. But the university does not offer guidance or support for PDS teachers who are novices at teaching adult learners. Finally, classroom teachers are routinely evaluated by their supervisors but not by their students, and such university level evaluations can be shocking, particularly when instructors get critiqued for things outside their control (e.g., logistical snafus). These difficulties indicate that while we have created opportunities for PDS teachers to connect more concretely to the university program, in the future we must support these connections in more effective ways.

Nonetheless, creating opportunities for CTs to participate in our teacher preparation programs has resulted in a more explicit programmatic focus on the urban context, how to understand it and how to be an effective teacher in it. Courses and field experiences have changed the topics covered, the focus of discussions, who instructs, and the number of hours devoted to urban issues. By connecting teachers to the process of program development, the overall knowledge base articulated through our programs has been enriched, and, at the same time, university faculty members have been afforded opportunities not previously available (e.g., access to classrooms). Further, by delving into teacher preparation issues, CTs have reflected on their own expertise and experiences—knowing better what they already know—in order to distill these into key programmatic recommendations. The benefits have been widely distributed.

Connecting Classroom Practice to the California Standards for the Teaching Profession and the Teaching Performance Expectations

Similar to many teacher education programs, our programs struggled with institutional and structural barriers to the full integration of theory and practice that could have resulted from tight alignment between field experiences and coursework and between the teacher educators (course instructors, CTs, and supervisors). Most PDS stakeholders viewed an Equity Network innovation, the CT model, as part of a viable solution to these challenges. In the CT model, the CT performed the majority of the supervision, mentoring, and evaluation tasks. Implementing this model, of course, created new challenges; the most pressing was how to prepare CTs for this role, especially since the College of Education did not have a formal practice of orienting or training host teachers for their role. The challenges associated with this enhanced role for teachers were particularly acute for one of our Centers where the majority of teachers at the three PDSs hosted candidates. In this Center, using the CT model posed many significant "capacity" issues related to the management of so many human resources on-site. The PDS model forced discussions of how to responsibly provide support to CTs in a systematic and formal manner. We ultimately developed a 15-hour lecture plus practicum course that was also combined with in-service training sessions. We adopted a flexible delivery model: the course has been offered as a traditional continuing education course at the university and it has also been tailored for specific sites according to their professional development hours and schedules. In one PDS Center, all teachers have participated in this course. At other PDSs, the participation has been more variable, shaped in part by other professional development demands and mandates.

Both the CT course and the in-service training sessions covered some key components. First, we introduced potential CTs to the Teaching Performance Expectations (TPEs), new standards for pre-service candidates that were created in 2001 but not disseminated widely in any systematic form to districts or schools. There are thirteen Teaching Performance Expectations, clusters of which align with the California Standards for the Teaching Profession (CSTPs), established in 1996 for in-service teachers. This portion of the training served an important educational function. Several of our partner districts had not yet incorporated the CSTPs into evaluation or professional development structures, so merely introducing these to teachers was important. In fact, using both the CSTPs and the TPEs generated productive discussion about effective teaching practices, especially for LI/RCLD pupils. Teachers quickly moved from discussing the standards conceptually to articulating the behaviors that could serve as evidence of meeting the standards during observations of candidates. This discussion in turn led to self-reflection about the role of the CT and to the importance of modeling—many teachers asked themselves and the group, "Are we sure that we are modeling 'best practices' for the candidates to observe?" When the answer was negative, their sense of professionalism and their commitment to the candidates' development propelled them to make adjustments in their own practice so that they better supported candidates to meet the standards of evaluation.

The conversation about standards also involved a critique of the standards, particularly from the perspective of teachers in urban settings. The dialogue frequently resulted in expanding the standards to include dimensions of urban teaching that were important to the participants but not addressed in the standards as written. Here, the professional development work associated with the PDS led to enriching the standards through including teachers' experiences and current research on such topics as English learners and metacognitive strategies.

A second important component of the CT training focused on the mentoring and supervision process. We introduce the clinical supervision model and use simulations and cases to help teachers understand how this process works. We share a range of different data collection tools that teachers are encouraged to use, including protocols for teacher/pupil-initiated interactions, gender interactions, wait time, teacher/pupil talk, and so on. As with the standards, the notion of using evidence to drive discussions of practice and the actual protocols themselves generate considerable dialogue, which begin with a focus on the candidate but inevitably loop back to the individual CT and the extent to which he or she is modeling expected practices. It has not been unusual for the CT to use a data collection protocol with the candidate and then request that the candidate collect the same data for the CT. Through this dynamic, we see a powerful example of how firmly connecting teachers to the teacher preparation process provides substantive opportunities for teachers to know better what they already know. In doing this, in a critical, reflective, and collaborative manner, teachers enhance their knowledge and skills about effective teaching and about how one supports colleagues (novices and veterans) to attain it.

The third component of the training focuses on the evaluation process itself—the assessments required, the formal and informal observations, and the role of the university liaison. We also raise issues related to "difficult" conversations and "difficult" situations that arise when candidates or colleagues do not exhibit the level of mastery expected.

Even with the support provided by up-front training and ongoing support from the PDS faculty members, the transition from host teacher to CT and primary evaluator created challenges for teachers. A brief case from one PDS illustrates some of the difficulties that characterized this transition. The initial training for the teachers occurred through a general convocation with follow-up meetings at each of the PDS sites, led by the LENS faculty (this chapter's author). Though pleased with the opportunity to play a greater role in the teacher preparation program, many teachers were not pleased with the actual amount of work that was necessary to move from a traditional supervision model to a CT model. In some cases, "too much work" and "union" became focal topics of conversations. Teachers also raised logistical difficulties related to placing a fairly large number of candidates (thirty in the first semester, sixty in the second semester) at the (then) two PDS sites.

Finally, they posed questions about how to distribute the candidates such that both their field experience and the benefits to pupils at each site were maximized. As it turned out, exceptional leadership from the PDS teachers and administrators successfully resolved all of these issues. This too is an example of the power of connections. Under previous arrangements, there would likely have been neither the opportunity nor the comfort level to squarely address these issues. The many connections being fostered by the PDS collaboration provided many more possibilities to work through issues large and seemingly small.

In the end, several powerful advantages emanated from this arrangement for both CTs and candidates. When candidates remained at one school for three semesters, they acquired a familiarity with the curriculum for each content area, the culture of the school, and the surrounding neighborhood, and truly became members of the school community. From the CT perspective, several advantages accrued. CTs got to know the candidates in multiple settings, and since the CTs were also evaluating candidates, they could be more effective mentors throughout the candidate's student teaching assignment. Also, CTs were more interested in investing their time and expertise in mentoring candidates since they contributed at the school site in a variety of ways and benefit children in a variety of classrooms. Overall, the supervision, evaluation, and support of candidates improved substantially. The CTs soon realized that there was "in-house" accountability. If a CT teacher passed along a weak candidate, colleagues at the school rather than someone at another school had to deal with it. Needless to say, this sense of whole-school responsibility for candidate growth and development encouraged CTs to do what was difficult but necessary rather than what was expedient when they had a weak candidate.

Over the years of collaboration with our CTs to prepare the next generation of teachers in LI/RCLD settings, a few choice reflections from teachers stand out. One teacher compares her PDS experience with the traditional university supervision model:

> I think one of the biggest differences is that we're their evaluators. And that was scary for a lot of the CTs to begin with. I was really comfortable with it because I was already evaluating my colleagues for my job. So that was really okay with me because I think it's really powerful to have some say in your own profession. Prior to that I would have candidates in my room; and they could be great candidates or really lousy ones, and pretty much what I said didn't count one way or the other—especially with the lousy ones. If their supervisor thought they should get a credential, by gosh, they would get a credential. It didn't matter what I said. The fact that I was

with them hours upon hours each day and they were with them four hours out of the entire semester, it was disturbing that their word counted over mine. And now it's flipped in a much more positive direction, where the person spending the majority of time with them is really making a decision on whether or not that person should receive a credential. And our voices are heard much more. I think that's been one of the most positive things.

A second teacher elaborated:

I think it has helped me become a better CT and a better teacher because when I'm doing a candidate's evaluation and I'm giving her feedback it makes you take a hard look at yourself—like wait time for example. My candidate may not provide pupils with enough wait time because maybe I need to be modeling more wait time. Very often they model, very much, what we do. So you can see yourself in them.

Another teacher reflected on the policy of placing candidates at one site for their entire student teaching experience:

I think the amount of time that they [candidates] spend bonding with the children, understanding the school's norms, and becoming a part of the school is a big positive. They know the kids. They're not just in their little classroom teaching. They walk down the hall; and, if it's a child whom they've had in the past or comes from another classroom into their reading group, they will say "hello" and make connections. So, I think they just have a bigger investment in the school. And our pupils really need the consistency of adults who care for them, love them, and stick around.

These benefits derive from connecting in-service teachers to the teacher preparation program in ways that are systematic, structured, and collaborative. The use of standards-based evaluations of candidates has spawned many important innovations including training and support for CTs, everyday use of standards and data collection protocols, promotion of dialogue among program stakeholders around elements of best practices in mentoring and modeling, and more effective coordinating structures to support K–16 PDS educators. These improved connections—across curricula, programs, and roles—enhances the operation of the system as a whole and not just its component parts.

Connecting Classroom Teachers to the Governance of Teacher Education Programs

The Equity Network has its roots in small, innovative efforts to bring teacher educators and school personnel together to design and implement high-quality teacher education programs for urban schools. As these informal relationships matured and innovations proliferated, additional collaborative forms of governance became imperative. Three primary opportunities for collaborative governance operate in our Network: PDS Site Steering Committees, the Tri-School Steering Committee (in the San Juan PDS Center only), and the Equity Network Governance Council.

Each site has a PDS Site Steering Committee that operates as a vehicle for multiple stakeholders to communicate about and formulate plans for PDS activities. In practice, because the PDS goals encompass so many different domains within the school and within the teacher preparation program, the site committees offer an effective way to integrate activities across these typically disparate units. For some of our sites, these committees functioned quite well as a democratic and participatory form of governance and this provided an ideal setting for educators to collaborate and create joint projects. At several PDSs, the steering committee included candidate representatives and parent representatives. The introduction of these two stakeholders into conversations about classroom practices, school programs, and teacher preparation programs was quite novel and, ultimately, very valuable.

In addition to the benefits that come from broadening participation, the steering committees helped to keep all stakeholders working toward the ideal of creating integrated practices across our programs and for the benefit of multiple constituents. At many sites, steering committee members led the charge in creating candidate handbooks (with information about school demographics, instructional programs, sample lesson plans, and sample evaluation forms), organizing lunchtime brown bag seminars, and providing special professional development sessions to candidates. Once again, immeasurable gains emanated from making explicit the connections among our goals and objectives across partner institutions. While grant resources were still available, the steering committees had ultimate responsibility for developing annual action and evaluation plans; committee members then collected and analyzed the data required for the annual report, submitted to the Equity Network Governance Council. Admittedly, some of the sites convened steering committees for very targeted purposes and did not reach the apex of collaboration and program integration that was desired. Often this was due to the complexity of the school (some of our sites operate year-round, multiple track programs that stymie broad-based coordination), distractions from other important mandates (e.g., responding to state sanctions due to "inadequate" academic performance), or the preference of an administrator for a more executive approach.

In the San Juan PDS Center, a Tri-School Steering Committee was created. During the development of the Center and after the addition of a third PDS site, it became obvious that some form of communication network had to be established for operations to function efficiently and with some degree of uniformity across sites. The Tri-School Steering Committee was composed of representative classroom teachers, principals, and university personnel, and handled policy issues that arose on a broader level throughout the academic year. For example, each semester some variation of a discussion about appropriate dress for candidates has occurred, and classroom teachers had the frustrating experience of communicating dress code policy to candidates. More significant discussions regarding the evaluation of candidates have been quite powerful, especially since the classroom teachers are the primary evaluators. Deliberations on how to assess candidates at midterm and at the end of the semester, using the same rubric for both assessments, have generated opposing views and rich conversations. The committee was crucial in opening doors for methods professors to work cooperatively with classroom teachers in content areas; teachers on the committee often served at the site level in content cluster groups for math, history/social science, language and literacy, and science in order to help facilitate the implementation of the strategies taught by the methods instructors. Meetings for the Tri-School Steering Committee are monthly and normally for two hours after the school day. The energy and commitment that teachers bring to discussions about the PDS teacher preparation program after spending the entire day with children in their own classrooms is truly inspiring, and reminds us that this collaboration bears fruit in multiple ways.

The Equity Network Governance Council convened twice annually and included representatives from all the partners of the Network: PDSs, district administration, teachers' associations, Sacramento ACT, and the university departments and colleges. At the fall meeting, participants reviewed annual plans submitted by the PDSs and made recommendations about funding and other proposed activities. At the spring meeting, PDS progress reports were made and data analysis on larger, Networkwide projects (e.g., teacher research, graduate exit surveys, etc.) occurred. Until recently, this council was the only entity of its kind at our university that brought this diverse group of educational actors together.

These formal governance structures provide yet another way for CTs to connect their professional knowledge to program and policy development for the teacher preparation programs. They offer another opportunity for leadership in addition to the more traditional service as union representatives or induction and peer mentors. Beyond the enrichments they bring to the governance dialogues and decisions, the CTs gain broader perspectives on their own profession and the trajectory of colleagues within it. CTs have another venue through which to know better what they already know about policy development, program formation and implementation, and the management of material and human resources. Their deliberations in these governance bodies sometimes confirm lessons already learned, but sometimes new knowledge gets formed.

Connecting Classroom Teachers to the Professional Knowledge Base

Presentations about the Equity Network PDSs have been made at conferences or meetings organized by the CSUS Bilingual/Multicultural Education Department, UC Davis CRESS Center's Voices from the Classroom, the California Association for Bilingual Education, the California Science Teachers Association, the California Council on Teacher Education, the Society for the Advancement of Chicanos and Native Americans in Science, the National Association of Research in Science Teaching, the International Association of Teacher Research, the Holmes Partnership, and the American Educational Research Association. At some of the conferences, we have presented general material about the goals and structure of the Equity Network. At others, the presentations have highlighted specific Network practices and projects.

These presentations have emerged from Network members' action research, formal research, and reflection on practice; some were prepared entirely by the PDS teachers, and others were collaborative efforts among the K–16 PDS educators. The life of a California public school teacher after 20 years of Proposition 13-driven budget cuts and other resource crunches includes little opportunity to participate in professional conferences, much less make presentations at them. Material support from the Teacher Quality Enhancement grant and direct opportunities to conduct research on practice provided teachers with valuable opportunities to connect with the broader professional education community in unfiltered ways that could meet their specific needs for professional development and critical knowledge.

During our six years as a Network, teachers have been involved in multiple forms of research and evaluation. Each PDS must submit an annual report that contains an analysis of outcomes for that year, and these outcomes often derive from our teacher research groups (usually six to eight operate each year), lesson study teams (about fifteen each year), and teacher research and policy advocacy projects (through our affiliation with Teachers Network Leadership Institute). These efforts, beyond producing important innovations for our programs that are now normalized as simply how we do business, also yielded important insights worthy of sharing in regional and national venues.

Preparing for such presentations consistently yielded important opportunities to reflect on the goals of the PDS and our progress toward them; to develop new goals based on a deliberate assessment of successes and challenges; to reinforce the centrality of data and evidence for the reliability and validity of our own assessments and self-reflections; and to dialogue about the different perspectives, interpretations, and conclusions emanating from our distinct roles and positions within the PDS. Attending the conferences and learning from keynote speakers and other presenters also provided access to current theories and practices; connections to regional and national projects and frameworks; and a sense of validation of our efforts as groundbreaking, in some cases, and normative, in others. It is important to note that none of the classroom teachers had previously presented their work to an audience whose background was primarily in research and teacher education. These teachers truly took center stage as teacher educators and practitioners who based their practice on data-driven decisions. Invariably, their presentations were well received; they had credibility with the audiences, and they fielded questions with expertise and finesse.

Research on teacher development and leadership points to PDS work as an important vehicle for connecting classroom teachers to the teacher preparation process in ways that are significant, authentic, and meaningful, for both university and school programs. Consistent with findings in the research literature, connecting classroom teachers to the multiple domains of the PDS effort has resulted in significant teacher learning, the flattening of governance structures so that the teacher's voice is more resonant, and the creation of new opportunities for teacher leadership and knowledge creation (teachers as evaluators, researchers, etc.). Consequently, "normal" leadership roles become viewed as eminently appropriate for classroom teachers. Moreover, these leadership activities have created a cadre of teachers with expertise and confidence to act deliberately in policymaking and program development venues, confirming findings by others (Gehrke, 1991; Gonzales & Lambert, 2001; Neufeld & McGowan, 1993). Such teacher empowerment is a boon to K–12 and university classrooms alike (Epperly & Preus, 1989).

Though energized by all that has been accomplished, we often fear that these interruptions to the traditions of K–12 teaching and of teacher preparation are an illusion that will one day disappear and allow the past to fully replace the present we have forged through much hard work. We think that our innovations have been sufficiently institutionalized so that classroom teachers will always be involved in teacher education at our university. But we worry about what will happen as external resources diminish and the inevitable waves of inertia set it.

In some respects, we fear that teacher education has put itself on a high wire by allowing or encouraging the participation of classroom teachers in such a rich partnership. Once classroom teachers are fully integrated into teacher education, the net could be removed by factors totally out of our control. Our program developed during a time of relatively healthy growth for our university and with the benefit of external funding; how will decisions be made during times of restricted resources? Will the teachers' role and the prominence of pupil learning objectives be minimized? How will classroom teachers respond if they are forced to be less involved in teacher education after they have had the experience of being more involved? In such a scenario, how will teacher education programs retain their credibility? I truly hope that our efforts are successful in making permanent the interruptions to the traditions. High-wire acts are fun to watch, but falls change everything.

Chapter Five

Beyond the Classroom

Candidates Connect to Colleagues, Children, and Communities

Jeanne Malvetti and Christie Wells-Artman

Through working with my CT on a collaborative partnership, I began to see opportunities to integrate the skills learned from my methods courses and professional development provided by the PDS throughout the credential program. I found my "teacher voice" and began to understand that I must be *willing* to take on leadership roles and be *eager* to share my specific talents with others. I also honed many other specific skills such as time management—and many dispositions such as confidence and assertiveness. As a candidate, I attended a professional development training session on "Differentiating Instruction—Infusing Depth and Complexity into the Curriculum," which inspired me to use these instructional strategies in the classroom. I found them to be so effective that I wanted to share this newfound knowledge. I delivered a PowerPoint presentation to my fellow candidates in our seminar class, and they, too, have used these tools to differentiate instruction and meet the various needs, interests, and readiness levels of their pupils. I have motivated veteran teachers to increase their knowledge of technology, providing information and step-by-step guidance (and even offering one-on-one tutoring sessions). (Rachel, PDS candidate)

The research literature and the media pepper their readers with stories about teachers whose first years of teaching were so grueling that they left the classroom, thus abandoning a dream that, for many, had been envisioned since childhood. Data indicate that 30–50% of new teachers leave the profession within the first five years (Henke, Chen, & Geis, 2000; Ingersoll, 2004). This turnover creates significant problems for all institutions connected to public schooling. Urban school–university partnerships, like the Equity Network, are particularly pressed to prepare candidates to be effective teachers in LI/RCLD settings such that they complete their induction years with their commitments to teaching for social justice still strongly intact.

We hoped that more and more of our candidates would have experiences like those recounted by Rachel and complete our teacher preparation program with confidence about themselves as teachers and with aspirations to become teacher leaders for urban schools. But in order to convert this hope into concrete reality, our collaborations had to construct responses to key questions facing urban teacher preparation programs nationally: What are critical skills and knowledge bases that will shape candidates' dispositions such that they commit to working in LI/RCLD communities, especially when they are typically middle-class, white females raised in suburbs? What key experiences will help candidates develop skills and knowledge needed for teaching effectively in these communities?

The research literature offers plentiful documentation of teacher preparation programs that have crafted innovative and bold responses to these questions (Haberman, 1999; Kershaw, Cagle, Hersh, O'Sullivan, & Staten, 2004; Leland & Harste, 2005; Quartz, 2003; Wong, Murai, Berta-Avila, William-White, Baker, Arellano, & Echandia, 2007). Although some important differences across these programs exist, there is convergence about the kinds of experiences and knowledge bases that best prepare candidates for effectiveness and success as urban teachers. Among these are the use of culturally relevant pedagogy, sociocultural learning approaches, sociopolitical consciousness, an ability to develop caring relationships with pupils, effectiveness as a team member, communication and collaboration skills employable with diverse groups (e.g., colleagues, administrators, parents), and skills and positive experiences in advocacy that boost confidence about the potential to create change and increase social justice (Corbett & Wilson, 2002; Haberman, 1999; Leland & Harste, 2005; Olsen & Anderson, 2007; Sanders, 2003).

These important components map nicely onto the deep expertise available through our school-based PDS partners. In applying the combined lessons from this knowledge base enriched by theory and practice, it became apparent to us that effective urban teacher preparation was not simply a matter of adding urban education content to coursework or providing diversity training at sites. Rather, we concluded that our candidates would flourish with opportunities that allowed them to experience the power of connections. That is, in addition to fully addressing the urban teaching context in our courses, we also created opportunities to connect candidates to the full range of resources in a school community that would bolster their efforts as classroom teachers. It was our contention that mentoring our candidates into understanding the full complexities of the urban school community was, in the end, as important as helping them master skills for a specific classroom. We amplified the opportunities for candidates to make connections across domains that, in our traditional program, had very rigid boundaries or were ignored altogether. Thus, we sought to redefine candidates' relationships with: the CT, his or her classroom and other classrooms and "spaces" in the school as a whole, the pupils, the school community, and the professional knowledge base. In redefining these relationships, we reconfigured existing connections and created new ones such that candidates ultimately did "more" in their student teaching, and with greater focus, purpose, and clarity.

After a brief description of our traditional program, this chapter recounts the many ways in which candidates became connected to the urban school ecology—beginning first with efforts to reshape the candidate-CT connection and then describing ways in which candidates became connected to the whole school and the community. Throughout, our PDS graduates offer reflections on their experience.

Earning an Elementary Teaching Credential in California: The Basics

Subject Matter Preparation

Until 2004, the pathway into teaching for prospective elementary teachers was either to earn an undergraduate degree in a subject matter of their choosing and then take a subject matter competency exam (in the five core elementary content areas) or earn an undergraduate degree in an approved waiver program, typically Liberal Studies or Child Development. In 2004, due primarily to requirements of NCLB, the means of verifying subject matter competence were reduced to only one option: passing the California Subjects Examination for Teachers (CSET). After this point, a typical prospective elementary teacher completing an undergraduate degree may be studying any major (with or without appropriate field experiences for future teachers) and will be making preparations to take the CSET, which is divided into subject-based subtests that can be taken separately. Once the bachelor's degree has been completed and the CSET is passed, the pupil can apply for the teacher preparation program, which is a post-baccalaureate program typically lasting two or three semesters.

New Teacher Preparation Programs

The year 2004 also marked an important transition point in our teacher preparation program as the three departments that offer a preliminary teaching credential began implementation of new programs tied to new Teaching

Performance Expectations for candidates and program standards for universities. Our basic teacher preparation program prior to 2004 embodied features that were the focus of the key critiques of teacher education programs leveled by such researchers as Goodlad (1990) and Sarason (1993)—namely, our program was organized to occur primarily on the university campus. Coursework focused discretely on different aspects of pedagogical theory; social studies methods were taught independent of literacy methods and science methods, multicultural education and social/psychological foundations delved into their own independent domains with little alignment to the methods being imparted.

In addition to fragmentation across the teacher preparation coursework, there were few structural and formal links between the coursework and the fieldwork required for the program. Field assignments in the coursework were limited and, when they were given, they were not tied to the overall structure of the student teaching experience. Moreover, the student teaching component of the program—though substantial at 24 hours per week for the first semester and 40 hours per week for the second semester—was fairly unstructured. The CTs, supervisors, and liaisons all played important roles, but without enough support, guidance, or integration into the program as a whole. Although most employers rated our graduates highly, the educators involved with the Equity Network knew that in order to prepare our candidates (mostly white, middle class, and female) for the challenges of teaching in LI/RCLD schools, we needed fundamental changes to our programs. Among these were more effective strategies to transmit the body of knowledge available about urban teaching and more authentic opportunities to involve our candidates in urban schools and communities such that they deepened the knowledge and skill base needed to be successful teachers in LI/RCLD schools.

As detailed in several chapters, the collaboration between school and university educators resulted in innovations that impacted the university programs as well as the school and classroom programs. As we "put our heads together" around the issues of enhancing the field experiences for teacher candidates, many important novel approaches emerged. In fact, many of the program changes that we instituted in 2004 to meet our new standards built on these PDS innovations, thus validating, at the college level, the significant work that our collaborations had accomplished.

The Equity Network Framework for Reorienting the Student Teaching Experience

The overarching framework for rethinking our program and the experiences it would provide for candidates stemmed from a central goal in the PDS model—improving pupil achievement, with progress toward the other three PDS goals tied into supporting this primary goal. This pupil achievement goal represented the most fundamental value shift for us and therefore required the biggest conceptual and practical changes. As noted earlier, the shift from a traditional teacher preparation program to a PDS model necessitated significant reorientation in our program, particularly in order to develop new collaborative strategies for enhancing pupil learning. This new focus on pupil learning required that candidates have new experiences that we predicted would increase their effectiveness including: developing respectful relationships with pupils and their families, acquiring skills to tap into community funds of knowledge, learning how to transform curriculum so that it connects with pupil experiences and interests, enhancing a disposition toward continual professional development and skills in collaborating with others at the site to share knowledge, resources, and support (Glass & Wong, 2003; hooks, 1994). Thus, as we refocused our program on pupil learning, we had to develop ways to build candidates' capacity in these other domains so that our new emphasis would not prove unrealistic. We next describe the ways in which these new connections provided candidates with space, knowledge, and guidance in developing their skills as future urban educators.

Enhancing Connections Between Candidates and the School as a Whole: Mentoring Candidates into a Professional Learning Community

The Equity Network's emphasis on pupil learning was central to the student teaching experience and the program's coursework provided the candidates with the requisite academic knowledge and beginning pedagogical skills vital to this important task. As the candidates and CTs connected around the goal of pupil learning, there was a subtle shift away from the apprenticeship model (which was the practice commonly used in the traditional teacher preparation program), where the teacher was the expert and the candidates in their entry semester were passive observers, to a more collaborative experience in which the candidates assumed specific roles in improving learning for all pupils.

This connection around a shared and central goal created an environment where the CT and the candidate developed a collegial relationship in which both grew and developed together in this micro professional learning community—the classroom and, often, beyond. We know that in schools, there are many talented teachers; however, it is extremely challenging to get them to "play together" in a truly collegial manner (Lortie, 2002), a dynamic that we hope is not subsequently passed on from mentor teacher to candidate. However, as the Network candidates acquired high levels of skills and expertise in teaching the content areas, they integrated the new ideas and learning into their daily lesson plans, always striving to help their pupils achieve academic success. As CTs observed these new techniques and strategies they expressed interest in acquiring these new skills. Such knowledge transfer happens naturally, but sporadically, in most in-service teacher/candidate pairings, but the PDS work actually encouraged formal structures for this process.

In the previous chapter, we described ways in which CTs assumed new roles in the teacher preparation process. The CTs received support for performing these new roles through training, mentoring, and other forms of feedback. This role shift made it possible for new opportunities to surface for candidates to broaden their experiences in classrooms and on school campuses. The PDS framework and our particular version of PDS implementation offered myriad venues for candidates and mentors to connect across a professional knowledge base, and to do so in ways that deepened the roots of a professional learning community that accommodated learners with different levels of knowledge and experience.

The idea that candidates could be contributing members of a professional community of learners, despite their status as novices, is a deliberate construction of the PDS, and is tied to efforts to make bridges across the theory—practice split and to the notion of continual professional renewal. Candidates and CTs strengthened connections within a professional learning community that had a shared focus—enhanced pupil learning—and was situated within structures made possible by the PDS. An important thrust toward deeper learning was the connection made for CTs between the candidate performance expectations (TPEs) and with the state's professional teacher standards (CSTPs), in particular, the emphasis in both standards on the "cycle of teaching": plan, teach, assess, reflect, and re-teach. As university instructors and K–12 partner teachers wrestled with how to better prepare our candidates for urban teaching environments, we identified more avenues for candidates to engage with this cycle of teaching—through our courses, through modeling in classrooms, through lunch-time discussions, and so on. These efforts helped us to develop the beginnings of a common language, spoken across institutions and status markers, with a clear focus on the pupil learning at the school. The knowledge from experience and the new knowledge generated at the university merged through these conversations between candidates and mentors and became structured into productive dialogue as both candidates and mentors applied this emerging knowledge base to analyzing and critiquing the implementation of the standards (TPEs and CSTPs) into practice.

While mentors were without question the experts on a host of important dimensions of teaching and learning (e.g., classroom organization, motivating pupil learning, and addressing state content standards), candidates also had exposure to new theory and practices that were not present in district professional development series, including such topics as cognition theory, elements of instruction for academic language development, social justice curriculum, and instructional technologies that had not been disseminated in our partner districts, most of them victims of the Digital Divide. This gave the candidates valued knowledge to share in the professional learning community. Thus, at several of the Equity Network sites, the candidates provided informal or formal professional development for the teachers at their site, and in one case it was available for all the district's teachers.

Formal collaborations emerged through curriculum projects and in-service professional development offerings. At Golden State Middle School, for example, candidates implemented a course-related service learning project jointly with the school district's technology coordinator. They identified the teachers' areas of interest and then developed and organized two workshops for district faculty, who received professional development credit. In other cases, individual candidates or small groups of them took the initiative to develop workshops and intervention programs at their school sites. Additional informal interchanges also surfaced. As the schools identified their needs, they looked to the candidates and their professors to help address them. Rachel, the candidate featured in our introductory quotation, encouraged her CTs to make the most of their technology grant by "dusting off" their LCD projector and modeling the use of PowerPoint daily in the classroom. A similar session was offered by candidates at Howe Avenue PDS and generated high praise from the principal there.

Candidates were a considerable presence at the PDSs in other ways and were deliberately organized to be an important resource for enriching pupil learning. At several sites, the candidates responded to the school's needs by organizing and teaching before and after-school enrichment or intervention programs for pupils, and in some instances, they did this without monetary or organizational support—just an invitation from the school principal and the university professor. At Sierra Gardens PDS, the children had the chance to attend weekly music/choir, sign language, and art classes provided by the candidates. Commendations and recognition from the school administration, the teachers, and also the parents were given to the candidates, which elevated their status and sense of belonging at the school. At other schools, highly structured intervention programs were organized by the teachers and the university liaison, and, after in-service training, were implemented by the candidates. One such program, at Greer PDS, resulted in significant learning improvements by pupils with pre/post gains in one grade as high as 29%.

Another powerful example of connecting candidates to the school was the planning of Curriculum Mornings, which were held once a semester at

John Bidwell School. A cohort of approximately twenty-five candidates in the first semester of their teacher preparation program developed an activity-based, hands-on lesson for a specific grade level. Based on the State Content Standards and the district and school pacing schedules, they designed a lesson plan for one specified content area, with support from the instructor for that content methods class. This lesson plan was reviewed and critiqued by the teachers with special attention given to the appropriateness of content and strategies for the school's diverse learners. The teachers offered suggestions for modifications, particularly in relation to pupils with special needs, and also shared some classroom management tips (especially verbal and nonverbal signals) that were used in the classroom. The curriculum morning was then ready to go—a full 3-hour block where all the candidates from a Center delivered the identified lesson, using appropriate grade-level material and strategies. Over several iterations, curriculum mornings focused on such topics as multicultural poetry, inquiry-based science, and math in our community.

The curriculum mornings provided a forum for meaningful collaboration among the stakeholders and were powerful for all. Pupils thoroughly enjoyed them because of the small pupil to teacher ratios and the departure from the usual routines. Further, teachers reported that pupils continued to request multicultural poetry activities following the curriculum morning that highlighted these literary resources.

The candidates experienced an authentic teaching experience that boosted their confidence in their teaching abilities and their decision to become educators. They polished curriculum development skills: during the planning process with teachers at the school, they learned more about strategies used by experienced teachers. They also honed classroom management skills as they successfully parachuted into new classroom situations and handled them with poise. The classroom teachers benefited from professional development opportunities connected to the curriculum mornings that were offered by a cadre of their own faculty, university faculty, and candidates. In fact, the sophistication of the preparation for curriculum mornings grew as time progressed. For example, in preparation for a curriculum morning on literacy, six of the candidates along with a literacy-focused faculty member designed and presented a 2-hour professional development workshop to the teachers. Each pair of candidates created an interactive presentation on the reading strategies that the children would be learning and participating in during curriculum morning. At the close of the session, teachers complimented the informational, professional presentation. One teacher even commented that she didn't realize that the presenters were "only pre-service teachers" because she thought that the training was of such high quality that surely it must have been provided by "real" teachers.

Yet a fourth practice of schoolwide connections can be seen at Golden State Middle School (a PDS featured in chapter one). Candidates in this

PDS worked with three different kinds of classrooms during their student teaching experience. With guidance from instructors and teachers at the PDS, they developed instructional projects to be used with pupils in a self-contained Special Day Class, in a Newcomer class for recently arrived, beginning level English learners, and in a Gifted and Talented class. Reflection on and analysis of these experiences focused on the similarities and differences in the classroom contexts, strategies used to provide these diverse groups of pupils with access to the core knowledge and skills in the projects, and the ways in which organizational forms (at the classroom and school levels) could be structured so that fewer disparities resulted. These sustained experiences with diverse groups of pupils and deliberately structured opportunities to confront issues of access and equality are rare in teacher education programs. Connecting candidates to the range of pupils and classroom arrangements at this school gave them an invaluable opportunity for understanding the school and its pupils in their full context and seeing the potential and limits of teachers' work in this context.

At Fruitridge PDS, candidates worked with the language arts specialist to produce materials and coach pupils on reading practices that had been identified in their curriculum and by their district as key to proficient reading. A group of eight candidates were completing their student teaching at this school. After a few training sessions with the language arts specialist, they created a set of visual aides that were provided to all primary classrooms and a set of intervention strategies that were either implemented by the classroom teacher or the candidate in his or her placement classroom. These activities supported the overall language arts program. Our candidates' experience with this project encompassed several dimensions. First, they were an integral part of an important instructional effort at the school; this helped them to see how teachers' work extends beyond a particular classroom into a collective effort that is coordinated and planned. Second, they developed additional expertise and were able to use that to exercise leadership, though in a small way, at the level of the school. Finally, their efforts shifted the perspective of many staff at the school who came to understand the potential power and benefit of relatively large cohorts of candidates for the school as a whole rather than just the classrooms of teachers considered, by some, as having been rewarded with candidates by the administrator.

While the previous examples stem from a dynamic in which candidates were organized as resources to the school as a whole, we encountered additional examples when CTs constructed programs that offered the resources of the school to the candidates as a means of connecting them to these resources and enriching their preparation as future teachers. In the San Juan PDS Center, teachers and faculty members created a pre-service teacher handbook as a result of a series of conversations and meetings in which they wrestled with identifying pivotal essential experiences for novice teachers, particularly given the time and schedule constraints inherent in meshing course and field experience requirements. These conversations always revealed the tensions between the teachers' primary desire that candidates be on campus for more hours, and the faculty member's responsibility to meet program requirements through course hours and other more traditional means. The process of addressing these tensions usually helped us to identify more clearly what was essential for preparing candidates, and, in the case of this Center, the initial result was a set of "extracurricular" activities that candidates completed on their own. These activities ranged from attending a family event (e.g., back-to-school night) to observing in the Language Development Specialist's English language development tutorials, to participating in an individual education plan (IEP) meeting. Over time, we have found ways to incorporate key experiences into coursework so that they are no longer relegated to the add-on status of "extracurriculars." These experiences have proven critical in connecting candidates to the various instructional support programs available on a school campus and to helping them think broadly about the multiple ways a teacher mobilizes resources inside and outside the classroom to support pupil learning.

As we analyze these various experiences, we note that a key factor in facilitating these innovations emanated from a program change initiated in the PDSs: prolonged placement at one site. In the traditional, postgraduate, two- or three-semester programs, candidates usually had two or three different field experiences that varied both in terms of school site and grade level (the latter is a state requirement). Since the candidates were placed at different schools each semester, it was very difficult for them to feel truly connected to the school or feel as if they had an authentic role to play or to have a voice in the school. Building connections and developing a comfort level at a school and within the community take time and the traditional model did not lend itself to the candidates making deep connections within the school or the community. However, as we looked at participation patterns at the Equity Network schools where the candidates "resided" at only one school for the duration of their student teaching, we noticed that this prolonged residence (up to 1½ years) was a crucial factor affecting the quantity and extent of school and community commitment and involvement.

This expanded level of participation took different forms in different PDSs. Several principals and CTs noted that candidates demonstrated more of an investment in the school. Candidates with year-long placements demonstrated an attitude that "this is my school and I will do whatever I can to support and be a part of it." As they progressed through the semesters, they had a clearer understanding of the culture of the school, a better understanding of poverty, and a grasp of the cultural differences and similarities among the children and the candidates. There became less of an "us and them" mentality, and more of a realization that these are kids who, although they have many special needs, can learn, when the educator acquires the skills and strategies to meet the pupils' needs. An additional advantage to this prolonged residence was aptly described by a CT at Greer Elementary, who noted that the pupils in her LI/RCLD school needed consistency from adults who would "stick around" in the child's life. The lessening of mobility among the candidates was an asset to the children as well as to the candidates.

We also found in many instances that, in prolonged residence placements, these candidates demonstrated characteristics that could be considered precursors to becoming future teacher leaders. We observed that our candidates were exhibiting a strong commitment to their pupils and their community, and that they were collaborative colleagues who worked well with their peers and shared their expertise with those who were willing to learn from them (Olsen & Anderson, 2007; Oplatka, 2006). It took time for many novices to find their voice, primarily because they had to learn the culture of the school and the community and they were initially awed and overwhelmed by the complexities and realities of LI/RCLD schools. However, with the passage of each semester and with more connections across key domains, their expanding knowledge of working in a Title I setting resulted in a growing confidence and a greater willingness to become involved and visible at the school. They participated in professional development opportunities, joined school committees, produced school newsletters, provided technology support and workshops to the pupils and teachers, conducted professional development sessions, and organized and developed several before- and after-school programs. The list is expansive and distinct for each novice teacher, but they all grew in their ability to provide effective instruction for low-income children and to become budding teacher leaders. Although these candidates did not necessarily "lead" in the sense of being at the head of a committee, they did guide and influence others by sharing their expertise with the pupils, teachers, and families of their school community.

To become an effective urban educator, one must engage in a variety of meaningful roles: catalyst and motivator for change, an advocate or supporter of the cause, collaborator, resource provider, and progress monitor (Haberman, 1999; Ladson-Billings, 2001). One must also be the leader and guide of the overall change process. What is distinctive about the Equity Network PDSs is that candidates—just at the beginning of their careers—proved able to exercise leadership and advocacy when opportunities to connect the myriad dimensions of the educational process were made available to them. In these settings, candidates not only find their "teacher voice" but they begin to see themselves as potential agents of change.

In all instances, whether the sharing of expertise was on a formal or informal basis, all of the candidates experienced a huge shift in their thinking about their role in schools; they were contributing not only to their individual classrooms, but also to the good of the school and the community—they had become an important part of a professional community in which all have something to offer, all have something to learn. This is somewhat different from an apprenticeship or teaching structure where one party knows significantly more than another—such a relationship has its appropriate moments, but the professional learning community can also accomplish things—like raising status and sharing new knowledge—that the apprenticeship model cannot. The professional learning community present in the PDSs connected these novice teachers to powerful norms of professionalism, collaboration, advocacy, and continual renewal.

Connecting Candidates to Pupils and their Communities

Although much has been written and documented that substantiates and validates the importance of establishing meaningful home–school partnerships, school–family relations in urban contexts take on particular meanings and confront specific challenges. On this issue, the work of Gonzalez and Moll (2002), Epstein (1995), and Sanders (2003) informs our efforts by highlighting an assets approach to LI/RCLD communities such that partnerships are formed around significant common issues and between partners with equal standing. Educators in the Equity Network fully recognized the importance that school, family, and community partnerships play in enhancing pupil learning, and several of the schools and university courses promoted, developed, designed, and participated in activities that fostered these essential connections. They were also eager to adopt new paradigms, protocols, and structures that critiqued and moved beyond persistent deficit notions about low-income parents and the ways in which they exhibited support for their children's education. And increasingly, strict adherence to curriculum scripts and state content standards exacerbated the "problem" by restricting teachers' time and constricting their flexibility with curriculum and instruction. Though the Equity Network had no extra resources or fail-safe strategies for engaging parents and the community, innovations at several sites helped us to rethink foundational principles and key assumptions about connecting communities and schools, especially their newest members—candidates. These innovations materialized primarily as outreach efforts and curriculum reform projects.

John Reith Elementary, a PDS school in the Elk Grove District, developed a door-to-door program called "Taking It to the Streets." It gave local community members and neighbors of the school pertinent information that provided a basic orientation to the school and also highlighted the achievements and school programs. Included were the names of school personnel, school schedules, academic programs such as the Collaborative Academic Support

Team (CAST) that met the individual needs of each pupil, additional child care opportunities, and academic and community partners.

This phenomenal program's goal was to engage the "community" that we knew was needed to educate children. This community included parents, neighbors, teachers, administrators, and candidates working together. Team members distributed brochures, business cards, and maps of local community centers and businesses to all of the residents in the surrounding school neighborhood through face-to-face, door-to-door encounters. This proactive outreach by the school helped to break down barriers and forged a stronger relationship between the neighbors and the school. Local residents learned about the school's commitment to continuous instructional improvement and made important personal connections. In turn, they volunteered for subsequent school events and identified ways to play a substantial role in fostering strong citizenship within the school and community culture. As this program grew through a collaborative partnership, the novice teachers were able to immerse and connect themselves in a community culture that promoted a diverse, enriched learning atmosphere for all pupils, with a purpose of encouraging them to become ethical participants in society. One candidate, who was inspired by the positive results of "Taking It to the Streets," led a team of other candidates and CTs to call on and reach out to local community members and business partners to establish a "Community Day" at the school. This event included a book fair with support from local libraries, information booths set up by various organizations to promote partnerships, city fire and law enforcement representatives, and an international food festival. This fair successfully drew support from the community because of the trusting relationship previously established between the various stakeholders.

The PDSs provided an ideal context for rethinking school and university curriculum so that community funds of knowledge became integral to the content and pedagogy, and offered new opportunities to connect candidates to the power of an assets-based approach to working with LI/RCLD communities. For example, the PDS team at three sites created community gardens (as detailed in chapter one). This initiative catered to the specific needs of the newcomer Hmong, Mexican, and Russian residents. Novice teachers assisted and led a variety of enrichment science lessons for the pupils and teachers to learn more about organic vegetables and a healthy diet. This collaboration enabled the Hmong residents to maintain their traditional diet by providing them with space to cultivate foods using traditional agricultural methods. Moreover, as the community of learners understood more about healthy and nutritious diets, they discovered the scientific and folk wisdom embedded in these traditional diets, all of which were far healthier than the American fast food approach to eating. With guidance from university instructors and teachers at the school, candidates built an outreach program around these community gardens that strengthened pupils' and families' strong and positive connections with the school and surrounding community, thus addressing school and cultural needs. Groups of teachers, faculty members, and candidates also developed science curricula for the school that placed the gardens and parents' agricultural knowledge as the central content to be learned. After 10 weeks of setup by the children, candidates, and teachers, the garden continued to be maintained by the families and pupils. As an extension to this garden project, a garden party was formed where families harvested and cooked delicious dishes to be presented and served at the school site. All pupils were invited to try the dishes and taste the vegetables from the community garden. This was a successful event, which demonstrated a powerful connection of a new culture to an existing community, highlighted for teachers the depth and relevance of community funds of knowledge, and built a relationship that enhanced and promoted pupil learning.

While the Bryte/Westfield PDS was hard at work with the community garden, across town, the teachers, candidates, and university faculty members at Bowling Green Charter School were immersed in developing the César Chávez community health fair (as detailed in chapter two). The purpose of this fair was to promote healthy lifestyles through prevention of risky behaviors. The focus was health care concerns identified in the school community, namely, diabetes, heart disease, and substance abuse. This project was part of the university science methods class and was the culminating activity for the semester. The candidates were responsible for teaching the related science content to the 4th, 5th, and 6th graders. The children's knowledge was demonstrated at the fair since they had learned to take blood pressure, created a bilingual brochure on diabetes, prepared a PowerPoint presentation on heart disease, and performed a health play. The community fair involved representatives from outside health, legal, and political agencies, many of whom provided in-kind services.

Although the three examples cited were very different, they were designed to meet the specific needs of their community. Each project contributed to the creation of an authentic, meaningful partnership between the school, the home, and the neighboring community with the purpose of ultimately improving pupil achievement. Candidates played important roles in these projects and learned firsthand the power of home–school connections and the vital role that they could play in fostering them.

Connecting with Pupils, Teachers, and the Community: Christie Wells-Artman's Story

As a candidate, I had many opportunities to plan, teach, and reflect in a supportive PDS community at John Bidwell Elementary School.

Over time (three semesters), I felt confident assuming leadership roles that promoted pupil learning and enabled me to collaborate with the principal, teachers, and other staff members. I began to understand the importance and need for effective leadership during my second of three student teaching assignments, when I was not only responsible for planning and delivering instruction, but also I was expected to participate along with the teachers in at least one school site committee. I found that by working on the PDS objectives and goals, and contributing to my school's educational development priorities, I developed my own dimensions of leadership. These ranged from being a vital member of the school's PDS Steering committee, participating in the Science Projects Related to Equity in Education (SPREE) Summer Institute at CSUS, attending various professional development seminars such as the Parent/Teacher Home Visit Project and Differentiated Instruction, infusing technology into lesson plans and instruction for pupils and teachers, and mentoring individual pupils.

An important step was to define the meaning of leadership and how it applied to a candidate. Leadership is taking initiative, with the capacity to take the guidance given in the school culture and use it toward the commitment to continuous learning. It is known that successful teachers can bridge the gap between theory and practice. To become a successful teacher, I needed to not think of myself as a teacher in training who met the university requirements, but as a co-teacher working collaboratively with like-minded educators who were committed to teaching in urban settings where excellence and leadership are needed most. John Bidwell PDS gave me opportunities that I might not have had otherwise, to connect across boundaries at the school site, with diverse forms of knowledge and experience—all of which helped me to develop my range of leadership as an effective teaching candidate.

Epstein (1995) argues that fostering school, family, and community partnerships strengthens school programs and environments, supports families, increases teacher effectiveness, and ultimately enhances pupil learning. John Bidwell School supported these types of partnerships. As an observer and participant in this kind of collaborative environment, I was able to become a "voice" and bring about change within my school community. There were several key experiences that shaped this process.

Prolonged Placement. The single most important element that influenced the development of my leadership skills was the length of placement at my school site. Most candidates are placed at different school sites each semester in the program. However, I was fortunate to be placed the entire three semesters at John Bidwell School. I became immersed in the school culture and community. I was able to build relationships and make connections with the principal, teachers, staff members, and, most crucially, the pupils and their families. I came to understand my classroom and my school in light of their complexities, strengths and challenges; and because I became more invested personally in all of the people at the school as time passed, I sought out more and more opportunities to play a role in strengthening and improving the school. These opportunities gave me the confidence to volunteer my services, and teach science to 5th and 6th grade pupils while also attending to my assigned responsibilities as a candidate in grade 1.

Steering Committee. In our PDS, novice teachers were encouraged to join the steering committee that governed the program. The steering committee offered an important environment in which teachers shared individual areas of expertise with candidates, administrators, and other educators. It also provided me with a genuine opportunity to exercise my "voice" as a representative of the teacher candidates. As I sat at these meetings during my first phase of student teaching, I was struck by the collegiality and the fact that my "voice" was as valued and respected as those of others with more experience or "expertise." Participation in the work of the steering committee enabled me to gain a broader perspective of the inner workings of the school, and to see how the four PDS goals played out in a "real-life setting." This, in turn, allowed me to connect pedagogical theories taught at the university to the school culture and teaching experiences. Suddenly, I became aware of how Paulo Freire's (1970) theory of enhancing *community*, building *social capital*, and leading us to act in ways that promote justice and humanity was being actualized in the school community!

Home Visits. Finding my "teacher voice" did not happen overnight. But as my involvement increased within the steering committee, I became increasingly aware of how my leadership skills could be used to meet the needs of pupils beyond the classroom. A key event occurred when I partnered with my CT to make home visits. We worked with a pupil's family to determine the best steps to take to impact the child's learning, and then ultimately we tutored him to meet his special needs.

I could see a definitive change occur as a result of the connection between the family and the school. Home visits allowed me to gain experience in communicating with parents of culturally, academically, and linguistically diverse children. This pattern of joining teachers and families together to meet the needs of pupils as academic, cultural, and social beings was very powerful.

Professional Development. During the summer prior to my last semester of student teaching, I represented my school site at a PDS summer institute at the university. SPREE was a collaborative project developed and implemented by faculty members in the College of Education and the College of Natural Science and Mathematics. This two-week institute focused on teaching standards- and inquiry-based science, in ways that supported English Language Learners and connected science learning to important community issues. The summer institute deepened participants' science content and pedagogical knowledge; interested participants were encouraged to continue their learning through academic year lesson study teams facilitated by the faculty members who taught in the summer institute. I was profoundly inspired by the SPREE Institute and the process of lesson study. With the principal's support and encouragement, I introduced the concept of lesson study to the faculty at a staff meeting, and later planned and developed a science lesson for intermediate pupils, with the collaboration of the principal, faculty supervisor, two teachers, and myself. After teaching the lesson once, the team provided feedback and we made modifications to the lesson. Ultimately, I had the opportunity to teach this lesson on atoms to four groups of 5th and 6th graders. The revision of the lesson each time enabled us to hone the content and optimize pupil learning and with each successive lesson, pupil achievement increased. And, the next year, nine colleagues joined me at SPREE and on lesson study teams.

The supportive, collaborative environment at Bidwell PDS enabled me to take risks that I doubt I would have taken had my experience at the school excluded any of the factors described above—tenure at the school, participation in work outside the classroom and opportunities for professional development.

The Power of Connections and Ideas for Future Directions

As teacher educators who place candidates solely in urban settings, the Equity Network educators contend that candidates need to develop feelings of "ownership" so they will work to transform the urban educational setting rather than feel defeated by it (Lane, Lacefield-Parachini, & Isken, 2003). In our experience, this ownership comes from thoughtfully structured opportunities to connect candidates to the multiple dimensions of urban schools, from stronger connections and joint work with mentor teachers to collaborative projects with pupils' families. These connections help candidates develop a sense of being a part of the school, having ownership over its successes and its challenges, and feeling emboldened by the knowledge that these connections generate to take action to transform classrooms and schools. Our experience confirms that candidates can become what Price and Valli (2005) describe as agents of change: people who "integrate" across boundaries, act proactively rather than reactively, and inspire others to do things differently.

Though we have not systematically compared candidates' preparation across models or instructors, one anecdotal comparison was offered by a PDS administrator: prior to implementing the PDS, her office was often the site of teary conferences with candidates in the midst of a two-week takeover, coming face to face with their inadequate skills and overwhelming anxieties. After the implementation of the PDS model, these kinds of encounters were a rarity—by the time the two-week takeover occurred in that last semester, the candidates were well prepared for the challenges. Data from a program exit survey provide some early measures of our efforts: candidates with PDS experiences are twice as likely as those with non-PDS experiences to indicate a preference for working in schools serving LI/RCLD pupils. These data and other research (Castle, Fox, & Souder, 2006; Ridley, Hurwitz, Hackett, & Miller, 2005) embolden our commitment to collaboratively designed and implemented urban teacher preparation programs that build on the power of connections. We contend that these deepened connections have contributed to growth in candidates' cultural competence, ability to develop relationships with pupils, colleagues and community members, capacity to advocate for fairness and equity, and analysis of school policies and programs.

We conclude with the following vignette and our analysis of it, as it relates to the notion of the power of connections.

> Paper airplanes fly, magnets adhere to metal objects and roll randomly on the floor, balloons pop, robots walk mechanically across the room, and 150 children, squished into the cafeteria, alternately yelp with glee and write poetry about flight, sound, and magnetism. Toss into this mix 45 candidates, along with a handful of substitute teachers and you have our first chaotic Curriculum Morning at John Bidwell School! Our initial intent was to provide an opportunity to two cohorts of candidates to plan and teach exciting, hands-on science and poetry lessons, so that the teachers at the school were "freed up" to attend professional development training from school district personnel. However good our intentions were, the reality was that the candidates were frazzled, the school site teachers felt disconnected from the event, and at best it was fun for the pupils, but there was little discernible pupil learning.

So, when the principal invited us back the following semester for another Curriculum Morning, both site teachers and candidates expressed a desire to become actively involved in planning the event. During several planning sessions, representatives from the teaching staff, candidates, university faculty members, the principal, and a grandparent from the school community worked side-by-side to design the event. Four Bidwell teachers provided a professional development session for their colleagues to provide science content knowledge for the teachers to help connect them to the content that their pupils would learn during the Curriculum Morning. Two other teachers assumed the role of providing technology and other resources for the teaching staff. The candidates on the committee were instrumental in providing feedback that improved many of the logistical issues. One example of this was to move the event from the multipurpose room to a more manageable situation where the teaching candidates rotated to classrooms and worked with between 20 and 30 pupils at one time, instead of 150 children. The committee also decided to provide each pupil with a science journal to record information and data from the demonstrations. This was in response to the desire to focus on pupil learning outcomes during the event. The grandparent who attended the meetings suggested a "hospitality room" where the visitors would congregate, and she volunteered to contact parents from the school community to staff this room. Each of the stakeholders made positive contributions to the success of this second Curriculum Morning.

Although this particular scenario might cause the faint of heart to shy away from collaborative activities on such a grand scale, we feel that this vignette aptly illuminates the power of connections, our theme for this section. In this vignette, candidates, CTs, the school administrator, parents, and university faculty members forged connections around the shared goal of providing pupils with an enriched science and language arts experience. To do this successfully, university instructors needed expanded knowledge of pupils, classroom teachers, and the adopted curriculum. The K–12 educators learned new strategies for scaffolding instructional experiences for novice teachers. Candidates deepened skills on all levels so that this innovative project would be successful. All honed important collaboration skills.

Ultimately, these kinds of experiences—where educators have an opportunity to know what they know better (e.g., school personnel have very vivid experiences with their own professional development that is key to informing candidate preparation) and to work across domains that challenge them to expand their knowledge and skill sets (i.e., university instructors and candidates putting theory into practice in K–6 settings and practitioners developing activities across grade levels and with innovative elements)—strengthen the practice and effectiveness of all involved. These experiences are probably most significant for candidates whose values and habits will be shaped by these transformative activities that place connections at the center of how they will act as professionals.

Chapter Six

Structural Shifts and Cultural Transformations

University Faculty Members and their Work in PDSs

Jana Noel and Deidre B. Sessoms

The power of connections for faculty members has created opportunities for myriad new projects, which have led, in turn, to significant role transformation and redefinition and new knowledge creation. Partnering with schools in collaborative relationships has not only given our Equity Network faculty members the opportunity to develop as leaders, but has also led to a considerable restructuring of our programs and the transformation of department and college culture. We have taken on new roles: liaisons to K–12 schools, coordinators of teacher preparation centers, leaders within community partnerships, administrators, grant writers, and advocates. We have, as a Center Coordinator stated, "become more relevant" to schools, community groups, and even candidates. Connections across roles, knowledge domains, and institutional boundaries have revealed new information, perspectives, and knowledge. Consequently, we have a broader understanding of how to work within the K–18 educational system to create reform, and we have deeper knowledge of how to work within local LI/RCLD communities to enact change toward equity. Our expectations of ourselves, our students, our K–12 partners, and our institution, have markedly changed. We now know better what we already knew, though we know it now through new lenses as change advocates whose full scope of vision includes CTs, pupils, families, district administrators, and community-based organizations.

In attempting to make connections across apparently separate domains, we are working against the grain, and, in doing so, we are sorting out the tensions between at least two competing and conflicting paradigms for teacher education, while simultaneously grounding our paradigm choice in authentic practices that have been collaboratively developed (Cochran-Smith, 1991). These innovative practices, grounded in a new (for our institution) paradigm of teacher education, were expressed in familiar and unfamiliar terrain. Our experiences illustrate how key factors—a clear focus on social justice goals, collaboration, negotiation, persistence, rigor, and reflection—facilitate important connections so that the system can operate more coherently and to the benefit of greater numbers of its stakeholders. We begin with a brief overview of the history of school–university relations, so that our experiences can be understood in their relevant historical context. Next, we describe some of the new faculty roles that have emerged as a result of PDS work. We then discuss the complexities and challenges of making role shifts such that connections are more fluid. Finally, we address the important conceptual and political work needed to solidify new connections for faculty members—across institutional status lines, departments, and disciplines and between the university and classrooms, schools, and communities.

Faculty Roles Historically: The Shift Toward Urban School–University Collaborations

Many postsecondary schools developed specifically to educate future teachers. Normal Schools were introduced in the 1830s. Generally credited to Horace Mann in Massachusetts, the practice of training teachers in Normal Schools spread throughout the country and lasted through the early 1900s. These institutions existed solely for teacher preparation and allowed many women, who were otherwise excluded from higher education, the chance to further their education and acquire professional training. While these Normal Schools ensured a more standardized, systematic, and scientific preparation for teaching, they have often been criticized for having lower standards of academic rigor than other professional education. These schools also reinforced discriminatory gender and class distinctions (Ducharme & Ducharme, 1996).

When teacher education moved into universities, contact with schools actually diminished. John Dewey's laboratory school at the University of Chicago, founded in 1896, was a harbinger of an early movement toward more involvement of university faculty in practicing elementary schools (Lyons, Stroble, & Fischetti, 1997). This model situated elementary schools directly on the university campus so that university faculty members could have more access to classrooms and teachers for study and experimentation. The lab school movement continues with active research and practice sites on universities throughout the country.

However, from the perspective of faculty roles, there are several short-comings within the lab school model that can be corrected through the PDS approach. First, the lab schools are isolated from communities and neighborhoods simply by virtue of being on university campuses. Even though faculty members spend time in the lab school classrooms, they are typically not involved in the daily community life of the children and families who attend the school. Second, the lab school concept does not broaden connections across roles, knowledge bases, or domains of action and expertise; university faculty members generally continue to function within their traditional roles, only superficially connected to school administrators, teachers, or pupils. Third, because the pupils who attend lab schools traditionally have been the children of university faculty members, this is a limited educational equity strategy.

In the 1990s, the Holmes Group (1990), John Goodlad (1994), and others proposed deep partnership collaborations across K–20 boundaries. The PDS principles address their goals and led university faculty members not only to become part of the school's community, but also to join with the K–12 sector in forging new processes through which the system could operate with purpose, coherence, and efficiency. Unlike other models, the PDS model has vast potential for intensifying, in positive ways, the connections across institutions and sectors in the educational system. Additionally, the traditional tripartite university faculty responsibilities of teaching, scholarship, and service take on new foci within urban PDSs. University courses are often moved directly into the K–12 school; scholarship is often expanded to include collaborative research with K–12 teachers; and, finally, service has expanded beyond university committees and disciplinary professional associations and journals in order to include a variety of duties in schools and community organizations. Often these new service commitments are linked with school reform efforts, and these in turn have become more prominent in faculty members' teaching and scholarship.

These shifts in primary faculty roles have responded not only to the aims of the PDSs but also to sentiment among K–12 teachers and the public that there is a lack of relevance in teacher education programs and a lack of connection between university, school, and community—the so-called theory–practice split. As Howey and Zimpher (1994) wrote, "Service by teacher educators has been neither widespread nor effective, at least in terms of direct contributions to improving elementary and secondary schools in urban and rural areas where problems are greatest" (p. 2). University PDS faculty members have explicitly taken on these challenges, but there continue to be even broader demands. As Ducharme and Ducharme argued, "the current teacher education faculty must add another urgent need to their efforts: they must expand their focus . . . in order to come to terms with their role in the larger issues of the transformation of schools" (1996, p. 706).

New Faculty Leadership Roles:
Liaisons to Equity Network Schools

In order to realize the Equity Network vision, we created a new faculty role: Liaison to an Equity Network School (LENS faculty). Faculty members in these positions had responsibility for fostering both broader and more in-depth interactions and collaborations with urban schools. Twelve faculty members who were committed to this goal became the first LENS faculty group. Some had previously been teachers at the schools with which they would work as faculty members; some had been involved in PDS work or other field-based collaborative programs through prior appointments. Others had been informally working in this role through modifications to the Center Coordinator role (discussed below) that had been supported by Stuart Foundation resources in the late 1990s. We were given a modest amount of "release time" from other duties in order to spend more time in the schools and this facilitated the trial-and-error efforts needed to redefine our roles as the LENS faculty. While the LENS role could include some of the duties traditionally performed by a Center Coordinator (especially if a Center Coordinator also worked as a LENS faculty member), the LENS role was envisioned to have other distinct responsibilities needed to further the PDS agenda, including: attending school staff meetings; serving on school site planning and/or governance teams; staffing an office within the Professional Development School; leading/facilitating teacher research groups at school sites; facilitating equity-related professional development activities for teachers; collaborating with teachers and principals on grant writing; conducting collaborative inquiry and research projects, including making presentations at professional conferences; facilitating candidate involvement in the activities and culture of the school and community; creating learning opportunities for K–12 pupils together with families and community members; and participating in the work of social service agencies within the neighborhoods of our schools.

Just as PDS teachers became connected to new knowledge and better connected to knowledge they already had, much the same was true for university faculty members as they embraced the LENS role. Though most of us had been K–12 teachers or had spent considerable time in classrooms and with teachers through projects and research, this LENS role required deep immersion in a school site and disciplined reflection on and analysis of the factors that contributed to success and to difficulty at the site and in its classrooms. We had to draw on knowledge bases related to all the social sciences in order to make sense of what we observed in schools. Then, we had to hone our skills in diplomacy, observations and feedback, and strategic decision-making to stabilize the emerging working relationships that ultimately gave us legitimacy in the school, community, and community agencies. As our knowledge and skills grew, these relationships were strengthened, thus greatly enhancing our capacity to be partners with the school in making equity changes.

LENS faculty members operate from a complex set of beliefs, actions, and dispositions in order to manage variables from multiple domains (organizational development; administrative and teacher leadership; informal communication networks; community involvement) and to build systemic structures that enhance organizational commitment and competency for the achievement of complex, long-term reforms. In other words, there are "important elements of the new knowledge, skills, beliefs, and dispositions used by this emerging type of bicultural PDS professor who feels at home, is effective, and is respected in both the university and PreK–12 settings" (Simmons, Konecki, Crowell, & Gates-Duffield, 1999, pp. 37–38).

As one LENS faculty member describes it, these strategic role shifts open the university programs to significant input from the K–12 partners, just as the PDS requires the schools to open up to university involvement and research-based practices:

> We have this monthly meeting and [another] one every six weeks to two months where we actually spend a whole day with the teachers and plan the program. So the teachers actually have votes about when the classes will be the next year, and what kind of times they want with the STs [student teachers], like do they want blocks of time or do they want some time each day, or all those sorts of things about the program, what the program should do for the school—these are all collectively decided. (LENS faculty member interview)

In this Network PDS, the LENS faculty member is intimately connected with key people at the school site and within the university; she has been able to effectively mediate deep changes in both contexts, while also garnering broad participation. She has managed to keep all the various partners "happy" or, at least, engaged. Few doctoral programs or junior faculty pathways are structured to prepare new faculty members for such a role, straddling as it does multiple worlds and knowledge bases. It is a challenge that our faculty members engaged because of their strong commitments to creating a teacher preparation program capable of transformation at both the university and school levels.

New Faculty Leadership Roles: Coordinators of Teacher Preparation Centers

After working as part of the LENS faculty, several faculty members decided to apply their learning to additional schools and settings. Though each had worked with a single school in the Network, their new positions as Center Coordinators (a role that predated the PDSs) brought their vision to a larger audience since multiple schools were connected to each Center. The principle of intensive field-based teacher preparation linked to the larger community and community agencies reshaped the programs even when a PDS was not formally institutionalized in every school in the Center. Center Coordinators with PDS experience broadened the impact, not only of the Network but also of the university's teacher preparation programs. The following sketches reveal how purposeful PDS-type changes in the Centers strengthened teacher preparation for LI/RCLD pupils.

Urban Teacher Education Center (UTEC)

One of the long-standing centers for teacher preparation at CSUS was called the Sacramento City Center, which placed candidates in schools within the Sacramento City Unified School District. This Center had the traditional structure with university courses offered on the CSUS campus and candidates placed at twelve to fifteen elementary schools situated in a range of low-income through to upper-income neighborhoods. Motivated by Center faculty members' work in the Equity Network, this Center was transformed into the Urban Teacher Education Center (UTEC) in fall 2004. UTEC emerged from multilayered discussions among the Network LENS faculty members and administrators in the College, the district and at one key site, destined to be the "hub" for UTEC. UTEC built on the strong relationships previously developed with Title I schools and drew those schools into deeper commitments to teacher preparation while further securing CSUS' ties to LI/RCLD urban schools and communities.

The UTEC description that is sent to candidates entering the teacher education program highlights the community-oriented, field-based, and LI/RCLD focus of the Center. A central UTEC principle is that effective education in urban settings emerges when teachers know how to teach in classrooms *and* learn about and engage in the communities of their pupils. Through activities that span spaces at the school and reach into those of the neighborhood and community groups and agencies, UTEC candidates access the funds of knowledge and assets within racially and ethnically diverse families and communities. With modeling and support from faculty, teachers, and parents, UTEC candidates learn to make solid home/community-classroom/school connections on personal, curricular, programmatic, and governance levels.

The debut of UTEC has had an immediate impact on the stated interests of the CSUS candidates who selected that Center for their preparation. In a study that queried incoming candidates on their choice of Center, 60% of candidates for the traditional program indicated that the diversity of pupils influenced their choice and 33% indicated that the poverty of the pupils is what drew them (Noel, 2002). Several years later, during UTEC's first year of operation, candidates voiced an increased interest in working with diverse pupils (73%) and in a poverty setting (65%), and, in addition, many were attracted to the focus on community involvement (33%).

San Juan PDS Center

The suburban San Juan Unified School District is an award-winning district that *Money* magazine lists as one of the "best" in the country. When pupils enter the CSUS teacher preparation program, many know of this reputation for excellence and request to have it be the site of their field experiences and student teaching (Noel, 2002). This image, however, obscures the needs of the many LI/RCLD pupils, clustered at the district's western edge, who have a substantially different achievement profile. In the case of this Center, much of the initial impetus for establishing PDSs came from within the district itself, which strategically viewed hosting candidates and becoming involved in new teacher preparation as central components in their effort to transform its struggling schools, and from two administrators who were acquainted with the PDS model and energized by it. Initially, a fundamental transformation was required: CSUS and district resources had to be prioritized for the two and eventually three Title I sites that became the hosts for a new collaboratively designed PDS Center.

The San Juan PDS Center quickly established a new reputation among CSUS candidates, enticed by such PDS activities as schoolwide curriculum projects, before-school tutoring projects, teacher research groups, brown bag speaker series featuring presentations by teachers on topics identified by candidates, and opportunities to present at local, state, and national conferences. In the same study previously mentioned, data revealed that candidate responses also changed with the shift in Center focus. After the PDS Center was created, new candidates still recognized the district's "reputation for excellence" (Noel, 2002), but 70% indicated that they selected the San Juan PDS Center due to its diverse pupil population, and 48% due to the number of pupils in poverty. Prior to this reorientation, only 33% and 20%, respectively, of candidates indicated these factors as preferences. Furthermore, candidates indicated an additional understanding that the Center's PDS structure provided "the opportunity to be fully involved with teachers on a regular basis" (Noel, 2005). Among other things, we can see that the change to a PDS Center oriented toward LI/RCLD communities furthered a central PDS and district goal: to attract candidates with positive dispositions and commitments to LI/RCLD settings (Haberman, 2000; Murrell, 2001; Weiner, 2000).

New Faculty Leadership Roles: Community Partners

Experience with school reform naturally led Equity Network faculty members to confront the limits of a schools-only approach to social justice, necessitating a search for ways to become more intimately involved in the communities where the PDSs were located. The traditional practice of staying safely on campus shifted along with a growing sense that they were becoming members of an "urban education community" (Noel, 2004). This understanding aligns with principles articulated by a number of other urban (Anyon, 2005; Lipman, 2004) and PDS educators (Holmes Group, 1995; Howey, 2000).

Howey (2000) laid out ten attributes of a high-quality urban teacher education program, including: "The involvement of prospective teachers in a host of urban community and community agency activities" (p. 13). Research conducted by the University of California's Center for Research on Education, Diversity & Excellence on successful urban education communities confirms this assertion. Other advocates for improving urban education and urban teacher preparation have emphasized connecting teachers with the families of their pupils, such as by conducting home visits with an ethnographic eye (Gonzalez, Moll, & Amanti, 2005). Teachers familiar with the community's and families' "funds of knowledge" will be better able to integrate the daily lives and values of the children into their classrooms and curriculum.

Equity Network faculty members have endeavored to embody these principles. Some have sought out or been recruited to become members of partner community agencies and organizations, even serving on the boards. The Equity Network's commitment to community engagement provided a springboard to broader involvements that reached beyond opening lines of communication or participating in meetings or activities. Network faculty members collaborated on funding proposals and shared other forms of leadership; one became a school board member.

One LENS faculty member has made connections with community the cornerstone of her sabbatical, during which she is working as the "community liaison" between an urban, LI/RCLD elementary school (the UTEC "hub" school) and the two public housing complexes served by the school. She takes part in community gatherings, resident meetings, a home-grown tutoring and mentoring center within the housing projects, and sits in on the planning sessions of the social service agencies located within one of the complexes. She helped create a "Community Outreach" committee of teachers and staff at the school, and is currently working with the school's principal to get a full-time counselor transferred from the neighborhood social services center into the school. School personnel and candidates have worked together to create a Family Resource Center. To ensure that candidates gain knowledge of both the strengths and needs of the community and make connections with parents, she has invited parents from the community to appear as guest lecturers in her Educational Foundations courses, which is taught at the elementary school.

Toward a Theoretical Orientation for What We Have Done

Much of the research literature on the roles of university faculty members in urban school–university collaborations focuses on initiating and negotiating a complex world of both bureaucratic and personal interactions (Bryant, Nechie, Neapolitan, Madden, & Rifkin, 2004; Hartzler-Miller & Wainwright, 2004; Howey, 1994; Lyons, Stroble, & Fischetti, 1997; Simmons et al., 1999). Howey (1994) examined how these complex interactions require "faculty development" in three areas: classrooms, corridors, and streets (p. 36). In collaborative contexts, an "ideal" integration can emerge, where the work in classrooms, corridors, and streets can be mutually reinforcing as the faculty members learn more about each domain and become more skilled in making connections across them. We feel we are making progress toward this ideal.

The creation of the LENS faculty role and the operationalization of this role by twelve to fifteen faculty members have deepened connections between "classroom" and other parts of the system, as detailed in many chapters in this book. While such collaboration is applauded in principle, deeper connections with "classrooms" force university faculty members to view their theoretical frameworks from an empirical and practical stance, which usually results in critical reflection on the implications of such theories for the lives of real children and teachers engaged in learning and teaching. This deep and critical reflection has necessitated work not just in classrooms but also at the department, college, and university levels. Here, Howey's notion of "corridors" is helpful since it invokes faculty work conducted within the university's physical space and organizational structure and culture. It was critical that we created a new role, the LENS faculty, in order to successfully support the PDS work. And while this "corridor" work is imperative, it is also often more difficult and less immediately engaging than the classroom work, as will be detailed in the next section.

Howey's notion of "streets" is meant to identify work that faculty members must do with partners and colleagues in other organizations from schools to community groups in order to effect change. In the previous examples, we revealed our tentative efforts to do this. LENS faculty members have shown that meaningful connections with communities bring a broad range of benefits to all the PDS partners—university faculty members, candidates, K–12 teachers, administrators, pupils, and parents. This kind of leadership extends far beyond the traditional conception of service among the professoriate. As faculty members bridge the divides among universities, schools, and communities, they are better able to meet the educational goals of teacher preparation and of the K–12 schools themselves, and even begin to work as allies to the parents as they unite together for social justice for their LI/RCLD communities.

Complexities and Challenges of New Faculty Roles

When we formed the Equity Network, only one faculty member was tenured. The remaining eleven faculty members were junior faculty. And while the commitment to urban PDSs was strong, the challenges seemed particularly daunting and the responses to them especially complex. It is worth emphasizing that a community of faculty learners—the LENS faculty and/or Center Coordinators with a PDS vision—provided important support and impetus for the initiatives described, which were bold because they were innovative and because they were led by junior faculty in the college.

A survey administered in Fall 2005 and completed by fifteen faculty members who all had been substantially involved in Equity Network activities sheds light on some dimensions of this community and its values. The survey presented a variety of items that were ultimately grouped into three categories: social justice (e.g., focusing work on opportunities and challenges in LI/RCLD settings), teachers and schools (developing teacher leaders, implementing the PDS model), and professional benefits (receiving assigned time, streamlining focus to one to two schools, opportunities for community service—important in promotion and tenure). While our motivation for participating in the Equity Network varied, there was significant agreement across the respondents regarding the most important and least important factors, with the least important being those factors extrinsic to the work itself (e.g., receiving assigned time in our workload or having the opportunity to combine our workload). All but one LENS faculty member ranked "Focus on low income students and schools" as a key factor motivating their work in the Equity Network and all respondents ranked "Focus on urban school challenges" in the top five most important factors. All but two faculty members ranked "Receiving assigned time for my work" as one of their lowest motivating factors.

Thus, the LENS faculty group, which has remained fairly stable over time, began with common values, which have only been strengthened as the group has experienced successful innovations and the prospect of continued success (because of deepening relationships with each other and schools, strong administrative support at the college, and increasing grant funding).

This has energized faculty members, particularly those in the junior rank, to take risks and assert leadership probably much earlier than if they had not been connected to this group. In addition, the deepened connections with teachers, administrators, and district staff associated with the PDS sites also emboldened faculty members, because these stakeholders were quite adamant about the importance of the changes.

Despite having strong, collegial support, considerable complexity still characterized these efforts to transform the structural, organizational, and institutional practices of the departments, college, and university context that housed our work. At a deeper level too, challenges emerged from shifts in values and priorities that the PDS work catalyzed, often unwittingly, as the LENS faculty members attempted simply to implement ideas that were consonant with their values and commitments.

Changing Values, Changing Priorities

The Equity Network pulled together a faculty group across departments (that had a contentious history) to focus explicitly on urban education. This seemed like an obvious step to take—after all, *Time* described our city as the most diverse in the country. Test score data, increasingly the *only* benchmark used to think about pupils and schools, demonstrated year after year that it was our LI/RCLD pupils who were consistently short-changed by our system. Moreover, the Bilingual/Multicultural Education Department (BMED) was founded on a commitment to social justice for LI/RCLD pupils and communities and the Teacher Education Department (TE) had a long history of faculty labor activism. Thus, we assumed that the apparent agreement about the "problem" (e.g., educational inequity due to institutionalized discrimination that required reform), also meant agreement about appropriate solutions (i.e., that university faculty members become involved, in role-appropriate ways, in urban school reform). In fact, we discovered that while people voiced much concern about the "problem," there had been little discussion about possible solutions or whether we had any role to play in enacting them.

Not surprisingly, as LENS faculty members began to address a central question of how best to design urban teacher preparation programs we bumped up against long-held department (TE) and college traditions and values about our programs and how they would best operate. Some of the many questions we faced included: What happens in an institution where "competition" between teacher preparation models is disallowed, where we do not discuss whether one approach or another will best serve LI/RCLD communities, where it is implicitly assumed "good" teacher preparation will serve suburban and urban schools equally well, and where involving K–12 teachers in substantive ways in implementing the program (e.g., as candidate supervisors or in designing courses) is viewed by some as giving up too much control to those who have been socialized by a broken school system?

As we embarked on discussing and acting on possible responses to these questions, we discovered that our efforts challenged the status quo in numerous ways. This led to confusion about our program and department goals, confrontations among faculty members, hurt feelings and fears among some junior faculty members about how their involvement in PDS work might impact the retention, tenure, and promotion process. Some of the tensions were an inevitable part of the change process—those coordinating existing programs were offended by the critique of existing practice implied by efforts to develop innovations and we have realized that more can always be done to try to facilitate smooth, informed transitions. But exposure of deep differences in values, priorities, and commitments, particularly at the level of action (rather than simply rhetoric), only exacerbated the inevitable tensions of the change process.

Changing Practices, Changing Structures

The research on teacher preparation strongly suggests that alternative educational paradigms—what we believe "counts" as knowledge or who we believe should have power in schools and classrooms—lead to teacher preparation programs with vastly different structures, activities, and goals. As we reflect on our work, we find much in the theoretical literature to help deepen our understanding of our struggles. In the behaviorist tradition of teacher preparation, candidates are assisted in developing specific observable performance skills that are assumed to be related to pupil learning. Critical reflection on the teacher's or school's goals or on the social context is not encouraged. In contrast, an inquiry-oriented program encourages its candidates to explore the contexts of teaching and learning and promotes certain dispositions, such as critical questioning and the value of personal versus school knowledge. In this view, the prospective teacher is an active participant in constructing knowledge about teaching and learning while critically examining educational goals and practices, in larger contexts (society as a whole or a particular district or school) and smaller (the individual candidate's daily teaching practices). Few of our college colleagues follow a behaviorist model and most operated from an inquiry perspective.

Cochran-Smith (1991) further subdivides this model into critical dissonance and collaborative resonance frameworks, offering a context for the struggles we experienced in implementing the Equity Network PDS model. In "critical dissonance" teacher preparation programs candidates experience dissonance between the critical university perspective on teaching and learning and the candidates' own generally less-critical school-based experiences—including the experiences they have as candidates. It is assumed that, without intervention, candidates inevitably become socialized into a conservative school culture that perpetuates inequities. Therefore, dissonant moments are structured in to facilitate candidates' development of a critical perspective toward those inequities (of race, class, gender, etc.) in order to interrupt the cycle. Cochran-Smith notes that critical dissonance programs have had little overall success, at least in part because programs with this ideology perpetuate the theory/practice split between the ideals of university faculty and realities of schools and teachers; studies indicate that candidates report being most influenced in their practice by their field experiences.

"Collaborative resonance" teacher preparation programs also aim to reform schools, and they too recognize that candidates' experiences in schools can be more powerful than their experiences in the university classroom. Therefore, collaborative resonance programs attempt to strengthen the connection between what candidates learn in university coursework and in local schools. Critical questioning of school practices or the culture of teaching is still vitally important, but it is done collaboratively, *with* the candidate, host schoolteacher, and university faculty member together examining practices and goals in school/site-based seminars or joint research projects. The dominant message of a collaborative resonance program is that school reform is possible when stakeholders collaborate, when power is shared, and the knowledge and experiences of reform-minded teachers and the greater school community are as important as that of university faculty members. Cochran-Smith (1991) argues that collaborative resonance programs are exemplars of participatory democracy and, as such, are more effective at assisting in teaching against the grain. We would argue that this collaborative democracy should extend to the design and implementation of teacher preparation programs, and therefore assist university faculty members in working against the grain as well.

Our work with the PDSs fit best with this collaborative resonance model, and, as such, represented an obvious break from paradigms used generally in the college historically. As LENS faculty members and Center Coordinators, we had authority with which to make program and course changes. In implementing changes consistent with our commitments to urban school reform and the PDS goals, we engaged in a public rethinking of key principles undergirding our college teacher preparation programs, particularly those in TE. As we crafted concrete responses to these questions, we had to tackle daunting structural impediments. Our successes and setbacks in this arena ultimately taught us how to act as change agents in our own institutional setting and honed our skills at negotiating the "corridors" of this difficult institutional terrain.

Faculty Members Taking Risks

Powerful institutional norms and simple inertia resist the changes needed for PDS faculty members to operate effectively and efficiently. Differing theoretical stances, discussed earlier, exacerbated preexisting tensions, whether these stances were explicitly or implicitly stated by faculty members. Complicating this situation was the fact that rarely did we openly discuss these teacher preparation paradigms, in general, much less the specific ones that we were each pursuing. And perhaps the most difficult situation related to the fact that the PDS projects were implemented by LENS faculty members, the majority of whom had not earned tenure during the most intensive period of innovation (to date) for the Network. Although the outcomes were mostly positive for the collaboration (as when the San Juan PDS and UTEC Centers were formed), untenured faculty members experienced significant stress.

The retention, tenure, and promotion (RTP) concerns are worth discussing in more depth, since they are the coin of the realm in all universities and play a powerful role in shaping faculty values, even when faculty members try consciously to resist such manipulation. In the survey described earlier, LENS faculty members also responded to two open-ended questions about their experience with the RTP process and the role that their PDS work may have played in it. A number of complications with the tenure process were described by respondents, as were perceived professional risks. They noted that PDS work is holistic and its teaching-research-service components are interconnected, while the tenure process at our institution keeps them separate. A number of respondents noted that their work in a PDS was overlooked, dismissed, or misunderstood by the RTP committee, department chairs, and higher-level administrators. One faculty member who recently received tenure noted, "At times, it appeared that you were always trying to explain your work to someone who would be evaluating you and deciding your future." Moreover, many PDS projects crossed domains that are evaluated discretely in our RTP process—one PDS project, for example, could address teaching effectiveness, scholarship, and service all at the same time but, in the RTP evaluation, each domain required a discrete set of activities.

While these obstacles were troublesome, some faculty members did note that work in the Equity Network assisted them in the RTP process by providing authentic opportunities for mentoring with one other. The Network also provided semistructured opportunities for involvement in the public schools; this was particularly important for newer faculty members without prior connections to the local K–12 community. Over time, there was also an increased understanding and appreciation by some administrators and some members of RTP committees about the nature of PDS work. Faculty members also said that they could not overestimate the importance of the community of practice that arose from our shared work. More than once at our monthly Equity Network meetings, one of us would say "What can they do, fire *all* of us?"

Learning, Leading, and Becoming Relevant

As a result of our participation in urban school–community–university partnerships through the Equity Network PDSs, we have become more connected to deeper and broader funds of knowledge, opportunities to lead, and possibilities for being more relevant in a number of struggles for social justice, both in and outside of classrooms. By being physically present and actively engaged in our partner schools, we are now seen as persons who have a legitimate and helpful presence in school-based decisions and activities. In our departments, we are regarded as having knowledge about the daily realities of the urban schools in which we work, thus increasing our viability as candidates for new administrative roles. And due to our participation in K–12 schools, teachers and candidates see us virtually every day and have come to have more confidence in us. Our courses have more immediate relevancy as we have integrated knowledge of daily school life and classroom structures and practices. Our learning process has paralleled that of other PDS educators. "Perhaps the most significant change in the work of PDSs is the new knowledge that faculty are constructing. Teacher educators are deepening their understanding of the dynamics of learning to teach" (Lyons, Stroble, & Fischetti, 1997, p. 96). We have also deepened our understanding of the dynamics of urban school structures and processes. Beyond all of this, though, we have developed a passion for who we have become.

Dream Keepers, Weavers, and Shape Shifters

Simmons et al. (1999) invoked three metaphors to describe the work of university PDS faculty members: dream keepers, weavers, and shape shifters. Each metaphor aptly captures the spirit that we experienced as Equity Network LENS faculty members. We served as dream keepers as we worked to stay the course, keeping the PDS work focused on enhanced learning for LI/RCLD pupils and improved practice for their teachers, present and future. As dream keepers, we helped make our collaborations a priority for busy teachers and parents, and we ensured that they renewed a shared sense of purpose to improve education for urban children. As weavers, we integrated a range of innovative activities in the service of our primary PDS goals (hosting university pre-service teacher education courses at the school site, creating after-school tutoring programs, participating in teacher research groups, initiating book clubs for in-service teachers' professional development, creating school–community resource fairs, becoming involved in home visits, co-teaching university courses with both university and school faculty, and collaboratively writing and presenting papers at academic conferences). We have also functioned as "weavers" connecting across multiple constituencies to create a common commitment to meet the challenges of urban education.

One of the LENS faculty members writes of such experiences in terms of "choreographing a ballet." She "tried to figure out which steps to take first. Should I talk to the Principal first? What about the Vice Principal in charge of candidate placement? Should I talk to the district administrator? Which one(s)? Should I even be the one gaining access?" Another LENS faculty member described the difficulties of weaving together a program in the face of constant changes, including changes in key personnel. So, reweaving became standard as various PDS partners and the external context evolved over time. In becoming adept "weavers," PDS faculty members must learn whom to talk to, how to gain access, arrange for meetings with multiple parties at university, school, and district levels, how to bring in community resources, and tie these all together in ways that equitably satisfy the needs, hopes, and desires of all.

The notion of shape shifters accurately sums up the complex ways that we interact with others to create and facilitate partnership activities. "Leader, follower, director, facilitator, listener, speaker, researcher, information provider, challenger, protector, counselor, secretary, designer, cook, teacher, and learner have all been roles taken on by us as PDS university coordinators" (Simmons et al., 1999, p. 42). And, as one LENS faculty member adds, "Sometimes [we] carry the groceries." We have felt like shape shifters in very significant ways throughout the development of our Equity Network. We are constantly listening to the goals and needs of our school partners, and trying to marshal the vast resources of the university in service of those goals. We sometimes initiate and design practices in our schools, at other times we simply document and record activities that are already occurring. We sometimes challenge all participants to push harder in meeting the goals of the PDS. And we have sometimes worked to protect the school from impositions by the school districts in which we work. And throughout it all we serve as researchers attempting to learn about what makes a successful urban school–university collaboration.

But we are also constantly learners. As LENS faculty members, we learn from each other, teachers, administrators, parents, community members, K–12 pupils, and our own students. We learn about good (and bad) teaching practices, about the lives of urban pupils and their families, about school district and state bureaucracies, about our own roles as faculty members, and about what families and communities want for their children.

Serving as shape shifters, weavers, and dream keepers is a conscious, ongoing, subsuming effort that requires "not standing on protocol or rank, not being afraid to take a risk, and not being distant and reluctant to get muddy or messy in a real-life situation that needs a collaborative response . . . [in fact] we often seem to be deliberately trying to demonstrate this friendliness, humbleness, willingness, and flexibility to do what is necessary to move collaborative reform forward" (Simmons et al., 1999, p. 42).

As emerging and developing leaders in our own institutions and across our PDS schools, we strived to embody a model of "transformative leadership" that "responds to such human needs as the desire for purpose, meaning, and significance in what one does" (Sergiovanni, 1990, p. 32). We have experienced our work to be a form of personal professional renewal. We are emboldened by the fact that our experiments in urban school reform and teacher education have been incorporated into the standard programs and operations of our departments, college, and university. And we have been able to see many of the activities that we helped initiate and facilitate become recognized hallmarks of our PDS schools due to the sustained efforts of leadership teams at the schools themselves. In short, we make a difference, which is why we entered the field of education in the first place.

Section Three

The Politics of Transforming Institutions and Institutional Relationships

Pia Lindquist Wong and Ronald David Glass

Cross-institutional partnership work is complex and messy, and must create an emergent "road map" that cannot be specified entirely in advance. The partnership dynamics are also subject to the unique combination of expertise and personalities of the players involved. Further, K–12 and higher education institutions do not typically have a history of egalitarian collaborative work and they are often structured in ways that make their relationships competitive rather than cooperative. In addition, local educational and political contexts shape actions and policies, and are themselves impacted by the broader state and federal policy and political environment. Equally important for the Equity Network, attempts to redirect resources and reorient effort toward issues of inequity and social justice threaten all the partners in the system, who both unwittingly or sometimes deliberately protect the status quo and depend on existing ideological frameworks for understanding teaching and learning.

As we established the urban PDSs of the Equity Network, we discovered unexpected challenges that exacerbated the already difficult issues that we set out to address. We had to face difficult equity and political issues embedded in the structural features of colleges of education and K–12 schools that produce competing demands and differing role expectations for education faculty members and school teachers. We also had to confront a variety of structural constraints that inhibited the realization of collaborative intentions, and these were multiplied by the personal factors that make cooperative work so challenging. Additionally, the politics of knowledge that create barriers between community funds of knowledge, university research-based knowledge, and teacher knowledge had to be deconstructed in order to reconstruct teacher preparation, in-service teacher

173

professional development, school curriculum improvement, and the university faculty members' research programs and professional growth.

Over the last two decades, educators and policymakers have sought to define new directions for teacher education in order to address widely perceived failures to prepare teachers adequately for the challenges to be faced in schools, especially those serving the poor and those without proficiency in Standard English (Clifford & Guthrie, 1988; Goodlad, Soder, & Sirotnik, 1990; Holmes Group, 1995; Howey, 2000). Yet the calls for commitments to equity and meaningful educational opportunity, to reflective practice and action research that critically examine the real context of teaching and learning in urban schools, and to collaboration within and across contexts have often been unrealized (Hawthorne, 1997; Murrell, 1998). Similarly, the standards developed for PDSs (NCATE, 2001) often receive more rhetorical than institutional support when their implementation challenges long-established institutional structures and practices (Johnston, Brosnan, Cramer, & Dove, 2000).

The barriers to substantive transformation of colleges of education and the formation of collaborative PDSs with urban schools are complex and each particular story of change has its own lessons (Hoffman, Reed, & Rosenbluth, 1997). Not only are the expectations for the new forms of relationship and practice at odds with the existing institutional cultures (Shive, 1997), but also the larger social and political context of urban education gets entangled with the specific reform efforts in ways that undermine their efficacy (Stone, 1998a). These larger political issues interact with the particularities of how individuals inhabit institutional roles and of how those roles inhibit or conflict with the change effort (Carnate, Newell, Hoffman, & Moots, 2000; Dailey-Dickenson, 2000; Steel, Jenkins, & Colebank, 1997), even when undertaking collaborative research projects with goals appearing objectively reasonable (Reed, Ayersman, & Hoffman, 1997).

The effort to build connections, as we saw in section two, requires all the partners to remake their professional work, to approach the other stakeholders with respect, and to see that many of the institutional barriers that inhibit collaborative work have not been cast in stone but can be remade. Despite obstacles and multifaceted resistance, the praxis that arises from the everyday reality of the PDS work provides the means of overcoming the challenges that appear to defy resolution at the theoretical and institutional levels. Even state-level standards for teacher preparation programs and professional competence, and the national policy demands for accountability by standardized test scores, need not be the crushing forces they can appear to be. Little by little, the open spaces within these frameworks can be harnessed to the local knowledge in schools and universities resulting in educational experiences for both K–12 pupils and candidates that offer genuine hope for schools serving LI/RCLD children and communities.

We found that it helped us to discover paths forward through the challenges of our work when we clearly identified the political and ideological issues generating the structural tensions and conflicts present in the effort to transform organizational forms and roles required to implement an urban PDS partnership. We especially became aware of how the political debates and contradictions present in the wider discourse of urban educational reform often erase class and race (Stone, 1998b), and that these issues were precisely the ones that were often at the center of our professional relationships, school and university dynamics, and the lives of the children we were teaching. Moreover, we discovered that these political and ideological issues get played out in a context of institutional inertia and action aimed at subsystem protection (Jones & Hill, 1998) so that the status quo gets maintained and the innovative objectives we sought got defeated. Despite the many forces at work that subvert the possibility for change, there are, nonetheless, effective forces that can sustain the reform processes and enable substantive progress against the obstacles (Dickens, 2000; Hoffman, Rosenbluth, & McCrory, 1997). We learned that when the power relationships and politics of our work were made an explicit part of our interactions so that they could be examined and deconstructed, then we had a greater chance of overcoming the structural barriers that hindered the achievement of our goals.

The Equity Network established new intersections and new connections among the systems with primary responsibilities for preparing teachers and for teaching LI/RCLD pupils, and the processes underlying this establishment revealed that issues of authority and legitimacy were entangled with the institutional rules, regulations, norms, and definitions that constrained and shaped the situations within which we worked (Rowan & Miskel, 1999). As we peeled away these layers of institutional practice to identify the governing purposes from which they were generated, we recognized that our own practices reinforced many of the structural obstacles we faced. This gave us some hope for change since we believed that we could help one another adopt new roles and form new spaces for our work, but it also gave us hope for making change more broadly since the socially organized environments that constitute institutions are created through the actions of others like ourselves. As we took action to reshape our environment, we were producing new forms of legitimacy that challenged the traditional ways of doing things in K–12 schools and in colleges of education, and that subsequently started to become normative for a reconstructed approach to teacher preparation and professional development. For example, the affirmation, through the creation of an organizational structure that expressed it, that both research and practice-based knowledge were legitimate in the Network PDSs enabled us to reorganize access to information and the distribution of resources within the Network. This reorganization empowered teachers and helped to overcome their skepticism that university knowledge could be genuinely helpful for their work in a standards and testing constrained environment.

The reconstruction of the power and political relationships of schools and universities through the PDS was no small achievement because the historically encrusted norms and practices of the traditional modes of teacher preparation and professional development are structured into inequitable dynamics that are part of a "world system" of educational institutions and discourse. However, we were able to take advantage of niches of open space created through the "loose coupling" (Meyer & Rowan, 1977) that occurs in these types of formal organizations. Given that "rules are often violated, decisions are often unimplemented, or if implemented have uncertain consequences, technologies are of problematic efficiency, and evaluation and inspection systems are subverted or rendered so vague as to provide little coordination" (Meyer & Rowan, 1977, p. 343), we could find sufficient space for experimentation even under the prevailing surveillance systems of the standards and testing regimes.

Although most theory of organizational change characterizes organizational actors as rationally pursuing interests, even though embedded in contexts constrained by regulations, normative obligations, and/or cognitive schemata that can be contradictory, our experience has been otherwise. Rather, we found that, through the pursuit of collaborative projects, interests emerged and were negotiated as we went along, and that these were not linearly structured by preexisting institutional positions or interests, or by consciously held principles or sets of beliefs. The conflicts became resolved through the power of the shared aim of serving LI/RCLD pupils. So consensus was achieved around technical matters (e.g., approaches to teaching reading), outcomes (e.g., test scores vs. portfolios), and resource distribution in light of what each participant in the PDS could contribute. This legitimated the expertise, knowledge, dispositions, and skills of all the professionals involved and produced an overall stronger PDS program. While we did experience the coercive pressures of the educational policy arena and the surveillance systems it enacted, and this pressure pushed the PDSs toward conformity to the very systems we were trying to change, we managed to be innovative and push back against these dominant narratives and norms. Moreover, our shared leadership legitimated the knowledge contributions of all the participants and helped us avoid the tendency toward hierarchical relations typical of complex organizations, though this required deliberate coordination among the many actors at the implementation level of the PDS and in relation to our context of hierarchical institutional structures.

The powerful ideologies that animated those of us involved in the PDSs—commitment to equity, democratic processes, valorization of the funds of knowledge of LI/RCLD pupils and communities, and to the highest quality professional development—shaped our responses and influenced our choices more than the seemingly predetermined situation with which we started. What we had in common in these deeper ways—the mutual goals, clear communication channels, shared practices—influenced us more than the imposed isomorphisms (e.g., similar institutional control mechanisms like standards and certifications), and thus the PDSs were more effective than might be imagined in overcoming the traditional isolation and tensions that hamper relations among the actors in the universities and the K–12 systems.

Reforming Teacher Education Through the Equity Network: Politics, Problems, and Promising Practices

Attempts to change historical and institutionalized practices test one's resolve about making authentic and positive change. In fact, after years of doing this, we observe that identifying the issues is the easy part—trying to address them is not for the faint of heart. Part of the challenge is due to the complex and politically charged nature of institutional reform, particularly when it offers a clear alternative to institutional relationships that are segmented, territorial, and exclusive. The chapters in this section examine the multiple layers of institutional transformation that can potentially occur with PDS work, while also identifying the palpable politics of these transformations. In doing this, we consider the politics within PDS sites, as leadership roles are altered and specific teachers or groups of teachers emerge as key partners with the university faculty and pupils. We address politics within districts and between the district administrators, site administrators and university faculty around forging a common vision of pupil learning and teacher development and competence. We examine the university politics and the strategic measures necessary to convert rhetorical praise for the idea of urban PDSs into material actions. We discuss these layers of ideological, strategic, and political struggle within the overarching theme of changing educational institutions structured to reproduce inequality into educational institutions designed to foster equitable outcomes for LI/RCLD children.

Though the three chapters in this section describe very different situations and initiatives, they are tied together by an underlying analysis of the problems and politics of institutional reform, and, taken together, they provide us with a sophisticated view of the systems-thinking and acting that must occur if change to components of a system are to ripple into meaningful change at the system level. While researchers like Goodlad (1990) and Sarason (1993) aptly describe the symptoms of the problems—fragmentation, discontinuities, and so on—we found that the root of the problems in urban teacher preparation is often found in other dynamics as well.

One of these issues, key to the chapters in this section, is the question of knowledge—what knowledge is worth knowing? Who participates in making this determination? Who knows that knowledge best? How do we know? These broader questions, when translated into urban K–12 settings, generate additional queries: Why is some knowledge valued more highly than others? What are the cultural, gendered, and social class dimensions of decisions about what is taught and how? How do we know what pupils know, and how do we know if we have given them the appropriate kinds of opportunities to demonstrate what they know? Transferring these questions to teacher education programs creates additional questions, including: What do teachers know and do they know what they "need" to know? How do we know what teachers know? If teachers need to know more, what is the "best" way to do this? And, finally, what kind of knowledge do new teachers need in order to be effective? What is the "best" way to develop that knowledge (through practice, transmitted from others)? How do we know if they have learned what we have identified as important? Any effort to respond to these questions, particularly if done in a collaborative and cross-institutional manner as we attempted with the Equity Network, must evolve through an ongoing process of open dialogue, careful planning, critical reflection, and evaluated action. To reach consensus, it was necessary to systematically uncover and analyze layers of historical practice, institutional policy, personal attitudes, and deeply held misconceptions.

In chapter seven, "Perspectives on Negotiation and Equilibrium in the Politics of Knowledge: Transforming the University and the School into a PDS Partnership," Hayes examines the views of teachers and faculty at three PDS sites as they reflect on the start-up phase of their PDSs. In this polyvocal account, we come to understand how one's role in making institutional change shapes one's perspective on it, learning that even with common goals that are strongly held, context still circumscribes how different players understand significant educational reforms. The PDS leadership, shared across the schools and the university, intensely debated the key elements of knowledge about teacher education, about what beginning teachers most "need" to become quality teachers for LI/RCLD pupils, and what those pupils most "need" from their teachers to be successful in school and in life.

In chapter eight, "Not Starting from Scratch: Applying the Lessons from a Thwarted PDS Effort," Hecsh describes two ambitious high school PDS efforts. The successes, particularly in contributing to pupil achievement and the overall academic culture of the school, as well as the significant challenges, are recounted. This chapter provides rich examples and ideas, but also offers cautionary lessons about the ways in which meaningful reforms can become insulated and consequently misunderstood, and about the importance of constantly expanding a base of support for reforms. This case reveals much about the disparate tensions that surround what is worth knowing and who makes this decision, and it shows how some of the deepest underlying conflicts in the S-TEC project stemmed from questions about how we know what we know, and whether what we know and how we demonstrate it counts with those in authority.

Chapter nine, "Bridging the Disconnect: The Promise of Lesson Study," examines a widespread initiative launched during the penultimate year of our TQE grant, a lesson study effort that involved faculty from the Colleges of Education and of Natural Science and Mathematics and lesson study teams at ten of our twelve PDSs. In this chapter, Jelinek and Porter tease apart the multiple layers of meaning and action in the lesson study effort—an effort that is both simple and elegant in its emphasis on collaboration around the design and teaching of a model lesson but also complex and subversive in its potential to transcend traditional norms of isolation in teaching and to confront more current tendencies toward deprofessionalizing teaching, particularly in urban settings. Through analysis of teacher work products and reflections, the authors conclude that the lesson study effort demonstrates how strong school–university collaboration, central to the PDS work, provides a base from which to transform mandated curriculum and instruction that had previously appeared impervious to local interference. In this transformation process, this section's thematic questions around knowledge all come into play. Lesson study teachers must ask hard questions about pupil knowledge while also being willing to reflect on and question their own knowledge.

Chapter Seven

Perspectives on Negotiation and Equilibrium in the Politics of Knowledge

Transforming the University and the School into a PDS Partnership

Kathryn Hayes

Though there is much to celebrate about our urban school–university partnerships, we are still well aware that our experiences in these collaborative efforts are shaped by the roles that we play and the primary contexts with which we identify. In our ongoing effort to understand the realities and dynamics of urban PDSs, like those in the Equity Network, we conducted three case studies of Network schools in 2002 and 2003. These cases highlight moments of negotiation and equilibrium in the evolution of the partnerships.[1] In their third year and becoming well established as PDSs, each school had dynamic programs that had arisen organically from the intersection of the Equity Network vision and the institutional needs and requirements of the university and the school, as well as the personal and professional needs of the educators.

Each PDS had experienced periods of equilibrium, often preceded by rounds of negotiation, prompted by one or more turning point that caused the various institutional actors to reexamine assumptions, goals, and practices. This ebb and flow dynamic swirled around a wide spectrum of issues, though the most intense and recurring negotiations were usually focused on the "politics of knowledge" at the PDS Centers, in which the stakeholders struggled with "whose knowledge matters most?"—the culture, approach, and perceived "theory" of the university or the culture, approach, and "practical reality" of the school. This dichotomy manifests often where schools and universities meet, and could also be perceived as a difference in perspective, with universities more apt to operate in two and three year cycles, at the shortest, and schools required to think in more curtailed time frames of months or one year, at the longest.

The politics of knowledge will be used throughout this chapter to highlight how each PDS balanced negotiation and equilibrium, and how (and if) any evolution in the collaborative partnerships occurred. In any collaboration, even the most superficial, tensions exist between aims, values, and practices. The PDS model is distinct in that the stakeholders chose to engage—to grapple with the tensions head-on in order to create a program that prepares candidates for the "real world," and, beyond that, to create the possibility for a true partnership between school and university. Therefore the university faculty and the school faculty and administration were compelled to communicate about knowledge. Where this communication has led them is illustrative of how each PDS site endeavored to achieve equilibrium.

This chapter first discusses the ways in which personal and institutional negotiation played out in two schools, Howe Avenue Elementary and Golden State Middle School, which struggled to gain equilibrium amid competing views of teaching, professional development, knowledge, and values. A third school, Greer, is then introduced where the spaces for dialogue within the PDS were large enough to encompass school knowledge, research paradigms, and other forms of university knowledge. Thus, at this site, equilibrium seemed easier to achieve and maintain, leading to a discussion of what factors influence the ability of people and institutions to form partnerships that are characterized by moments of equilibrium, and finally what factors in that equilibrium or negotiation might lead to institutional change.

Howe Avenue Elementary School

Howe Avenue Elementary School is a large K–5 school located on the western edge of a large, mostly suburban district. The district's "west-side" schools, of which two are PDSs, resemble those of its urban neighbor next door (Sacramento City Unified School District) with poverty rates and numbers of English learners that are higher than those of the rest of the San Juan Unified School District, historically characterized by high test scores and a pupil population that is middle- to upper-middle class and white. Howe Avenue sits in a neighborhood that is an anomaly for this district—dense residential development characterized by apartment buildings past their prime and retail space that either houses discount stores or struggles to keep tenants. The sense of transience is punctuated by the hectic traffic that speeds up and down Howe Avenue, traveling between one of the major east-west arteries or to the nearby freeway. Though a large park with a small creek is adjacent to the school, pupils and their families use it warily, always taking care to go in full daylight when conditions are safest. Howe Avenue has over 550 pupils, the majority of whom are pupils of color and low income. In addition, because it is a district "language center" over 40% of its pupils are English learners, with Spanish as the predominant home language. It has a split staff—at least two-thirds can be considered veteran and have spent the bulk of their careers at Howe or schools like Howe. It does experience a fair amount of turnover each year, though this trend has been minimized since the PDS began operation. In an attempt to address years of sub-par pupil performance, the school has adopted a range of programs.

Howe Avenue teachers and administrators supported the PDS and recognized that the university-based knowledge contributed both conceptually and practically to the work of the school. The PDS structure enabled active communication about theory and practice and provided venues to identify and integrate the knowledge of the two institutions. According to the founding principal (since retired), this was, in fact, "one of the underlying goals" of the collaboration, and she was especially pleased that she and the teachers were able to "work with instructors to get a curriculum that is far more reality based" and thus strengthen the preparation of the candidates at the site. The LENS faculty concurred that the redesigned courses had made the assignments "more closely connected to the field" so that what candidates "experience in the school is just related totally through that theory/practice connection that the PDS helps with." Teachers also appreciated that the PDS provided better preparation for the candidates because of the continuity between what they learned in university courses and what they were doing in the classrooms.

However, the forms of knowledge and modes of communication that underlay the cultures of the university and the school did not always mesh smoothly, and the ideals, no matter how strongly shared, proved difficult to put into practice. The principal commented that the university "had a whole different way of organizing and thinking" that sometimes made the distance between the cultures seem large. Similarly, the LENS faculty person sometimes experienced frustration when teachers at the school rebuffed suggestions for action research and for research-based professional development that were seen as too much in the theoretical realm: "I would like my CTs to be doing more, but I don't know how to push them into that. I think having a school person introduce some of those ideas is going to be important for my program, because they associate me with a certain role."

This cultural clash got defined in reference to the "source" of knowledge that could prove its value in the classroom; some regarded everyday experience as the key foundation, and others regarded "best practices" as validated by research as the key foundation. One teacher identified the candidates' coursework as an obstacle to their obtaining the right kind of knowledge for the classroom, even though the courses were field-based and taught on site: "Professors seem to put so much emphasis on what they are asking the candidates to do that it sometimes even gets in the way of what they're supposed to be doing here; time here with actual children outweighs any coursework they can get." Despite the fact that the PDS university faculty members were often spending more time at the schools than they were at the university, they had to overcome deeply engrained skepticism about the basis and value of their knowledge. As one teacher alleged: "They haven't seen the inside of a classroom in so long, they don't know what these candidates are dealing with, they don't know what we deal with on a day-to-day basis. They do what they do based on what they've done in the past." This kind of lack of faith in the efficacy of university knowledge led some teachers to believe that the courses for candidates should be taught at the school only "by people who work here, or are here on a regular basis." In a related vein, some even asserted that teaching candidates how to use the school's adopted curriculum would allow for the smoothest transitions into their positions as new teachers.

While a range of processes and structures created opportunities for constructive dialogue, the dynamics between the teachers and site administrators and the university faculty members weren't always imbued with mutual respect and trust. Both sides of the "divide" could be arrogant and hold onto a dichotomous way of thinking about school and university knowledge, and this made it all the more difficult to achieve the kind of partnerships that the PDSs were attempting to embody. Such dichotomous thinking about the sorts of knowledge that was valuable for improving classroom practice presented a serious challenge to the PDS partnership at Howe Avenue. Over time the quality of the collaboration began to bridge the chasm between the two sides, as various members had experiences that helped them to broaden their perspectives and rethink their positions. For example, one faculty member noted, "I think the district knows a lot more about their schools than we know. And the more I'm hanging with the district, the more I think they might be right. And then we have an attitude about it: 'Hey, we know what we're doing and you don't.' Personally . . . I don't think that we do. And there's not a lot of humility on our part." With gradual shifts in perspective like these—by both university and school educators—Howe Avenue moved toward a state of equilibrium. Recurrent projects and attendant communication structures shaped a lived experience of working together to improve both teacher preparation and pupil achievement, thus generating trust and contributing to the overall stability of the PDS. The ongoing discussion of the value of disparate forms of knowledge itself became a valued part of the PDS as teachers and CSUS faculty members continually sought to work together, using all available resources, toward common ends.

Golden State Middle School

Golden State Middle School (GSMS) is the only middle school in this city
(West Sacramento) which was once a sleepy neighbor of the state capital
and has recently experienced a metamorphosis fueled by rapid agricultural
land conversion and aggressive business development, punctuated by the 2005
opening of a new IKEA store. Golden State is a large middle school whose
administration and teachers gamely attempt to juggle multiple and often
competing goals related to educating a high proportion of English learners
from Mexican, Russian, and Southeast Asian backgrounds, pupils raised on
nearby farms, and children of lobbyists and other state workers. The school
itself has worked in partnership with faculty and graduate students from UC
Davis and from Sacramento State University for decades; in fact, a few of
the graduate students at UC Davis became faculty members at Sacramento
State and continued working in collaboration with Golden State.

As a subsequent chapter reveals, establishing a PDS at the secondary level carries specific challenges not encountered in similar efforts at
elementary schools, which tend to be less complex (relatively speaking), less
compartmentalized and departmentalized, and smaller in pupil and teacher
numbers. Many would argue that middle schools, junior high schools, and
senior high schools are designed to atomize faculty; and that to attempt
collaboration across departments or between middle schools and other
institutions rocks the secondary structures at their core. For example, in our
interviews with GSMS staff, stark divisions (possibly shaped by content
or grade foci) emerged in their own ideologies of how best to work with
LI/RCLD pupils as well as prepare novice teachers for that work. Here the
politics of knowledge were far more pronounced, the stakeholders greater
in number, and the voices more strongly disparate. Not surprisingly, rapid
flux in the negotiations between stakeholders and persistent strains between
the cultures of the university and the school as well as those within the
school itself created obstacles for the PDS. The politics of knowledge were
clearly recognized, and the partners experienced only tentative agreements,
which were easily disrupted when issues and events brought tensions in core
values and principles to the fore. Some of these differences related both to
which knowledge was most valuable *and* to perceptions about the needs and
wants of their "constituency" in relation to knowledge transmission.

For example, some GSMS teachers expressed skepticism toward the
PDS approach to such teaching/learning domains as classroom management
skills, lesson preparation, and instructional modalities. The lead teacher illustrated a typical doubt about how the candidates were being prepared in the
PDS: "Collaboration, technology, and standards are aspects of a whole, but
the whole is that you have to get control of the classroom—these candidates

have less skills in that way and they're not carrying them into the classroom with them." Another teacher lamented that in the PDS, "We do a whole lot of philosophy and not enough of how it's going to apply in the classroom every day." A fellow teacher concurred with this critique of an alleged "lack of realism": "There'd be two adults—two candidates working with maybe three to five pupils—how realistic is that? When is that ever going to happen? This is my fourth year. Unh unh; it's never happened." These comments reflect old and familiar debates in the field of education; not surprisingly, they played out in the PDS too.

In fact, even complimentary views about the PDS contained this prioritization of teachers' practical knowledge. For example, some teachers regarded the PDS courses for candidates as better than the standard university courses precisely because active teachers participated as co-instructors. These co-instructors could be trusted to know the real foundation of teacher knowledge: "I know there's coursework they have to do but to me the more time they spend in the classroom the better." For these teachers the key was finding the right balance between theory and practice, and they expected the PDS faculty members to be critically aware of that balance. "To me the benefit was that it was always a more practical program. You don't want to lose that practicality and get so theoretical that they're not able to work with kids when they get through. And I think that's been pretty well handled so far."

Certainly it is common to believe that the most important knowledge for candidates to acquire in their preparation programs is that which enables them to manage or control the class and to lead whole group instruction for thirty or more pupils. And the current realities of scripted instruction in many schools that are under "program improvement" strictures leave few, if any, opportunities for constructivist projects with small groups of pupils, the approach valorized by the Equity Network and the larger community of PDSs. Nevertheless, there was a core group of GSMS veteran teachers who were active in the PDS *because* of the constructivist, inquiry-oriented, and innovative preparation it provided candidates.

Two EL teachers who had worked closely with the PDS candidates believed it was fantastic to have them facilitating instruction with small groups, and they believed that their pupils benefited in multiple ways from this kind of focused adult attention. One of these EL teachers enthusiastically recounts: "The candidates took the groups out to do soil temperature experiments. It was small groups, maybe two candidates to five kids. At the end of the day each group gave a PowerPoint presentation. And this room was filled! These suits—even the superintendent was here—and my kids just went, 'Hi! Welcome, come on in!' "

The other EL teacher commented, "We were studying buoyancy and we took people out to the river and now they're doing solar ovens and things like that. That didn't happen before and it certainly didn't happen where you could have teachers in training working with three or four pupils." The teachers thought the academic benefits from working with candidates and small groups of pupils were real and significant, and far outweighed the benefits that could be derived from giving the candidates more experiences that would transmit knowledge of how to control a large class. One teacher elaborated on this:

> I mean, you could look at it and say well, sure they're getting out and working with small groups of kids, but . . . they have to take over the class of thirty-two—well that's true, they still have to do that, but there's something about it that gets them connected to the kids, and it's a very positive experience. Because they're in smaller groups they can kind of deal with pupil thinking and help them work things through as opposed to pure classroom management and crowd control.

For a number of the teachers and for the school administration, the partnership with the university was less about an agreement to the principles of the PDS model or to resolving decades-old conflicts between theory and practice, than it was a pragmatic calculation of costs and benefits. Instead of a long-term commitment, for these educators, the agreement rested more on an "I'll scratch your back if you scratch mine" realism. As one of the teachers put it: "The teachers also get benefits and the administrators recognize and support those benefits, as far as everybody working together to make it keep happening and to keep those benefits in the forefront—to me that's the ideal."

While various teachers involved in the PDS staked out their positions on either side of the knowledge divide, the GSMS administration had no doubt about its agenda and just what the PDS should be emphasizing. As the principal said, "All that theory stuff is great, but I've had candidates who never see what a grade book looks like. [In the PDS] they get an actual experience, and theory, they get a theoretical experience which may or may not match." He further noted, "a lot of myths come out of the ed program and it's good to dispel some of those"; he thought the PDS approach could do this. He also wanted the PDS to respond to the immediate needs of the school in relation to professional development as these needs were revealed in standardized test scores and the resultant larger political pressures on the school and the district. He recognized that this would put his goals some-what at odds with the university's aim with establishing the partnership. "It's a yearly specific. If we're working on math this year and I need all math in-service, I can't ask Sac State to do all math this year and then switch over and do all Social Studies next year." At the same time, he observed, "Evolving, I think, is good. There has been more and more learning to it each year, and I think Sac State has done a wonderful job putting a good program together for the kids."

The principal also weighed the situation in relation to the larger context of a teacher labor market that typically put LI/RCLD schools at a severe disadvantage. So he viewed the PDS in the light of its creation of a hiring pool: "Advantages again—in a competitive world you get first crack—it's a recruitment deal. If it's not a benefit to the school, the school wouldn't do it—or the district—so the number one benefit for us is the access to the candidates. What I've needed the support on is to get quality teachers, to have a quality school. So far, if the results are for the last three years, it's working."

The university faculty tried to mediate the needs and perspectives of the teachers and administrators, but at the same time they had their own views on what knowledge needed to be transmitted to candidates. Unlike the teachers, there was generally more unity among the university faculty about the merits of a constructivist, inquiry-oriented program that grew its roots deep in the pupils' community and cultural funds of knowledge. The LENS faculty member who coordinated the PDS described her ultimate goal as creating a teacher credentialing program that grounded theory in practice more deeply than the typical university-based program, "to do teacher education very on the ground, kind of from the teacher perspective." Yet because she was critical of much of the current practice in LI/RCLD schools whose instructional programs were dominated by the testing and accountability regimes required by national and state policies, she felt it was her duty to prepare candidates with a wider range of experience and teaching skills that were aligned with research-based best practices. She saw a value in the challenge of negotiating this kind of preparation for the candidates in the actual context of the GSMS because "it makes us honest" about the conditions the candidates would soon be facing. As she explained: "Most of us at the university are not thrilled about the testing and standards craze. It's very easy to sit at the university and criticize it. But when you're out in the school—a school that is committed to raising the test scores and the teachers have to be committed to that to keep their jobs—we still can be critical but we have to think about it in more real terms. Our candidates have to prepare those kids for the test; they can't just resist it. They won't get a job. They won't be able to even function in the school as it's functioning." Many of her GSMS colleagues would agree, as we have seen earlier.

The political tension produced by this "reality" of schools serving LI/RCLD pupils and the pressures confronting their teachers and administrators forced university faculty members to balance their theoretical commitments with their commitments to ground the PDS in the lived experiences of teachers and pupils in those schools. The faculty members had no choice but to negotiate in an environment that seemed to work against the very possibility of the PDS principles they so desired to enact. They were left with having "to be kind of honest with the administrators and teachers" and at the same time, with the candidates, they felt they couldn't "say a different thing that would contradict" the message delivered by the administrators and teachers. Finding an equilibrium point that allowed the faculty members to be "honest" across the board was not a simple achievement.

Instead of the PDS becoming a vehicle for collaborative planning for the curriculum in its programs as well as the school classrooms, the university faculty members had to structure the program for the candidates within the initial parameters established by the school and then slowly identify "cracks" that opened the way for more constructivist and culturally relevant activities. For example, the university science faculty person recalled that she "had to weave in and out of those projects" that she experienced as "very constrictive." "Normally there's certain things I would present in a teacher preparation science class and I don't do those activities anymore. I have to change my activities every year based on what the teacher's doing." These limitations were accepted in the trade-off of having the PDS situated at the school site, with its many opportunities for broader and more sustained interactions between the candidates and "the real kids." Although the university faculty had to adapt to the existing GSMS curriculum more than they would have liked, they nonetheless found ways to make the most of the "cracks" that they did encounter for implementing classroom instruction. They kept to their commitment to give the candidates experience in the research-based constructivist models of instruction that they valued. They developed an approach that enabled them to "model project-based learning that they may not otherwise be experiencing in their student teaching, but in a service learning context where the kids get to experience it too, and that also models it for the teachers, so it becomes an indirect in-service." They also found ways to integrate other core principles of the Center, especially the integration of community funds of knowledge into the standards-based curriculum (as detailed in chapter one).

Organizationally, the faculty recognized the struggle to balance these strong and disparate voices. As the Center Coordinator herself commented, "This is a really smooshy Center to try to figure out who's doing what . . . a PDS is an extremely political animal." There was the voice of the teachers: "The teachers actually have votes about when the classes will be the next year, and what kind of times they want with the candidates . . . what the program should do for the school—these are all collectively decided." Balanced with that were the needs and desires of the administration: "If we leave these people, like some of the teachers [and administrators], out of the loop, we get into big trouble."

Faculty members facilitated negotiations among all stakeholders—teachers, administration, candidates, and the university faculty. Balance between teacher empowerment and university needs was a particularly difficult issue that came up repeatedly. As the Center Coordinator recalled, "We were involved in a whole semester negotiating about redesigning our program to meet these new state guidelines at the university—but we didn't until the end of the semester bring it to any of the teachers . . . the teachers were infuriated, because there were things that got designed in there that wouldn't have been their choice. And then we've had to have several days of negotiation with them . . . So they feel very strongly empowered." A Center faculty member concurred, "Our CT's are involved in everything from placing candidates to telling us what we should teach in our courses—they're really adamant . . . out there."

Within this environment of direct negotiation and occasionally open tension, moments of equilibrium surface, enabled by a mutual focus on common goals. The GSMS principal valued the ability to contribute to the teaching profession. "One of the things that we talked about when we first started this is my belief that we should put back into the system that has given to you. So, all of us have benefited from a candidate program at one point or another in our lives. We should put back, and we should also change the things that we thought were wrong . . . I think we're turning out better candidates. I think we're turning out a more realistic view of what education is than what others are doing."

In the end, perhaps the story of this dynamic PDS can be best captured in a summary of an exchange between two graduates, one who voiced consistent concerns as both a candidate and an alumni, and another who exhibited enthusiasm about the program. The first graduate reflected, "I think the only thing that it [Middle Ground PDS] did was introduce me to . . . the culture of the school and the culture of the community. But it's like when I've got all those standards to get through—two posters full, I've got kids who are below 7th grade standards, I don't have a whole lot of time for that. I'd like to have a project for every single concept, but it's just not going to happen . . . that's a scary limb to go out on when your performance as a teacher is based on how well they do at the end of the year!"

The other graduate offered a different perspective, one that perhaps was based on a more long-term view of the teacher preparation program goals. She stated, "Well, I think this program has a paradox. Because in a way it doesn't really matter that the teachers learn how to lesson plan because in the elementary schools it's going to be scripted for a long time. So I can see how maybe they wouldn't spend a lot of time giving language arts methods instruction just because why spend a whole year on LA methods when you're just going to be handed a script anyhow and that's how you're going to teach it."

The two graduates' comments reveal the underlying tensions felt by all actors in the program, from candidates to instructors to teachers and administrators. The politics of "knowledge" in this case played out in terms of what constitutes valuable knowledge for teachers—contextual knowledge about pupils and their communities or technical knowledge about how best to get those pupils learning. The first graduate probably represents the mainstream approach to teacher preparation and more attention to the technical aspects of teaching that she needed might have quelled her concerns and those of some of the teacher partners of the PDS. At the same time, we are struck by the graduate's comment that the *only* thing she learned was about the pupils . . . this highlights an important paradigmatic conflict that will continue to play out in these kinds of partnerships. There is no one "best" answer to what is most important—knowing your pupils or knowing effective strategies and techniques. The truth is that both are critical. The challenge, which the Middle Ground PDS educators tackled courageously, is how to create a program where candidates value both elements and can skillfully practice them. With much persistence and patience, the GSMS partners engaged in negotiation, particularly if it provided opportunities for pupils. They did not often allow a wide berth for their negotiation and, as a result, it was an ongoing process with few shared values except those connected to pupil success, and even this definition was contested. Nevertheless, the long-term PDS aims provided an anchor point to work things through in practice even if disagreements in theory remained.

Greer Elementary School

Greer is just down the street from Howe Avenue Elementary School. Greer is a smaller school, however, and does not have the same programmatic complexity as Howe Avenue since it does not operate a language center. Nevertheless, its pupils are from predominantly low-income families and the school has a high proportion of ELs. Various factors have led to the creation of a very tight-knit professional community. Effective and stable leadership has created a professional culture in which reflection and action research factor prominently in professional development efforts. Though this made the site ideal for a PDS, the tensions between theory and practice could still be found, but avenues for moving the dialogue forward to productive projects had been identified. Unlike Middle Ground PDS and Howe Avenue, the small size of the school and the relative unity of the staff also created fewer stakeholder groups among which to negotiate. The majority of teachers, a mostly veteran group, had prior experience with many of the activities that the PDS would support (teacher research, mentoring via professional standards, etc.). This made them particularly open to embracing the opportunities that the PDS brought.

Two teachers at the site exemplified this ability to appreciate theory while still remaining practical. One teacher taught the seminar course for candidates in their first semester, and could evaluate the PDS from the university and school perspectives. She observed, "I like having the theory and the practice together—all of my methods classes were at Sac State, completely separated from the classroom entirely, and I think it's fabulous for them to learn and see and do within the environment as much as possible."

Another teacher, who taught the second semester seminar course, had even further insight on standardization and the issues of teaching courses to meet the current needs of the school. The theory/practice debate was quite vivid for her, without being generalized into a school versus university debate. "Curriculum is so much bigger than just being able to pass the test.... We're not, hopefully, as silly or misinformed as the rest of the public that a standardized test tells us what we can do, but we also know that that is what is speaking right now for the world of our kids.... When they get out of here in 6th grade, they may be doing well in all of our performance assessments, but it's that standardized test that puts them ... in a lower math grade.... They'll get in those groups and be pushed up, but the score is what is going to make it for our kids." Her concept of equilibrium would entail "some of the time the university instructors should have our materials in their hands, and find the time to connect what they are teaching them with what the candidates are seeing in their student teaching classrooms."

These two teachers, who were actively involved in the PDS by virtue of teaching program coursework among other leadership duties, saw room for improvement. One idea was for "teachers [to have] input into the methods classes. So that when they're teaching methods they're emphasizing the types of math that we're teaching, and they're emphasizing the types of things that we're emphasizing ... on a scale of 1 to 10, it's [the PDS] probably meeting the needs of people entering Title I schools at maybe a 7 or an 8, and I'd like to see it a 9 or 10." A third teacher echoed these thoughts: "It would be really neat to see the professors sit down and plan as a team. Here's our common ground on how we're going to talk about classroom management ... [or] about how we're teaching standards." She added, "The whole reason [this] whole thing started is how does this benefit our kids."

While these teachers echoed many of the concerns identified in the other two cases, and they did so as vehemently, a key factor related to the equilibrium achieved at this site may have been the core values that motivated teachers' participation as well as a willingness to resist dichotomizing the variables, seeking instead avenues where a broad range of useful knowledge could be accessed. One teacher noted, "I like the control of knowing that I am impacting my own profession. I like having input into my own profession. I think that is the reason why I am passionate about it and why I like to do it." Another teacher recalled her reaction to the idea of the PDS: "I ran asking, can I? Can I be on the development team? I want to be here, I want to help." A third offered, "The philosophy of the program. How it totally benefits our kids. It benefits future teachers, and it benefits me as a teacher. It's highly effective."

This framing of the PDS, with all its potential tensions, as a win-win for the pupils and their teachers spilled over into the kinds of innovations teachers embraced. One teacher, with multiple candidates in her room, observed, "It's really allowed me to differentiate learning and really trust that person to be able to take a group and do a good job." Another concurred, "One of the big advantages—and it's very obvious—is differentiation. When I've got a group of kids and [the candidate has] a group of kids, so much more can happen ... more pupil engagement [and] more pupil interaction than there would be without that extra body in the room. . . . [We] use the candidates to differentiation's most glorified definition."

Faculty perspective on the same set of issues was mostly congruent. Greer's LENS faculty member asserted that collaborative work had proceeded and negotiations had resulted in positive contributions from both sides. "I think the major difference would be that there's input from principals, the school staff, faculty, about certain things that they want implemented in the coursework ... to be current, to have a certain amount of legitimacy as a professor, you have to know what's going on in classrooms. So there hasn't ever been a time since I've been here that I was divorced from the classroom and didn't know what the district curriculum was and didn't know what teachers were doing because it just doesn't work well for me to do it that way. . . . But as I mentioned before, I think that's an area that needed to be looked at more in the future."

Negotiation and Equilibrium: Charting the Possibilities

Howe Avenue genuinely supported the presence of the PDS; however, they were steeped in a milieu that emphasized the disparities between university and school and the deficits of each. Therefore, they had to continually reconsider the positive contributions made by stakeholders, resulting in ongoing negotiations in the struggle to define knowledge and values. GSMS had an internal culture of tension in which the stakeholders' own positions within the power structure played out in a push away from equilibrium. Here the politics of knowledge were far more pronounced, the stakeholders greater in number, and the voices stronger in their dissonance. The equilibrium became harder to find amid many negotiations between stakeholders, and ultimately between the philosophical divisions apparent among staff members and between the university and the school. One faculty member observed: "I think we're in an ongoing process in trying to figure out what our beliefs are and what the teachers' beliefs are about teaching and learning. And how to really explore the origins of those, and how to get more on the same page. And that's a tricky business." One of the graduates summed the situation up quite well: "I didn't know any of this happened in the school system. I didn't know it was so political."

Despite the disparate stakeholder viewpoints, the program generated positive feedback—and a vision that was occasionally aligned. One of the Center faculty members commented, "In fact, that's my vision—that we really have a program at the university that's really meaningful. A program that works in the real sense of the word. Now some people in the schools would think that all the courses that we are teaching here are just theory—it's not practical. But I think the work of the PDS, where there's a better connection between the university and the schools provides an opportunity for communication, collaboration and discussion." The Center Coordinator also saw success in one of the important components of the PDS—that teachers would grow to believe they themselves were teacher educators. "I think our teachers have a real belief in the program. We occasionally have conflict, but I think that overall it is an enrichment to them too, and the other thing that has grown over time is that they really consider part of their job is that they are teacher educators." After expounding on their tensions and disagreements with the PDS, teachers and administrators had generally a positive vision of the program and that their differences, when handled productively, could actually provide a kind of balance in perspective and approach. Finally, the principal assessed that the PDS "continues to evolve into something that's very good for my pupils. And for the candidates."

Greer continued to maintain a more steady state of equilibrium, bolstered by a strong administration. Greer administration and teachers had already created an internal culture of research and professional contribution, which aligned to the PDS philosophy more closely, and eased communication between university and school. All school staff interviewed mentioned this strong school culture, anchored by commitments to diverse urban children and leadership within their profession. One teacher commented, "The principal is completely immersed in meaningful professional development for teachers—so that culture was already established here before the PDS was even thought of. And I think that's one reason why the PDS fits very well at this school, because we are a school of learners. . . . So when the PDS came I think we were already walking the path."

One faculty member, key to the PDS at Greer, shared some insights on factors that contributed to the general feeling of equilibrium in that PDS. He observed, "Well, I think probably one of the bigger challenges was building a sense of trust or building a relationship of trust between the principal and myself. And that's been an amazing experience as far as working with someone on a daily basis or a weekly basis and their sensing that I have an investment in the kids at that school and the teachers at that school, and wouldn't do anything to harm or exploit them, and on the opposite way to look at it, that the principal and the faculty there are committed to our candidates and wouldn't do anything to exploit them. . . . And it didn't happen overnight. And it's been a challenge—learning how to speak to each other and discuss things and work out problems, and when problems occur, being able to have a sense of trust that the problems can be worked out."

One of the school's teachers offered her own praise for the program. "I look at where we started from, and we've come so far already, it's hard to believe we started back where we started, and it's almost hard to envision ultimately where it could go. Because right now I feel like it's working pretty well." Another teacher quipped, "I want a denim shirt that says—Greer and Sac State collaborating PDS!"

As we have discovered again and again during our PDS work, like most of the dynamics in teaching and learning, PDS projects live and die, so to speak, based on the people that are involved. The case of Greer highlights that certain kinds of structures and processes certainly facilitate *how* people begin and sustain their involvement. But at the heart of the PDS work are people who must solidify their connections to each other and to a common project, founded on mutually held principles and values. In some cases, this process is slow and must be repeated often to achieve equilibrium; in other cases, the road to equilibrium has fewer bumps and is shorter. This is not a sprint; it is one's endurance that counts in the end.

Note

1. Data for this chapter come from surveys administered to every graduating candidate from Middle Ground in 2002 and 2003 and interviews with all key stakeholders at each site. The interview protocol included questions about the rewards and challenges of working with the PDS; how well, comparatively, the PDS prepared candidates to work with diverse pupils; the effects of the PDS on the school environment and teacher practice; and areas for improvement. Interview transcripts were coded and themes identified.

Chapter Eight

Not Starting from Scratch

Applying the Lessons from a Thwarted PDS Effort

Janet I. Hecsh

This chapter charts the evolution of our efforts to establish a high school PDS. We recount the creation of a PDS at one high school, where significant reforms were envisioned and put into motion but were ultimately thwarted by conflict and miscommunication. With insight from this experience, a PDS was launched at a new high school. The process for initiating the PDS work, building a base of support, identifying the PDS projects, and sustaining the work is compared across the schools. This chapter provides rich examples and ideas, but also offers cautionary lessons about how meaningful reforms can become isolated and consequently misunderstood, and about the importance of constantly expanding a base of support for reforms.

This narrative begins with a more general discussion of urban high schools, urban high school reform, and how high schools, particularly urban high schools, differ from the elementary and middle schools discussed thus far in this book. For decades, large-scale and smaller scale examinations of high schools have been conducted. Beginning with Conant's 1959 report, *The American High School Today,* urban high schools have been under the microscope of qualitative and quantitative researchers. Anthropologists, sociologists, economists, educators, political scientists, and historians have dissected high schools and reported on them in a variety of venues. Urban high school research in the 1970s and 1980s, in particular, highlighted a set of dilemmas, competing ideas and ideals, and structural challenges that are specific to schools in urban settings. In studies of high school reform initiatives of the 1980s and 1990s, researchers and theorists concur that the persistent and problematic characteristics of urban high schools stem from competing ideas about the purposes and emphasis of a high school education (Apple & Beane, 1995; Fullan, 1991; Gibboney, 1994). Additionally, structural features of high school organization influence reform efforts: size, organizational complexity, pupils' movement within the school, and tracking by ability (Chang, 1992; Foley, 1990; Grant, 1988). Size makes interventions costly, departmental structure often results in conflicts and competition over pupils and resources, and ability groups and other tracking mechanisms become more difficult to resolve in high schools, usually more decentralized than their elementary counterparts (Fullan, 1991; Hampel, 1986; Louis & Miles, 1990). Large-scale studies of high schools by Boyer (1983), Goodlad (1984), and others document the experience of life in schools for pupils and teachers while documentary films (Wiseman, 1970) and other Hollywood high school movies illustrate, and even mythologize, the "daily grind" and discrepancies between pupil values and ideas and the expectations of teachers and administrators. Furthermore, in-depth examinations or "portraits" (Cusick, 1973; Lightfoot, 1983) of high schools reveal what have come to be described as "dynamic complexities" of high schools that have tended to confound reformers. The latter, in particular, reveal that high schools have their own "DNA" and their own particular cultures. Moreover, pupils and communities in which schools reside have changed over the past decades while public school structure, teaching practices, and practitioner preparation have remained relatively static despite thoughtful recommendations for reform.

Typically, reform initiatives that have occurred in comprehensive high schools have been supported by grants, therefore limiting prospects for sustainability. More often, the initiatives are concentrated in one department or segment of a high school, and therefore do not address the overall "grammar" of high schools (Tyack & Cuban, 1995). Most recently, districts, with large-scale philanthropic support, have pursued the "smaller is better" approach, building on successful demonstrations publicized in the 1990s (Meier, 1995; Sizer, 1993, 1996). Small high schools (whether schools within schools or actual small high schools) show promise in personalizing the often-overwhelming scale of the comprehensive high school, giving all stakeholders better opportunities to "know" and respond to each other and to participate in the core activities of the school. Similarly, the pathways and linkages between high schools and universities, where they occur, have become clearer in recent years, though their improved articulation is more often focused on transition to college and outreach activities. Though other "archipelagos" of collaboration between schools and universities, such as professional development in the content areas through such networks as the National Writing Project, for instance, are evident, educators have not yet fully situated the high school as a training site for professional preparation programs (Fullan, 1991). Even in our case, our teacher preparation program has historically reflected a habitus that was hierarchical, insular, and entrenched in a quarter century of practice that viewed high schools as institutions that were "used" to place candidates.

Given these structural and organizational challenges, it is not surprising that the PDSs have had less traction in high schools than elementary schools. In preparation for writing this book, a comprehensive review of more than 800 studies on Professional Development Schools was conducted. Of those studies, high school PDS partnerships constituted fewer than 5% of the total. High schools make up part of the data set in a few studies on mentoring in PDS settings (Mantle-Bromley & Foster, 2001, e.g.). In studies of teacher preparation programs within a PDS context, high schools are quite underrepresented (Sandholtz & Wasserman, 2001) and with few exceptions (Quartz & Oakes, 2003), there is little evidence of studies that describe the work of developing PDS partnerships in high schools or consider high schools as a unit of study within the universe of PDS and other school reform initiatives.

Organizations such as the Holmes Partnership and the American Educational Research Association's Professional Development School Special Interest Group provide forums for the examination and discussion of university–school partnerships; however, the relatively few high school–university partnerships that have been described in the last five years have focused on subject-specific collaborations and/or descriptions of decentralized supervision models of preparing candidates. Exceptions exist, for example, the Knoxville, Tennessee Fulton High School PDS, but, for the most part, high school PDSs tend to be generally absent from research literature and underrepresented in venues aimed at showcasing such partnerships. The absence of models at the high school level is somewhat understandable given the challenges described earlier. Therefore, this portrait of the Secondary Teacher Education Collaborative (S-TEC) PDS and its reincarnation as PULSE addresses significant gaps in the PDS literature.

This is the story of a pilot project within our Single Subject (secondary) Teacher Preparation Program (SSTPP) to establish a PDS partnership with Florin High School, a large comprehensive urban fringe high school serving a low-income, racially, culturally, and linguistically diverse (LI/RCLD) pupil body. After three years, it became necessary to end that project and initiate a new PDS partnership with New Technology High School, a much smaller urban high school serving a similar pupil body. First, the stories of these two collaborative ventures are framed in terms of vignettes or "structuring activities" (Mehan, 1978) that describe the school and university contexts and the processes for entering the two high schools, establishing a base of support for PDS work, designing the PDS projects, and sustaining the work. Next, using a comparative lens, I will highlight positive examples and ideas that may be useful to PDS-style reformers as well as cautionary lessons about how reforms may become isolated and consequently misunderstood. The chapter concludes with several recommendations for research and praxis and proposes a model for collaboration between secondary schools and secondary teacher preparation programs (TPP) that is transformative and ultimately adds value to the work of all stakeholders in the educational enterprise.[1] It is not easy to describe "objectively" one's own practice, and perhaps it is even more challenging to write about it when one reveals mistakes or missteps, and when the events are relatively recent (in this case, within the past five years). The author is still considering the complex series of events and the following narrative is the most current iteration of this analysis.

The Florin High School Secondary Teacher Education Collaborative-S-TEC (2000-2004)

Set in the "velvet ghetto" at the southern edge of Sacramento's city limits, Florin High School, home of the Florin Panthers, appears to be a typical comprehensive high school. It has the traditional suburban brick and steel low-slung buildings, with plenty of acreage that stretches across what were once strawberry fields farmed by Japanese families until Executive Order 9066 removed them to internment camps. In the decades following World War II, the fields in southern Sacramento County were converted into tract homes. Opened in 1989, Florin High School (FHS) was the third high school in the Elk Grove Unified School District and within three years of opening, it served more than 2000 pupils, many first generation immigrants from South East Asia and Mexico (Hecsh, 2001). While the external features of FHS resemble the traditional high school (large playing fields, traditional classrooms, traditional schedules, bells, etc.) described by Goodlad and others, the overall organizational structures and practices had more in common with progressive school reform efforts of the late 1980s (Meier, 1995; Sizer, 1993, 1996) in that the school had a relatively flat decision-making structure with committees operating on the Effective Schools model (see Sizer for more details).

Instead of the traditional subject-centered departmentalization organization, FHS was organized into divisions with several departments oriented around the explicit goal of curriculum integration and collaborative planning within and across subjects. In response to the research on the negative effects of tracking and ability grouping, all pupils were enrolled in college preparatory classes. Honors and Advanced Placement courses were accessible to all interested pupils via an open enrollment policy and extensive tutoring services were established to support pupils in meeting high academic expectations. Teachers engaged in ongoing professional development to hone their ability to deliver instruction in heterogeneous settings. During its first five years, FHS received a set of grants to support professional development activities in the areas of curriculum and instruction. These funds supported faculty release time and stipends to design and implement a series of authentic assessments, including one of the first Senior Projects in the region. Additionally, funding had supported the development of the first small learning communities (schools within schools) in the region.

FHS had a strong reputation as a school with a high degree of faculty participation in professional networks, including the California Writing, Math, and Literature Projects. Faculty members who participated in summer institutes also engaged in teacher research linked to these networks. FHS was also well regarded for its English learner program and services to pupils who were the first in their families to pursue secondary and higher education. The ethos of the school reflected a strong value and commitment to lifelong learning, a willingness to experiment and reflect, and a celebrated respect for cultural diversity through a myriad of cultural clubs and an annual multicultural faire called the Kaleidoscope of Cultures.

By the end of its 10th year, FHS had experienced a demographic shift such that its pupil body had become more racially and ethnically diverse, poorer, and more academically challenged. The trends of the day had shifted away from interdisciplinary teaching and learning and authentic assessment toward curricular intensification and performance on standardized tests. The third principal (the two previous principals had been "founders") was in his second year of what would become a four-year term.

I was a social studies teacher for 10 years at FHS. During the period of change described, I was beginning to become acclimated to my own changing role as a university professor and, along with other colleagues in our college who were involved in innovations for teacher education, had identified several ways for my association with FHS to continue. Because I had "insider" status and knew well the school ethos of collective decision-making and collaboration, getting started was relatively easy. Our first meeting was in spring 2000, preceded by a "call" for participation in a dialogue to discuss the preparation of new teachers. Approximately twenty teachers across the disciplines along with a counselor and one vice principal attended our first meeting, held in a local restaurant. I began by posing open-ended questions about what made a good teacher preparation program, what roles public school educators currently play and how those roles might be redesigned, and what their perceptions were of the strengths and weaknesses of the current CSUS TPP. The majority of those at the meeting had received their credentials from that TPP and many had hosted candidates in the traditional structure. During the discussion, veteran teachers expressed interest in taking a more central role in the preparation of new teachers. Some expressed their sense of being out of the "loop" since the university supervisor was the "authority" in the triad of pupil teacher, teacher, and university supervisor. There was some discussion of the benefits of holding the credential courses on the school site, and the value of having candidates experience the whole school year instead of moving from school to school each semester. We closed that first meeting by developing a rough draft of a proposal for S-TEC, slated to "open" in fall 2001.

About six weeks later, the group met again and reviewed the final draft of the proposal. We opted to adopt the Collaborating Teacher (CT) model recently created for elementary schools (see chapter four). In addition to adopting this model, we discussed ways in which team members could collaborate on curriculum issues. The student teaching seminar, slated to be taught on campus, seemed the logical place to start and several teachers volunteered to "co-teach" specific sessions. Several other collaborations emerged: one teacher developed a set of candidate guidelines that was eventually adopted for S-TEC, a special education teacher developed a school orientation for candidates, and various other teachers (across disciplines) offered their classrooms for different activities. By the close of our second meeting, we had created the framework for what we hoped would be our first cohort of candidates. It included substantive activities for the candidates and multiple possibilities for teacher participation.

S-TEC was endorsed at the district level, due to familiarity with the two elementary PDSs already in the district, my former roles as a teacher and small schools coordinator, and the support of a then-Associate Superintendent, who was once a principal at FHS. The Equity Network's focus on the California Standards for the Teaching Profession and the district's great need for new teachers (the fastest growing district in the nation at that time) also made S-TEC a compelling collaboration. Finally, the opportunity for more resources (from the TQE Title II grant) directed to one of the less well-resourced schools might have been an additional consideration.

In the S-TEC pilot, the seminar for candidates was taught on the FHS campus, and the syllabus for that course and the course sessions were jointly constructed and facilitated by the teachers and me. All of the candidates were placed in FHS classrooms with CTs. Candidates were to be considered part of the FHS community, present from "back-to-school" through the close of the school year. Their work in classrooms was to look more like the developmental and co-teaching model designed to maximize pupil learning, but more commonly found in the elementary school.

Several other innovations characterized the S-TEC effort. The Coordinator of the English language development program was able to train our candidates to administer the required placement test (CELDT) for ELs, and every candidate had the experience of teaching these pupils in a variety of settings. Candidates reported the value of having so many mentors interested in their progress and willing to share their expertise in everything from curriculum to problem-solving classroom management dilemmas. The CTs and other FHS teachers were extremely hospitable, and they included the candidates in professional development opportunities, field trips, and even monthly "bunko" games at a teacher's home.

In year-end reflections and semistructured interviews, CTs described the mentoring of candidates using metaphors like "mirror" and "sounding board." The diagrams they created to characterize their work with their candidate depicted them in close proximity and in the middle of the process, as compared to their prior expressions of being "sidelined." Our CT meetings were lively; teachers shared stories, offered suggestions for refining the program, and organized a way to observe each other's candidates. Their activities and enthusiasm generated both new CT applications and offers to contribute to the TPP and candidates' experience. Having the program centralized in one school was more efficient in terms of transportation—candidates carpooled, I could visit many candidates and CTs in one trip—as was communication and other transactions typical of the TPP. By the time the third cohort was completing their program, learning to teach had become a normative activity at FHS. For the candidates, learning to teach urban kids, poor kids, and English Learners in a well-organized school with committed and caring teachers demonstrating best practices had become normative as well.

From 2001 to 2004 three cohorts of candidates (thirty-five candidates working with seventeen CTs) participated in a three-semester teacher preparation program in S-TEC at FHS. With one exception, every candidate was hired and is currently working as a teacher in an urban setting, thirteen have been hired by the district, eight at FHS. There were some definite strengths and successes in the S-TEC program. It built on an already-established ethos of collaboration and inquiry. It was a grassroots effort that was implemented within the already-existing structures of the school and meshed well with the spirit of experimentation that characterized FHS. In addition to preparing new teachers, S-TEC had made some headway in engaging its stakeholders in professional development activities, had begun to institutionalize some specific practices (targeted tutoring, mentoring for Senior Project, mentoring for Science Olympiad) aimed at improving pupil learning, and had continued to develop teacher research/praxis groups for teachers and candidates.

One of the more successful endeavors was the Art Partnership, a multifaceted collaboration between S-TEC art teachers and art candidates and an elementary PDS school nearby. The high school ceramics teacher visited the elementary school and did some ceramics instruction with the teachers and his candidate took her class to the elementary school to teach the pupils to work with clay. The photography teacher had several of his pupils do their Senior Project at the elementary school, working with the after-school program pupils on making cameras and doing "pin-hole" photography.

Another candidate worked with 4th and 6th grade teachers to design art projects that were connected to the math concepts the pupils were learning and brought those pupils on a field trip to the high school to visit a high school art class and make art with the high schoolers.

It would be satisfying to report at this point about how successful and smooth this experience was and to describe the success of subsequent years of S-TEC. Yet after three years, S-TEC was discontinued. What caused this seemingly successful program to be terminated? Despite the promising practices and successes at the grassroots level, conflicts and miscommunication at the level of the school, the district, and the university's Single Subject Teacher Preparation Program made S-TEC vulnerable and ultimately led to its disbanding.

A significant barrier to institutionalization of S-TEC was the conflict that developed between the Single Subject Program Group (SSPG) members and me as a result of my single-minded (and unfortunately single-handed) actions in support of establishing and implementing S-TEC. New to my job at the university, I did not understand or appreciate the institutional culture and was less attentive to the norms of practice within my own program group. When I joined the faculty, I entered into a group that had been together for decades and had developed norms and procedures that appeared to be quite adequate. Though my work was not meant as a direct critique of this history, it implicitly and explicitly did raise questions about the priorities, values, and practices of the program group because it represented a departure from what was normative. When my work was simply conceptual, it was tolerated. At the point of implementation—that is, when I asked for a group of candidates from our overall pool or to teach classes in a certain way—then the situation became extremely contentious and, in retrospect, created a level of enmity within the SSPG that situated me in opposition to the traditional power brokers in the group.

My proposed pilot at S-TEC did significantly depart from past practice. For example, S-TEC involved placing a cohort of candidates at a single school for their entire student teaching experience, though they were still slated to have different grade-level experiences. In addition, S-TEC was predicated on a commitment to educational equity in urban schools—who S-TEC candidates were and their dispositions and knowledge base mattered. However, my first cohort was actually selected by zip code! I endeavored to gain more control over the composition of future cohorts. And, finally, I had hoped to structure the credential courses in ways (on-site, blocks, modules, etc.) that better matched the school realities. Up to that point, the most important course scheduling questions focused on whether courses would follow a Monday and Wednesday or Tuesday and Thursday pattern.

A new dean of the college, knowledgeable about PDSs, and the presence of a solid core of faculty members in the Equity Network ultimately facilitated the implementation of the S-TEC pilot project, though it proceeded over the objections of the SSPG. The intercession of the dean had consequences, however, in that I became even more isolated from my more senior and more politically powerful colleagues who labeled this as an "end run" and me as a "solo flyer." So, although S-TEC moved ahead, I was isolated and felt more kinship with my former colleagues at the high school than with my university colleagues.

In addition to conflicts with faculty colleagues at the university, another barrier was the insularity of S-TEC and the disengagement of the FHS administration. According to NCATE (2001), promising PDSs align their work across institutions—university with school and vice versa. Though the PDS was welcomed initially at FHS and the core group of CTs and other teachers embraced candidates, S-TEC never became fully integrated into the life of the school. Some of the barriers seem clear, with hindsight. For example, more attention could have been paid to governance. Similar to other Equity Network PDSs, we had a PDS steering committee, although it met infrequently and seemed a low priority for the administration. Without this formal governance structure as a strategic vehicle, other efforts to penetrate the school beyond the initial FHS enthusiasts were thwarted. For example, despite frequent offers of support (funding, release time) for professional development and collaborative activities with the university, generally S-TEC came to be viewed by nonparticipants as a candidate program exclusively rather than a partnership between the school and the university of which one element was preparing new teachers. Additionally, turnover in administration at the site created slippage, resulting in the PDS work being delegated to a vice principal already overwhelmed with other demands and duties. Unfortunately, these factors led CTs to conclude that S-TEC was only a segment of their world and work; eventually, the testing regime and academic intensification became increasing barriers for forwarding the S-TEC work at FHS. Even the most ardent S-TEC enthusiasts, including the coordinator of the English language development program, were unable to raise enough colleague support to continue the PDS.

There is no easy way to describe the end of S-TEC. The immediate cause was tied to a misunderstanding that developed in a feeder middle school associated with S-TEC, and this resulted in a conflict between the vice principal, a teacher, and me that escalated to a point that made it clear that S-TEC would not be a good match for this school. This incident highlighted the lack of attention given collaborative processes in establishing the work with a new school. Although the entry was legitimate, it did not engage the school's critical stakeholders in the process of negotiating and participating in the development of the PDS. The middle school incident also highlighted my "solo flyer" status vis-à-vis the operation of S-TEC.

In retrospect, I understand why large comprehensive high schools are challenging places in which to forge partnerships like the S-TEC PDS. Elementary schools typically have better structures to ensure whole faculty and faculty/administration cohesiveness. Many high school teachers have a long list of adjunct duties (before school, after school, weekend coaching, etc.) that make securing collaboration time difficult to impossible. High school administrators have tremendous responsibility for a diverse set of programs, but often wield little authority. In our specific case, the combination of size, competing interests, and increasing distractions for the site administration resulted, unfortunately, in the mission and the goals of the PDS remaining localized to the CTs and a few other FHS teachers. Thus, S-TEC became insulated and eventually isolated to the extent that there was little will to advocate for its continuation as a PDS. In 2004, when the third cohort graduated, I left my work as LENS faculty and S-TEC ceased to operate.

Interlude: Reconceptualizing the Single Subject Teacher Preparation Program

During the years of the S-TEC pilot at FHS, the SSPG in the College of Education was undergoing its own transformation. New faculty members had joined the group, and these faculty members had taught S-TEC candidates, had done some collaborative work with FHS teachers, and were familiar with and supportive of the PDS model. At the same time, several senior faculty members retired.

As irony would have it, just as the conflict with the middle school was unfolding, a new opportunity emerged. Though in the heat of the moment, all my S-TEC efforts seemed to have evaporated in a poison cloud, deeper reflection revealed that many important insights had been gained. Many of the innovations from S-TEC reflected "best practices" and had yielded significant results. Serendipitously, new state-mandated standards for our program mirrored many of the projects tried in S-TEC, legitimizing, on some level, that pilot effort.

The SSPG spent more than a year planning our new teacher preparation program. This was the first reexamination of the SSTPP in more than a quarter of a century. Past practice, so deeply embedded, was seriously challenged at the institutional level for the first time in many years. Not surprisingly, the planning cycle involved debate, discussion, disagreement, and, ultimately, compromise. During this period, the S-TEC pilot project provided some exemplars of assignments and experiences that would meet the expectations of the new standards, including holding courses at school sites, clustering candidates at sites so that they could make contributions to the school's academic programs, and following the school calendar rather than the university calendar.

In addition, the SSPG adopted a structural model that created clusters with coursework and faculty members that would be assigned to teach in those clusters. Candidates would apply to the clusters, which were designed to have particular emphases and be associated with specific regions in the metropolitan area. Consequently, there was a need to develop a cluster in the urban core of Sacramento. Thus, S-TEC served as a template for the reconfiguration of our secondary teacher preparation program, especially for this proposed urban cluster. As the framework for this urban cluster emerged, it became evident that it was a good match for me, given my experience with S-TEC and my own status as a member of that urban community. With encouragement from my Equity Network colleagues, and with a short list of things to remember from my S-TEC experience, I applied to become the coordinator of what I called PULSE, Preparing Urban Leaders in Secondary Education.

Take Two: Sacramento New Technology High School and the PULSE Teacher Education Collaborative

In a memo, "Notes to Self," I constructed a reminder of the do's and don'ts that I had learned from S-TEC and was committed to applying to the development of this new PDS. These included the following: (1) Do my homework at each site; (2) Build coalitions within my group; (3) Wait before acting or speaking on a controversial matter; (4) Begin by establishing a site steering committee; (5) Integrate candidate work with work of the school; (6) Structure collaboration and reporting between stakeholders; (7) Hold candidates more accountable for "legacy" or service learning projects; (8) Structure inquiry and mentoring/observation into PDS activities; and, (9) Develop coaching and receiving feedback curriculum.

With this list in mind, the process of gaining entry to this site was initiated in a much more structured manner. A colleague, with close ties to school district administrators, served as an intermediary and mentor, arranging introductions with various administrators. In addition, because this effort was part of the new cluster structure, I could count on other faculty colleagues to forward this PDS work. Together, we prepared a description of our proposed program and submitted it for review to several teacher colleagues from city schools. We also worked with our mentor to learn as much as we could about various high schools and programs in our area. Through these activities, we created a program vision for PULSE that included: an emphasis on preparing urban community teachers who would be interculturally competent as well as capable of teaching in their subject area; opportunities for candidates to student teach in nontraditional settings including continuation schools, small schools, charter schools; and, an expectation of adding value to the learning experiences of young people.

A meeting with small schools principals at Sacramento New Technology High School (SNTHS or New Tech) proved pivotal. We met in a classroom—at least they said it was a classroom, but it was twice the size of a regular classroom; it had conference tables in the middle and at least forty brand-new computers along the walls. SNTHS, it turns out, was one of the first Education for the 21st Century schools in the district, funded in part by the Gates Foundation, and it constituted one component in the district's restructuring efforts to make high schools more engaging and powerful learning institutions for young people. Though there was broad interest from the group, New Tech was the most viable site of the group. Fortuitously, the principal invited us to set up shop as soon as possible. We left elated by the welcome and excited about our next steps.

Though my initial idea for a high school PDS was to have everyone at the same school, like Florin, the work with small high schools predicated a different approach. Ultimately, we initiated relationships with five high schools, and identified New Tech as our home base. We maintained a flexible approach, buoyed by the faith that the PULSE PDS would develop its own character over time and that we would begin by doing the same things that went well in S-TEC: building relationships with teachers, spending time at the school sites, getting to know the pupils and the community, asking questions, observing, experimenting, collaborating.

The choice of New Tech as a home base proved a prudent one. Though anxiety levels ran high when the initial principal took a health leave, his replacement was excited about the PDS and revealed additional details about New Tech that made it even more attractive. Rather than the "shopping mall" model of high school (Powell, Farrar, & Cohen, 1985), New Tech was part of a national network of reforming high schools and used Project Based Learning (PBL) and the latest technology as a tool and a text to enhance pupil learning. In addition, the school featured elements of the progressive reforms of the 1990s: a block schedule, curriculum integrated across content areas (e.g., English and Social Studies), team teaching, a weekly Critical Friends common planning time to discuss curriculum and instruction, and a daily advisory. (For more information, see www.newtechfoundation.org, www.essentialschools.org, and www.bie.org.) Moreover, unlike some other small charter high schools, SNTHS was committed to accepting every pupil from within its attendance area—a LI/RCLD community—so the pupil body reflected the city's ethnic, cultural, and linguistic diversity. It also served pupils grades 9 through 12.

When PULSE joined New Tech the school was in its second year, and the teaching staff was inexperienced. However, two teachers had been in the S-TEC program at Florin, and several others had been in a MAT program at a neighboring institution and were willing to mentor new teachers in a PDS model not dramatically different from their own experiences. The first year we placed five candidates at New Tech and held two of our courses there. I regularly attended Critical Friends meetings (faculty meetings) and was enrolled in the Lotus database, giving me broad access to school life and facilitating communication. I attended meetings for their national network and the principal and staff members attended the annual Holmes Partnership Conference and the Equity Network Retreat in 2005. In addition, we had success in integrating our candidates into the life of the school, even when their primary student teaching placement was not there. At the end of the first year, the principal hired two of our candidates into full-time teaching positions. These elements afforded frequent communication among key stakeholders. Over time, I felt like a member of the faculty and the school-based educators had increasing clarity about the potential of the PDS. Moreover, the painful lessons about the politics of transforming institutional relationships learned during the S-TEC experience had been successfully implemented in PULSE; I had addressed items 2, 5, and 6 from my "Notes to Self."

In year two, we continued to have PULSE's home base at New Tech and to place candidates there. New Tech teachers became involved in additional Equity Network projects, expanding their capacity for leadership at their site and for the PDS. We added a powerful component to our work for both teachers and the TPP curriculum, Home Visit Training, which supported candidates' in-depth community studies and our PDS goal of creating urban community teachers. We established and continue to maintain a tradition of welcome receptions, winter receptions, and graduation receptions to celebrate our collaborative work.

During this second year, more items on the "Notes to Self" were addressed. My mentor was invaluable in opening doors and advising me about the norms of collegiality and protocol that defined the culture of the district. As a result, we continued to develop and broaden relationships with the stakeholders in the district and with certain principals in our partner schools. We made presentations to district administrators, met with new principals, and sought out common ground. Our PDS efforts were multi-faceted and tailored for each site.

The third PULSE Cohort has now begun. Though we have come to accept that, for the present, it will be impossible to place all the candidates at the same PDS site, the faculty associated with PULSE has expanded, resulting in more human resources with which to cultivate collaborative projects at our several sites. Some exciting examples include the following: PULSE candidates now work with pupils and the counseling faculty at two high school sites on career and college activities that will provide support for LI/RCLD pupils to transition to college or other postsecondary options and PULSE candidates are working with teachers in an innovative program for English learners at another site. We are developing a vision for PULSE that is a *cluster* of PDS sites, each with its own character and projects, but with a common purpose, a commitment to educational equity for adolescents who are at risk of being left behind.

Looking Back, Looking Ahead: Implications and Recommendations

In retrospect, it seems clear that S-TEC was unsustainable as it was originally constituted. It was framed as a pilot, and it was an almost completely "solo" operation. While the Equity Network provided material resources and offered a community of practice, the actual day-to-day work of the PDS was isolated, disconnected, and therefore generally misunderstood by the SSPG who viewed it as rebel cause. The innovative nature of the pilot intensified the politics of transformation, inevitable with any kind of serious change, and led to conflicts and further misunderstanding of S-TEC's processes and goals. Ultimately, the initial ease of access, the collaborative ethos, and the strong relational support that characterized the successes of the S-TEC PDS were not sufficient to overcome the increasingly disengaged leadership and the consequences of my working alone at the university SSPG level.

As the reinvention of the high school PDS in PULSE indicates, one cannot overestimate the politics of transformation. This effort underscores the importance of actively engaging the school leadership. Creating deep norms of collaboration across various roles is also essential. Access can be negotiated in a number of different ways, as we can see from this account, but "solo" work is not sufficient to build an enduring base of support for long-term joint work. The PULSE PDS Cluster now includes five faculty members with 25 or 50% of their assignment in the PDS, in contrast to the work with S-TEC that I did on my own with less workload credit. Finally, time and resources must be invested in developing a broad community of practice that includes frequent communication among members (e.g., CTs and faculty members), an ethos of collective support for candidates, and efforts to integrate in increasing levels of intensity the university and school programs.

As I revisit my "Notes to Self," I offer the following enhancements:

1. Work with others: have at least one partner from your unit, department, or college to share your ideas with, to give you feedback, to divide the workload, to talk sense when you are faced with a controversial matter. Also, identify a mentor or advisor who has strong familiarity with the schools and the local educational milieu.

2. Do your homework: be a participant observer in the school, listen and ask questions, figure out the organizational (explicit and implicit) structures of the site, and find a mentor to assist with your entry and acculturation to the site.

3. Keep in close contact with the principal or designated contact person and participate in the life of the school as fully as possible.

4. Work with key teachers to build a core group of teachers, counselors, and others who are enthusiastic about the PDS work.

5. Constitute an advisory group and meet regularly, build coalitions across the site, and link with existing networks, organizations, and associations.

6. Be patient and be respectful of the realities and dilemmas inherent in public high schools. Think of this work as long term and consider the work in schools as service to the school and ultimately to the university.

7. Keep an open mind and be willing to consider possibilities "outside the box."

As I complete this narrative, I take away a more complete understanding of the depth and magnitude of the work with S-TEC and PULSE. What began as an idea and a pilot project to democratize the structure of teacher preparation and to intensify a partnership with a high school that was "working" for urban kids has become, not without adversities and setbacks, institutionalized into the Single Subject Teacher Preparation Program. This program now reflects innovations in the structure of schooling and teacher preparation, valorizes the importance of "joint work" (Little, 1982), and emphasizes educational equity in both rhetoric and practice. These innovations interrupt the traditions in high schools that have inadequately served LI/RCLD pupils, their teachers, and their communities.

Note

1. As the perspective in this chapter is primarily that of the author, the reader will note a change in perspective and voice throughout. "I" refers to the author and "we" will be used to refer to the group of school-based faculty (teachers, counselors, administrators) and subsequently to the university faculty members (teacher educators) who were engaged in the PDS partnerships, with clarifications as necessary to distinguish between the two groups.

Chapter Nine

Bridging the Disconnect

The Promise of Lesson Study

David Jelinek and Jenna Porter

Teachers and pupils in urban schools experience a wide range of disconnects, many of them emerging from the very structure of the school system and the units that support it. In this chapter, we look at one initiative, lesson study teams in science, that we designed to address two significant disconnects—between teacher learning (from pre-service to in-service), teacher practice, and pupil learning, in general, and teachers' science knowledge, their science teaching, and pupils' science learning, in particular.

In recent years, many reforms have been instituted to address the disconnect between what teachers know and how they teach, and what pupils learn and how they perform. The problem with many reforms is that they are politically driven efforts that boost voter confidence but fail to address the underlying issues related to improved teaching and high quality pupil learning. These reforms generally leave teachers disconnected from one another's practice, perpetuating their isolation and adding to the demoralization of the profession as teachers wait for yet another mandate to fade away. Another reason reform efforts often fail is that the institutions from which the reform emerges have minimal contact with the schools, teachers, and pupils where the reform is to be implemented. Against a backdrop of artificially important outcomes and structural disconnects, it is easy to lose sight of the questions that should be asked: What do we need to do in the classroom to address the real teaching and learning issues; who develops the curriculum (and why); and who uses the curriculum (and for what purposes)?

Lesson study stands out from "yet another mandate" because it puts control into the hands of those most closely connected to the action—teachers—and focuses on the questions that drive improved teaching and learning. Its success lies in its utter simplicity: teachers meet, they design lessons to address agreed upon goals, they teach and observe each other and the pupils, and then they refine and reteach their lessons. "Learning at its best" in the words of Alfie Kohn, "is a result of sharing information and ideas, challenging someone else's interpretation and having to rethink your own, and working on problems in a climate of mutual support" (Kohn, 1993, p. 214).

In our case, it was also significant to focus our lesson study efforts on science education. Elementary teachers generally receive minimal preparation in science, particularly given the wide range of science disciplines they are expected to teach. In addition, candidates are typically exposed to traditional didactic university science instruction, and in-service sessions on science usually replicate this model. Compounding this situation in recent years is the virtual elimination of science from the K–6 curriculum so that more time can be devoted to language arts and mathematics. As we have argued consistently throughout this book, this is especially true in schools serving LI/RCLD pupils. Keeping science in the elementary school curriculum was one powerful way to address a troubling equity issue that was bound to further disadvantage pupils in Equity Network schools. It is important to emphasize, however, that we were interested specifically in an inquiry-based model of science education. This emphasis was particularly significant given the pattern of curriculum choices made by our partner districts in language arts and mathematics—in both cases, highly scripted curricula were in place. While using an inquiry-based science curriculum would depart significantly from the "teacher-proof" approaches being adopted, we felt it was essential that science education not follow this trend. We began our lesson study project two years before science content debuted on the California Standards Test. We hoped that this head start with inquiry-based, community-related science would build a cadre of teachers who could use their record of work with lesson study to advocate at their schools and in their districts for a science curriculum adoption that did not mirror the scripted curricula of mathematics and language arts.

Like any worthwhile effort, lesson study encompasses a range of goals, all of them connected to the broader goal of strengthening teacher practice and improving pupil learning. Our primary objectives were to:

1. Establish a culture of collaboration among participating teachers and university faculty members and facilitators. This was significant in that both College of Education and College of Natural Science and Mathematics faculty members participated (ushering in a new era in collaboration for our campus) and that we connected with Equity Network teachers who had not been active as CTs previously.

2. Deepen teachers' understanding of science content as reflected in state and national content standards.

3. Improve teachers' pedagogical repertoire, especially those strategies needed to teach inquiry-based science successfully to LI/RCLD pupils and to assess pupil learning authentically.

As the lesson study project has evolved (from six teams in the first year to sixteen teams in the third), we have also delved deeply into researching the effects of lesson study. In particular, we have looked at: How do "research" lessons change with each iteration in relation to being responsive to pupil readiness, interest, self-efficacy, and characteristics? What benefits from lesson study do teachers identify? What are the challenges associated with lesson study—from the teacher and university faculty perspectives?

Theoretical Framework

Lesson study fits within the open systems perspective for changing educational settings, a perspective that argues that change must take place within the school organizational structure because change is taking place within the larger environment. In order to survive, an organization must know how to adapt. History reminds us, however, that school systems struggle to adapt successfully. Part of the problem lies with the nature of public school organization, which dates back to the machine metaphor (precision, predictability, centralized authority, and specialization) of the early 1900s. Frederick Taylor's scientific management approach promoted the theory that by mechanically analyzing tasks, productivity could be maximized and input of energies and resources minimized. Fayol's administrative theory worked to rationalize the organization in a "top-down" approach, then Max Weber's theory brought organizational structure to its most highly developed form of bureaucracy (Scott, 1992). A typical organizational model from a traditional school setting will include top-down control from the district to administrators to teachers to pupils, leaving the teacher as "information giver," relying on textbooks and other procedure-driven systems of teaching. Goals are specified and standardized and the teacher is encouraged to "follow the rules."

The downside of this kind of hierarchical system is that it rewards conformity and punishes innovation and initiative (Garcia & Garcia, 1996). "Modern education arose from general scientific thinking and is built up around scientific theories of socialization, with rules of sequencing, of curricular structure and interdependence, and of pedagogical method" (Hallinan, 1987, p. 158). Thus, a "standardized processing system" is preferable to creative and critical thinking by teachers or pupils (Hallinan, p. 157). This replication of the scientific management model in education affects how and what young pupils learn as well as the kinds of commitments and capacities they develop. It also affects teachers' strategies, school organization, administrative structure, and the whole construction and evolution of the educational system.

Darling-Hammond (1989) and others challenge the "scientific management" principles that "standardize and rationalize the process of schooling." Under this system, argues Darling-Hammond, schools are mere agents of the government, slotted into a hierarchical decision making structure where policies are made at the top, handed down to middle management to be translated into rules and procedures for the teacher to follow and enforce. Pupils are processed according to class schedules, curricula, textbooks, rules for promotion, and so on, with "[a fostering of] equal and uniform treatment of clients, standardization of products or services . . . to prevent arbitrary or capricious decision making" (Darling-Hammond, 1988, p. 75). It is assumed pupils can be sufficiently standardized to respond in predictable ways, that treatments can be prescribed and generalized to all educational circumstances, that standardized rules can be operationalized through regulations with systems for reporting and inspection, and that administrators and teachers will faithfully implement the top-down mandates. This ideologically based framework represents one attempt to address the loose coupling in the education system, which creates vexing disconnects between policy development, policy implementation, and policy outcomes. But, we would argue, it is only one framework for tackling these disconnects. We think that lesson study is a promising alternative that, if implemented in a comprehensive manner (which was not within our purview), could prove an antidote to many perennial reform issues in schools today.

Interrupting Tradition: The Promise of Lesson Study

Against this backdrop of artificially important outcomes where "reform again and again" has dominated school culture for decades, it is easy to lose sight of the questions that should be asked: What do we need to do in the classroom to address the real teaching and learning issues, particularly for LI/RCLD pupils; who develops the curriculum (and why); and who uses the curriculum (and for what purposes)? Lesson study mitigates many of the typical reform shortcomings because it addresses teaching and learning issues at the heart of teachers' work, strengthens their connections to their pupils and to their colleagues, and has the potential, as in our case, to connect classrooms to intellectual and pedagogical centers outside the school structure. In short, teachers participating in lesson study bridge the traditional disconnect gap inherent within schools and between administration and teachers. In our model, lesson study has also served to bridge the disconnect between schools and institutions of higher education. Even districts that insist on stringent control mechanisms still grant broad latitude with regard to lesson study, thus situating lesson study as an ideal catalyst for a new kind of reform—characterized by an organizational structure in which administrators "delegate to the group of professional employees considerable responsibility for defining and implementing the goals, for setting performance standards, and for seeing to it that standards are maintained" (Scott, 1992, p. 254). Lesson study has the potential to become a functional mechanism in service of the educational objectives of bringing quality education to a diverse population under a wide variety of programs and methodologies.

In the lesson study process (see Figure 1), groups of teachers meet regularly over a period of time ranging from several months to a year to work on the design, implementation, testing, and improvement of "research lessons" (Stigler & Hiebert, 1999). Research lessons are actual classroom lessons, taught to one's own pupils, that are (a) focused on a specific teacher-generated problem, goal, or vision of pedagogical practice, (b) carefully planned, usually in collaboration with one or more colleagues, a content specialist and a methods specialist, (c) observed by other teachers and specialists, (d) recorded for analysis and reflection, and (e) discussed by lesson study group members and other colleagues (Fernandez & Yoshida, 2004; Lewis & Tsuchida, 1998).

Figure 1. Japan's Professional Development Model

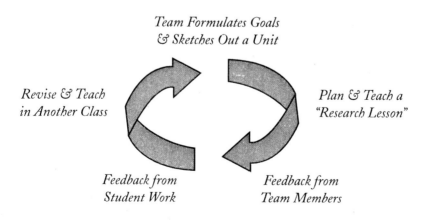

Team Formulates Goals
& Sketches Out a Unit

Revise & Teach
in Another Class

Plan & Teach a
"Research Lesson"

Feedback from
Student Work

Feedback from
Team Members

Originating in Japan decades ago, this successful professional development model has developed an extensive following in the United States. As a form of professional development, it enables teachers to teach effectively within a culture of mutual respect. Through lesson study teachers achieve common understandings of pupil thinking, expectations for pupil learning and production, and the strategies needed to maximize pupils' educational experiences (Wang-Iverson, 2002).

Thus, when analyzing why the system does not work as well as it could and should for LI/RCLD communities, we determined that there are competing interests across sectors within the system, that there is only superficial isomorphism, and that structural disconnects are managed with tighter control and authority at the top, often pulling teachers further away from their pupils and school communities. Moreover, such dynamics underscore the intense negotiations at the heart of the politics of transforming institutions to better serve LI/RCLD pupils, emphasizing the critical questions about which knowledge, whose knowledge, and how knowledge is transmitted and learned.

Lesson study has the potential to reverse these dynamics. It situates the key activity of reform squarely in the classroom and makes teacher knowledge of pupils and teacher thinking the primary foci. It reinforces the importance of evidence, as lesson observation concentrates less on teacher "performance" and more on data about pupil engagement and learning collected by observers (also lesson co-designers). And finally, it is predicated on the notion that teaching is an iterative act, best characterized as a craft where deeper learning (content and pedagogical knowledge for teachers, content and process knowledge for pupils), continued attention to detail, careful observation, reflection, and collaboration lead to improved practice and results.

Lesson Study and the Equity Network

Our lesson study effort had modest beginnings. We were concluding our third year as a Network PDS and, for the third time, survey data indicated that CTs wanted increased support in the area of educational equity and teaching English learners. Their feedback identified a possible weakness in our structure—we held firm to the principle that our PDS projects needed to emerge from the local contexts of the schools, resulting in each site pursuing different projects based on local needs and the expertise and interests of the actors involved. Thus, while all of the PDS projects addressed equity issues, they did so with varying emphases. In an effort to craft a suitable response to these data, the Network faculty members began exploring possible new initiatives, considering lesson study and a coaching model as options. Meanwhile, colleagues in the College of Natural Science and Mathematics were considering resources from the California Postsecondary Education Commission to provide science professional development to K–12 teachers and were also contemplating a lesson study initiative. A chance encounter brought us together and we jointly fashioned a proposal that included a summer science institute and academic year lesson study teams intended to support teachers as they endeavored to implement the science learning and teaching from the 10-day summer institute. Much to our delight, our proposal was funded and with our new partners from Natural Science and Mathematics, we initiated our Equity Network science education project, slated to be a three-year effort.

Echoing themes in other chapters, this too has been an effort in which we have "made the road while walking" (Horton & Freire, 1990). In this chapter, we describe our first large-scale effort, the year after we piloted lesson study with six teams. In this first year at scale, our structure included an online "workbook" and resource guide for lesson study, a basic process for identifying, training, and supporting lesson study teams, and a nascent support and training system for lesson study facilitators, most of whom were faculty members in either the College of Natural Sciences and Mathematics or the College of Education. We had hired a full-time lesson study coordinator, who had been an active teacher leader at a PDS site.

Teams were located at the same site, but often members came from different grade levels, a mix that proved productive. They began by thinking about the *aspirations* they have for their pupils, the *gaps* between these aspirations and where the pupils currently stand, then moved to formulate *goals* to address at least one of these gaps. Each team set about designing a science unit in light of these goals, out of which they selected a single lesson to focus on. Before actually planning and teaching the lesson they were asked to *justify* how the lesson related to the lesson study goals. Referencing content from the summer institute, team members also linked the goals to the California K–12 Content Standards in Science and, where possible, to pressing community issues that they knew could have a scientific application. During the planning portion of lesson study, members were required to incorporate effective instructional practices and assessment strategies modeled during the institute. We drew heavily from the NSTA framework of the "five E's" (engagement, exploration, explanation, extension, and evaluation) and the "five standards for effective pedagogy" identified through research conducted by the Center for Research on Education, Diversity, and Excellence. Lesson study teams were supported through an initial training session, a comprehensive set of resources and protocols provided in the online resource guide, and regular collaboration with their facilitators (who both facilitated and provided content support and expertise needed for the lessons).

Each team implemented two cycles of lesson study. Once the planning phase (described earlier) was completed, the research lesson was taught by one member of the team, with other members observing for particular aspects of pupil engagement and learning during the lesson. It is important to clarify that each team focused on one lesson in particular—not because it was such a critical lesson that it had to be taught, refined, and retaught to make sure the pupils would "get it," but rather because it allowed the teachers to focus more deeply on aspects they could not possibly identify until after trying it out and revisiting it. After the lesson was taught, the team met to analyze the data that were collected, discussing the lesson's effectiveness and identifying what could be done to improve it next time, including using different strategies or accommodations. Then another teacher taught the revised lesson, observations were conducted, and the team again debriefed and refined their lesson. Throughout this entire process, the methods and science content faculty served as team members, collecting data and even co-teaching in some cases.

While teams operated independently for most of the year, a Lesson Study Final Reflection Meeting provided an opportunity for all of the lesson study teams to meet across sites, share their lessons, and reflect as individuals and as groups on the outcomes of the process for themselves as teachers and for their pupils as science learners. This event builds a strong community of teachers who appear to be growing increasingly committed to lesson study as a powerful vehicle for professional development and to teaching science, despite the various constraints that conspire to keep it out of the curriculum for LI/RCLD pupils. In our three years of supporting lesson study, we have collected a wealth of data. We collected and analyzed "study" lessons, team planning minutes, observation notes and logs, pupil work and other evidence of pupil learning (observations of pupil science talk, digital images, pre- and post-assessments, tallying of pupil response and engagement, etc.), observations of team deliberations, year-end reflection survey, lesson study questionnaire rated on a Likert scale, and guided reflection prompts. Evaluation rubrics were created and used for each team to assess their lesson study artifacts; two independent evaluators also rated the artifacts of each lesson study team using this rubric. In the next section, we discuss what lesson study and our analysis of these data have taught us about teacher learning, teachers' science knowledge, teachers' science pedagogy, collaboration, and pupil learning as well as what the process has revealed about the challenges of redefining whose knowledge counts and why.

As stated earlier, we pursued multiple objectives with lesson study. We wanted to deepen teachers' science content knowledge, based on the belief that knowing something well is not only important but can also provide the confidence to experiment and innovate. We were also committed to introducing teachers to models of teaching science that put learners at the center, structured planning around their needs and interests, and employed assessments that accurately captured what they were learning. Finally, we were confident that deepening a culture of collaboration—within sites and between sites and the university—would foster effective and innovative teaching and strengthen teachers' resolve to teach inquiry-based science to their LI/RCLD pupils.

Our concern about teachers' science knowledge does not stem from ideologically driven critiques of teachers or candidates as deficient in intellectual capacity. There are many roots to this issue. Gender inequity in mathematics and science education in the K–12 system is certainly one of them. Such inequities can lead to poor performance and/or continued confusion about science and scientific thinking; these factors combine to lower candidates' confidence about their science knowledge, often making them reticent to teach anything but the basic facts displayed in their textbooks (if they have them). In addition, most of these teachers will have had Liberal Studies/Arts or its equivalent as an undergraduate major. This major, in most of its configurations, includes coursework that exposes candidates to the subdisciplines addressed in the content standards (basic earth science, physical science, and chemistry), but these course sequences simply allow candidates to touch the surface of science learning. Moreover, only in the most innovative settings are these courses taught in an inquiry-based way, modeling effective pedagogy for future teachers. These factors combine with two recent phenomena in schools. The first, prevalent in the early to mid-1990s (thus for teachers with 8 to 15 years experience), is the use of science resource teachers that may have strengthened the science programs in schools, but also truncated science learning for the regular elementary teacher who came to rely on the science resource teacher to teach science to her pupils. The second is the more recent phenomenon of the "disappearance" of science from the K–6 curriculum. Many teachers at the beginning of their careers have simply not taught science . . . yet. *Most of our teachers, because they teach in LI/RCLD settings, have never had science texts or resources in their classrooms.*

In fact, on a number of different data collection tools, teachers have revealed, with little hesitation, that science is an area of weakness for them. In reflection on the lesson study process and during our summer institutes, teachers' comments included:

> I have been most thrilled with the opportunity for a deeper understanding of the science. I have a lot of general science knowledge and I like having more depth.

> Science is fun . . . I have taught K and 1st for my whole career, so I have not had to go beyond my science comfort zone. . . . There is so much that I do not know in science.

The most challenging part [of teaching science] will always be the lack of knowledge and exposure that I have.

Physical science is a concept that has always felt foreign to me. Looking at energy, I am still vague on the different kinds.

Coupled with teachers' lack of confidence about teaching science and genuine gaps in their science knowledge is their lack of familiarity with science pedagogy, though such deficiencies are not surprising given all that has been described previously. Though scripted curricula and the like give the impression that anything can be taught if a well-designed textbook is available, most scientists and science educators bristle at the notion that pupils would learn science from a textbook and worksheets alone, especially since careful analysis identifies many errors in textbooks. Nevertheless, our work in lesson study has emphasized a pedagogical approach (inquiry, community connections) that is also new to teachers, thus we destabilize them at every turn! Several teachers remarked:

I found that science is never going to give you a direct answer. It is hard to explain that to your classroom when you can't grab that yourself.

My 'aha' moment was related more to the process of science, specifically to a more insightful view of carefully selecting the right science activities/experiments for a lesson so as to avoid (hopefully) misconceptions regarding the learning goal. [Also] . . . it was challenging not getting an exact answer.

The challenging part of learning science was not having 'all' the answers and having to predict a lot about different processes. These ultimately resulted in many 'aha' moments.

Most challenging is to take the science that I know, but I don't think of it as science, and relate it to everyday life, especially my (young) pupils' lives.

With these self-assessments as a backdrop, we turn now to the emerging outcomes of our lesson study project. Our narrative here focuses on results from the evaluation of lesson study artifacts (lesson plans, meeting minutes, reflections) and a lesson study participants' survey.

In terms of the impact of lesson study on teachers' science content knowledge and confidence in teaching science, the survey results reveal positive gains in both. Teachers were asked to rate their knowledge of the target standard before and after the lesson study process, as well as to assess their confidence in teaching science before and after lesson study. In both cases, they indicated that knowledge and confidence grew as a result of lesson study. For example, the majority of teachers rated their confidence with teaching science as low prior to lesson study, but as high after lesson study. Similarly, teachers expressed anxiety about pupils' questions during science lessons prior to lesson study, but were much less anxious about this possibility after lesson study. And, finally, teachers made similar shifts in terms of their confidence in using hands-on strategies for science.

Several factors may account for these positive changes. Teachers identified collaboration with peers, the CSUS facilitator, new resources, and planning time as important contributors. Similar to the results on science content learning, teachers indicated that lesson study helped them to develop new science pedagogy knowledge. Here, they identified new instruction techniques, collaboration with peers, opportunities to observe lessons, support for trying new techniques, and new assessment strategies as important components. Teachers predicted that the combination of increased confidence in science teaching, deepened content knowledge, and the acquisition of new instructional and assessment strategies would lead to the following changes in their practice: (a) more hands-on learning; (b) less direct instruction; (c) more exploration; (d) more self-reflection; (e) more pupil led discussions; and, (f) greater ease and encouragement to seek out peers.

The assessment of lesson study artifacts enhances our understanding of how the lesson study process impacted teacher practice; it also highlights some areas of concern. Four criteria were evaluated for each cycle of lesson study. A rubric was used to evaluate two sets of artifacts from each team—each iteration of the lesson, meeting minutes, pre- and post-conference notes, and observation data from the first and second rounds of lesson study. Our primary objective was to identify areas of growth, that is, dimensions in which teams improved their lessons from the first round to the second. Our analysis is briefly summarized next, by criterion.

Criterion One

"The learning objectives articulated in the lesson plans are meaningful, measurable, and connected to identified standards and specifically address a range of EL learners." While no teams submitted artifacts that were assessed as exemplary for these criteria, each team showed improvements in their lesson study work, moving to either "partially addressed" or "fully addressed" by the second round.

Criterion Two

"Instructional plan utilizes strategies and resources that are appropriate to the tasks, learning outcomes, and learning styles of pupils." Teams made the most progress in this domain of their lesson study work. It appeared that the opportunity to observe pupils during the first teaching of the lesson sharply focused teachers' sights on the extent to which lessons were designed to truly meet the academic needs of the pupils. Second round lessons for most teams included significant changes in the kinds of strategies used (e.g., more strategies to scaffold content for ELs, etc.).

Criterion Three

"Interactive and collaborative activities provided." Teams were assessed at relatively high levels on this criterion, with one team achieving the "exemplary" benchmark. We are not surprised by this since the notion of "hands-on" science has been stressed repeatedly with our teachers.

Criterion Four

Our last criterion required "varied use of assessments that match the learning objectives." Here no change was evidenced and the lesson study efforts were rated as relatively weak, with most teams showing only "partial evidence." It has become increasingly clear that although the teams developed pupil goals before designing their lessons, many teachers lacked the skills or experience necessary to provide effective assessments for their pupils. Several of the pre-conference forms indicated that, especially in the first cycle, there was little or no thought on how to collect evidence of pupil learning. In some cases, teams made improvements in this area, possibly due to focused encouragement from the university facilitator.

Finally, additional data sources provide us with insight into the ways in which lesson study contributed to a culture of collaboration within a site and between the PDSs and the university. While the fact that several teams had already had experience working together confounds our analysis on some level, we can say that survey data and teacher reflection narratives indicate that this new domain for collaboration—science with an explicit focus on evidence of pupil learning—was much appreciated. Because there is little room to debate content, concepts, process, strategies, or outcomes, most collaboration in schools is very task-oriented. Teachers at the same grade level plan activities together and then divide up the tasks of getting the activities ready for implementation—one makes copies, the other finds supplies, and so on. Lesson study demands a deeper level of collaboration and one that requires difficult conversations about how teachers conceptualize pupil learning, what they are willing to try, and how they want to evaluate the success of their combined efforts. It also requires that teachers follow a protocol and proceed in their collaboration in very deliberate and mindful ways. We are encouraged by the fact that this kind of deep and substantive collaboration is so valued by the lesson study participants. In fact, one lesson study member, recently selected as County Teacher of the Year, remarked: "Lesson study is the single most powerful professional development I have done in my decades of work as a teacher."

We entered into new territory with the training and provision of university faculty members as lesson study facilitators and with the introduction of science faculty members as resources to the Equity Network. We anticipated that consistent support from the university, through science content specialists and facilitators, would strengthen lesson study team productivity. Faculty members received release time so that they could be present and available to work with each team as they worked through the goal setting and planning stages of their science lessons. Their role was to ask the "hard" questions—about science content, about accommodations for pupils, and about assessment. Specific protocols guided their efforts; monthly meetings among facilitators also provided extra support, particularly for those new to this role.

The reflection survey given to participants at the end of the 2004–2005 school year indicated that lesson study had been a beneficial and team-building experience. Teachers ranked several different aspects of lesson study on a scale from 1 to 5, with five being most positive. The mean rank for the university facilitation aspect was 4.42. When asked to rank the effectiveness of the university facilitator, participants commended them and ranked them at a mean of 4.29. Open-ended questions about the support of facilitators yielded comments like "Facilitators were very effective in giving structure and purpose to our study." They were given reasonable scores (3 out of 4) in terms of their ability to engage all team members, listen actively, contribute to the dialogue, and keep the team "on track." Teachers described faculty facilitators as "supportive," "effective," and "helpful."

Discussion

Overall, the evidence from our lesson study effort indicates that it has increased understanding on many levels, including addressing pupil needs and more effective strategies to teach standards and content. Teachers reported increased enthusiasm for teaching science as a result of lesson study's winning strength: collaboration with peers and opportunities to watch and receive feedback from other teachers: 57% of the group felt confident to teach science at the beginning of lesson study; 6 months later 81% of the group felt this way. They also gave high positive ratings to focused planning time. They felt the process as a whole gave them new instructional techniques, better understanding of science content, and opportunities to work with other teachers. In particular, they felt more likely to design lessons that would include pupil-led discussions and they felt greater ease in seeking information and encouragement from their colleagues.

As we reflect on our efforts with this lesson study project, we consider our work at the level of the specific and the general. In terms of our specific goals and objectives, our data reveal that there is still a good deal to do. While we are encouraged that teachers find this a powerful form of professional development and that they rate lesson study as having improved their science knowledge and confidence in teaching science, we see room for considerable improvement when we look closely at the rubric assessments of the lesson study artifacts. While these paper assessments cannot tell us everything about the quality of the science that was being taught, we suspect that because the scores did not move as much in this area that there is still much more to do to deepen teachers' science content knowledge and to improve the structures (facilitators, summer institutes, etc.) that we have developed to support lesson study. We are buoyed by our own prediction that, given what we know about the work ethic of these teachers, their increase in confidence will likely lead them to seek out professional development and further science content knowledge. Nevertheless, this dimension of their practice remains a concern that we will continue to try to address, both through lesson study and other means.

Though teachers appeared to incorporate increasingly more hands-on activities for pupils, a trend that we see as positive because it means that the pupils are doing science rather than reading about it or watching someone else do it, our assessment tool did not give us a fine-grained measure of whether those hands-on activities were also "minds-on" activities. When we view this uncertainty in light of the difficulties that teachers had with identifying or designing tools for authentic assessment of pupil learning, then we gain further clarity about the tasks ahead. The lack of depth in teachers' understanding of pupil assessment is particularly troubling, as it could potentially point to the fact that a gap still remains between what teachers teach, what they want to see from pupils, and the extent to which pupils understand expectations and are supported to meet them. Again, this is certainly an area for further work within our partnership.

When we consider our lesson study project from the more general lens of school reform, we again see both successes and areas of concern. On the surface it is clear that each team articulated its own set of aspirations for its pupils, and then identified gaps between these aspirations and where the pupils currently stand. To the extent these gaps were sufficiently identified and understood, the teams were able to formulate goals, units, and lessons to help the pupils (and teachers) narrow those gaps. But even though the response from the team members indicates that lesson design was improved, the underlying question is: *Did this help you narrow the gap?* Did it bring the teachers closer to grappling with the reform questions posed earlier—questions about what they need to do in the classroom to address real teaching and learning issues, about who develops the curriculum (and why), and who uses the curriculum (and for what purposes).

On the one hand, lesson study sounds simple and straightforward, but in a world of conflicting viewpoints between teachers, administrators, unions, and school boards, where instruction is increasingly scripted, where standards define what and how much to teach, and where teachers are pressed for time both in the classroom and out, reform is never simple and straightforward. To stand a chance, reforms must find a way to peel away layers of distractions and keep attention focused on pupils and their learning. Moreover, they must make sense to teachers and relate to the core issues that keep them energized about their profession. In this way, lesson study serves as an antidote to the current rash of overly prescriptive "teacher-proof" curriculum and the corporate model of rationalized inputs and outputs, while, ironically, working within it.

A key factor in school reform failure has been the coercive pressures school districts have placed on unconventional innovators in an effort to cease their nonconformity (Kozol, 1967) while a strong variable of success has been district-level support (Fullan, 1982). Lesson study is innovative and collaborative. It takes risks. It is unique. It assumes its own personality and characteristics, bearing in mind that environmental interaction and adaptation are crucial to its survival. Innovative lesson study teams are possible within the public domain because they do not diminish the standards of education nor threaten the existence of an organized educational system.

One of the salient features of lesson study is it lets teachers become curriculum innovators through a rigorous process of reflection and inquiry, all in the name of improved pupil learning. New ideas are encouraged, participants' needs and concerns are important, and change is possible if the situation requires it. Lesson study takes the whole into account, including both teachers and pupils within the context of the particular class. Lessons change as a response to external environmental factors, and this ability to adapt to the environment and implement changes assures lesson study's success within the complexities of the school structure as a whole.

As we've emphasized, in order to survive, an organization must know how to adapt. The innovative nature of lesson study places it in a perpetual process of adaptation because this improves its chances of survival on many fronts. Lesson study participants are aware that they are not an entity unto themselves, but a unit within a much broader environment, and they know that engaging in exchanges with that environment is a condition of survival. This makes them *active* in survival strategies, utilizing whatever resources and services the environment has to offer to better their chances of success. Thus, they create and build connections both within and outside of their school structure—in short, they bridge the traditional *disconnect* gap inherent within schools and between schools and institutions of higher education.

Making History by
Creating New Traditions

Concluding Reflections and Future Directions

Ronald David Glass and Pia Lindquist Wong

The six years of Equity Network PDS projects that are described in this book constitute an impressive body of work and chart the creation of new traditions that will, we hope, address the more persistent educational equity challenges that have been a part of the history of public schooling and teacher preparation to date. In the preceding chapters, we have showcased our work while offering critical and honest reflections on the limitations and missteps that have also been integral parts of our experience and our learning. In this chapter, we situate our accomplishments and our challenges within the broader historical context of reforms in teacher education and for educational equity in the K–12 sector. In analyzing the interplay between tradition and our attempts to interrupt it through the Equity Network PDS projects, we are able to identify key themes that we hope will frame our future collaborative projects as we use a model of engaged pedagogy to create new and more equitable traditions in teacher education and urban public schooling.

Themes in the History of School Reform and Teacher Education: Toward a New Tradition

As those who spend time in urban settings quickly conclude, public schools are not working well for LI/RCLD children. In fact, historical analysis reveals that schools have always produced mixed outcomes for the poor, providing a modicum of opportunity for the few while exacting a heavy psychological price from the many who suffer its ranking and sorting assessments with little hope of success. For people of color, these processes were made all the harsher by decades of discriminatory segregation and paltry funding for their schools, with few social and economic opportunities awaiting even the best and brightest. After World War II and the vast expansion of schooling for the poor and working class that flowed from the generosity of the GI Bill of Rights, new obstacles were placed in their way in the form of broader applications of standardized testing. Not surprisingly, LI/RCLD students found themselves again at a decided disadvantage. Consequently, closing the test-score gap and pursuing educational equity have been consistent themes in education policy discourse since *Brown v. Board of Education* broke down some of the primary legal props upholding segregated schooling.

Nationally, several trends have surfaced. Increased and more equitable distribution of resources are perennial demands, and while simple fairness would seem to require the provision of adequate resources for all students to have an equal opportunity to learn, this has proven astonishingly difficult to achieve. The issue remains much debated but rarely addressed in a systemic manner (Hanushek, 2003; Levin & McEwan, 2002). Lawsuits to address funding injustices have made little headway, and even the victory achieved in the *Williams* case in California was limited because it was settled without redressing the underlying structural discrimination against LI/RCLD children and their communities. Despite substantial moral, political, and legal pressures on public education nationally to provide equitable and adequate resources, the discrepancies in funding between school districts in a community can amount to literally hundreds of thousands of dollars per classroom, and, even in California, where there are limits on such gaps, it typically amounts to tens of thousands of dollars per classroom (Peske & Haycock, 2006).

Similarly, one can find a substantial gap between rhetoric and practice when it comes to honoring a curriculum that embodies the contributions and perspectives of the multiethnic and multiracial realities of U.S. life. The democratization of content and fostering of anti-bias skills and dispositions in students has fallen victim to the narrowing of curriculum caused by the push toward greater emphasis on standardized testing (Jones, Jones, & Hargrove, 2003). The push back against the post-*Brown* gains has been relentless, and over the last 25 years it has been the dominant driver of school reform.

The anemic responses of the educational system to the most serious challenges of the past 50 years to its dominant "grammar of schooling" betokens the power of institutional forms to resist substantive transformation when they have become absorbed into the taken-for-granted cultural frame of reference (Tyack & Cuban, 1995). Although a confluence of historical, economic, and political forces can produce tectonic shifts in schooling, even these changes have had limited effect in altering the foundational social structures of inequalities tied to race, gender, language, and class (Katznelson & Weir, 1985; Tyack, 1974). For the most part, however, over the last 100 years, reformers have tinkered with the system with minimal effect on the core structure and the underlying assumptions and values that shape schooling. This has led other analysts to view the battles about schools as embedded in larger power struggles about resource distribution and representation in the social and political sphere (Bowles & Gintis, 1976; Carnoy & Levin, 1985). They argued that broader social forces perpetually shift alignments in an uneasy coexistence in the midst of fundamental conflicts structured into the contradictions in democracy and capitalism, and thus historically evolving coalitions compete for control over school policy decisions, from curriculum content to instructional strategies to governance and contract issues. The ideology and discourse of school policymaking swing from a pro-democracy stance, in which concerns about representation, opportunity, and equity are paramount, to a pro-capitalism stance, in which workforce preparation, efficiency, "excellence," and standardization dominate.

Recent national reform efforts are reflected in this analysis. Reform advocates in the 1950s and 1960s focused the nation's attention on the unequal educational outcomes and opportunities that sorted children by social class, gender, and race, producing schooling outcomes that reproduced existing social relations. Many of their demands focused on issues of access—for students and communities—and on the content of the school curriculum. Still concerned with this equity issue, reformers showcased "effective schools" in the early 1980s as the model to follow for improved educational outcomes, particularly for LI/RCLD students (for example the Accelerated Schools Project and Comer School Development Project). But the creation of effective schools proved more difficult, and the staying power of the old system more persistent, than anticipated. Administrators and policymakers soon discovered that conditions needed to replicate effective schools for LI/RCLD students on a systemwide basis required considerable investment, that policy and program mandates did not always translate into projected behaviors, and that the same combination of factors in different contexts produced varying results. Not surprisingly, the momentum for change waned.

As support for the effective schools approach faded, calls were issued for new reforms focused on the management and administrative structure of schools, and on imposing measurable standards on schools and teachers in order to make them "accountable." The Reagan-Bush era *Nation at Risk* report decried the "rising tide of mediocrity" engulfing the nation, and called for the return to basics that could enable the nation to compete in the rapidly globalizing economy. When the politics of blaming schools and teachers for a weak economy played well with voters, schools became harnessed to the corporate effort to retool the workforce and restructure the economy.

Corporate and industrial models of management and decision-making became predominant, and business leaders again exercised explicit influence over school policy matters, whether at the local level through Chambers of Commerce or at the state and national level through organizations such as the Business Roundtable. Reforms such as site-based management teams were touted because of their success in improving efficiencies and profits for corporate giants like Toyota (or General Motors' Saturn plants, which mimicked the Japanese forms of management) (Emery & Ohanian, 2004). The argument was that these proven industrial modalities would transmute the inefficiencies in schools to produce better teaching and learning (i.e., higher productivity and profitability). Aligned with these demands were market-oriented reforms (charters and vouchers) intended to promote competition, which in turn was supposed to yield increased excellence in school performance (as measured on standardized tests). To make this restructured system work, schools had to conform to uniform curriculum and outcome standards and adopt prescribed accountability systems to measure progress toward the standards. These initiatives, launched a quarter century ago, have become the transcendent organizing principles for public schools, and have imposed an especially heavy burden on those who serve LI/RCLD students and communities (Orfield & Kornhaber, 2001).

In 2000, the reauthorization of the Elementary and Secondary Education Act, known as "No Child Left Behind"[1] or NCLB, launched a standards- and testing-based assault on the test-score status quo in schools. NCLB dramatically increased federal activism in local education matters, with unprecedented mandates related to testing instruments and protocols, curriculum adoptions, teacher certification, and teacher training. On its surface, NCLB appears to prioritize the education of students who have historically been marginalized, and it calls for accelerated implementation timetables for schools serving the nation's poorest and most diverse students. At the same time, NCLB has been widely criticized by scholars for its reliance on invalid measures and inappropriate test-score targets. Its implementation has been fraught with difficulties caused not only by the faulty logic of its mandates, but by severely inadequate funding of key legislative provisions. NCLB's exclusive dependence on standardized tests to measure what a "child knows and can do" ignores the realities that these tests do not and cannot fully measure student learning and achievement, they are often misaligned with adopted state content standards, they fail to provide accommodations to students whose learning cannot be accurately measured by current tools (e.g., tests in English for recently immigrated students), and they do not provide informative data for subsequent teaching and learning decisions. Furthermore, NCLB imposes arbitrary proficiency targets that do not reliably or validly capture student growth in learning, and it exaggerates testing requirements as a performance measure, which channels significant resources away from a wide range of important teaching and learning needs toward simply raising test scores. This reorientation of instruction is driven in part by insufficient funding to enable quality teaching, and it creates disincentives for professionalism and creativity among teachers through a growing reliance on highly scripted curricula geared into the tests, which cannot simply be ignored because NCLB provides for serious sanctions that are often hastily applied and/or applied based on invalid data. The resultant narrowed curriculum for those who score low on tests most severely impacts schools serving LI/RCLD students, once again putting these children at a disadvantage. Sadly, NCLB requirements and consequences ignore solidly grounded research findings that contradict the political agenda behind the act (such as when decades of research showing negative consequences of retaining children for low test scores is ignored in favor of supposedly "higher standards").

Many educators of all political persuasions see a broader agenda underlying NCLB that explains its imperviousness to these very substantial criticisms. Though the Bush-Cheney policymakers' propaganda about NCLB heralds it as a significant attempt to transform a failing public school system and make it more fair for LI/RCLD students, the legislation's discrete actions and mandates indicate that the end goal of this transformation may well be an education system that is decidedly in the hands of private and entrepreneurial education providers. Schools facing five successive years of "program improvement" status must cede their operations to state control, to a private firm, or pursue charter status. Local control cannot include the pursuit of practitioner-created programs that reconstruct organizational, managerial, and teaching systems to expand local capacity and meet a variety of locally determined learning goals rather than test-score improvement. Similarly, schools in chronic "program improvement" status must allocate funds to contract with private tutorial programs to provide interventions for profit, rather than extend the instructional day through programs taught by the certified publicly employed teachers who already know the school's students and its curriculum. Not surprisingly, this national policy push toward the dismantling of public education is not warranted by any research that demonstrates that for-profit corporate approaches achieve any better testing outcomes, and some recent research actually shows that the public schools serving LI/RCLD pupils outperform their charter and private competitors on this most simplistic and meaningless of measures (though the only one legitimated by these policies).

These various corporate or industry models of management appeal to that faction of the policymaking community concerned foremost with reforming schools to meet efficiency goals in relation to workforce preparation, and the testing regimes provide easy information (though not always accurate) to the public at large and permit policymakers to make what sound like objective claims in the pursuit of a broad political agenda that cares little for public schools or the LI/RCLD children who are most dependent on them. While these approaches may mollify the business sector, professional educators and advocates for children worry deeply about the effects, particularly for children who are already disadvantaged by virtue of their home language, socioeconomic position, race, or abilities. Yet the prevailing policy environment goes forward with its programming no matter how often critics of NCLB point to the logical and technical flaws in transferring corporate-industrial models to schools, where human beings learn, develop, and teach but cannot be manufactured and engineered to specification. The fact is, the stated aims of these reforms are in some ways beyond reach, but meanwhile the evidence of negative consequences continues to mount.

Fortunately for LI/RCLD students and communities, human beings are resilient, unpredictable, and capable of subverting the intention and practices of even the most inhumane environments, so teachers, parents, and students have been fighting back with growing force against the globalized standards and testing regimes. More and more people are calling for schools to return to their democratic purposes, and demanding that adequate resources be provided so that all students can learn and have a fair opportunity in school and in life (Oakes, Rogers, & Lipton, 2006; Shirley, 1997). A sophisticated strategy for enhancing the social, economic, and political context in which public schooling occurs for LI/RCLD families—job prospects for parents, availability of health care and affordable housing, safe neighborhoods, accessibility of cultural and educational opportunities—must accompany any serious effort to improve public education (Anyon, 1997, 2005; Lipman, 2004).

At the same time, while many of the barriers and challenges facing LI/RCLD schools cannot be overcome by the professionals within them but rather need the allied forces of the larger community that are now getting in motion, there remains much that can be done with high-quality teacher preparation and development. Recent research affirms the centrality of quality teaching as a significant and necessary ingredient for producing educational success (Amrein & Berliner, 2002; Peske & Haycock, 2006), and particular characteristics of highly qualified teachers and conditions needed for high-quality teaching have been identified. These factors include strong subject matter preparation, pedagogical knowledge and competence, analytic skills, interpersonal skills, organizational skills, and the ability to work across disparate groups of stakeholders who vary in age and in their objectives for being involved with schools (Achinstein, Ogawa, & Speiglman, 2004; Darling-Hammond & Youngs, 2002). Critical educators also cite the importance of anti-bias knowledge, sensitivities and skills, an ability to negotiate between multiple cultural and identity worlds, a commitment to education for social justice, and advocacy and leadership skills (Cochran-Smith, 1991; Glass & Wong, 2003; Ladson-Billings, 2001; Oakes, 2003). The university clearly has an important role to play in preparing and supporting such a high quality teaching force. But, without a clear and current understanding of K–12 teaching and learning realities in LI/RCLD schools and sophisticated strategies for how to prepare new teachers to be successful in this context, universities could easily and widely miss the mark in their teacher preparation efforts, particularly when it comes to dynamic and complex urban settings.

Despite the shortcomings often noted about teacher education, specific preparation programs have been shown to positively impact the subsequent performance of its graduates (Darling-Hammond & Youngs, 2002). Such programs usually focus on particular aims and outcomes, are built on clear unifying principles, and often are relatively small. Still, many conservative commentators and pundits condemn the quality of the teaching force and call not just for the reform of teacher education in general, but for the virtual elimination of university programs, suggesting that credentialing programs be replaced with hiring criteria related to verbal acuity and subject matter knowledge (Walsh, 2001). Others take a more studied approach and focus on improving several factors that appear to plague college- and university-based teacher education programs across institutions and regions (Goodlad, Soder, & Sirotnik, 1990):

1. The absence of teacher education from the shared mission of the institution, often despite what the proportion of education-focused students might actually warrant.

2. Fragmentation across the teacher education curriculum creating a situation in which future teachers take subject matter and pedagogy courses in a number of departments, none of which claim full responsibility for their ultimate preparation.

3. Discontinuities in terms of the kinds of values being transmitted to future teachers.

4. Tensions between knowledge-theory and practice, with knowledge-theory often taking a backseat to practical concerns because of district pressures, hiring forecasts, and candidates' own anxieties.

5. Lack of attention to the distinct challenges of preparing mostly monolingual, dominant culture women for highly diverse and poor urban education settings.

6. Efforts by the state to standardize and narrow teacher education to the most basic technical concerns.

Not surprisingly, the calls for eliminating teacher education understandably find few supporters in colleges of education or among the ranks of certified teachers. There, a deep understanding of the emotional, cognitive, and social complexities of classroom teaching makes it easy to dismiss the notion that teaching is merely about being verbally adept, "loving kids," and knowing some subject matter. Rather, most teachers and teacher educators recognize and affirm the set of critiques offered by Goodlad, his colleagues, and others (Sarason, 1993). They agree that teacher preparation programs and university structures need to be profoundly reconceptualized to address the major challenges that face not only the field of teacher education but the reform of schools serving LI/RCLD populations. Programs must enable new teachers to emerge with the knowledge, skills, and dispositions to work productively with diverse learners in ways that are respectful and rigorous, to engage families and communities in school life, and to reorient the organizational life of the school toward goals of equity and quality.

Sarason (1993) argued that reformed teacher education was the logical and more efficient first step to K–12 reform, and could *prevent* problems by changing attitudes and practices before they became socialized into the existing routines of schools, which are so resistant to change. He also recognized that the *repair* of schools must be undertaken concurrently and symbiotically with the *prevention* achieved with the restructuring of teacher preparation. This could be achieved by having future teachers engaged in structured experiences that allow them to understand the full complexity of working in classrooms, schools, and school districts. In his vision, candidates would have early undergraduate experiences in which they would interact not only with teachers, but with other school personnel active in the lives of children and they would learn about other aspects of the school system such as policymaking, curriculum development, parent relations, and collective bargaining. These integrated course and field experiences would help foster the knowledge, skills, and dispositions required for success in these complex systems.

Goodlad and his colleagues call for a much more ambitious agenda that reconstitutes teacher preparation through a wholesale reorientation of universities. Teacher education hovers at the bottom of the priority list even when teacher candidates comprise a substantial percentage of the overall student body, and even when the universities began as teachers' colleges or Normal Schools. The diminished resources, power, and status afforded to teacher preparation leads to a range of difficulties associated with fragmentation and to a lack of coherence in the socialization of students into the teaching profession (Goodlad, Soder, & Sirotnik, 1990). Goodlad and his colleagues argue that the institutional barriers that prevent equitable and sufficient funding for teacher preparation must be eliminated, and that new pathways that cross traditional boundaries between academic units must be constructed around shared goals and a consistent vision of what is needed for high-quality teacher education. As they argue,

> A reasonable expectation for teacher education programs is that they be oriented toward a conception of what education and teaching ideally are and what schools are for. A further reasonable expectation is that this conception be shared and continually examined by the faculty group responsible for each program—not just the tenure-track professor but everyone, including cooperating teachers. (Goodlad, Soder, & Sirotnik, p. 30)

This kind of collaboration both within the university and between the university and the K–12 system can help overcome the fragmentation and discontinuities that plague traditional programs. But more is needed, including providing incentives that create a consistent group of teacher educators (including content, pedagogy, and field-based faculty members) who can be engaged in maintaining the vitality and vision of the program across the many contexts and institutions that are loosely coupled in the K–16 structure.

To realize this conception of teacher preparation, a core challenge is to foster a productive dialogue between research-based and practice-based knowledge. The traditional vision of "a fresh stream of knowledge and ideas flowing down into the ponds of practice" has never, and never can, overcome the mismatch between the university realm of theory and the classroom realities. Suspicion and disdain are unsurprising by-products that pollute the flow of this stream: university faculty members publicly defer to district and state practices while distancing themselves from them in the privacy of their discourse with student teachers; student teachers publicly defer to their professors while grabbing for any teacher-endorsed strategy that promises help with survival in the classroom; cooperating teachers publicly appease the university faculty members while assuring student teachers that the true knowledge is only to be found in the classroom; both professors and teachers publicly claim allegiance to "best practices," but are not firmly integrated into communities of reflection/inquiry that enable the critical examination of practice and generation of warranted knowledge about what truly is best. Most often, the working relationships between university faculty members and K–12 classroom teachers is congenial, but it is rarely collegial. As a result, teacher preparation lacks consensus on professional norms of conduct, on necessary skills and dispositions, and on accepted bodies of knowledge about pedagogy. This situation is not inevitable, despite being historically entrenched, but without its transformation at a deep level, there is little prospect of reconstructing teacher education to meet the needs of LI/RCLD students and communities.

Many researchers and practitioners agree[2] that the needs of LI/RCLD students and communities require specialized attention in teacher preparation because of the profound challenges that go beyond those already identified in our review of themes in the history of school reform and teacher education. These challenges are especially acute in urban areas and urban teachers consequently need preparation that differs in some ways from that for their rural and suburban counterparts (Cochran-Smith, 2001; Howey, Post, & Zimpher, 2002). The majority of students in U.S. public schools reside in urban areas and these areas continue to be the most diverse in terms of race, ethnicity, language, family structure, and social class, even as more people of color move into suburban areas (Anyon, 1997). Yet the overwhelming majority of teachers today is still white and female (National Center for Education Statistics, 2005), and these women will be working with cultural, language, and income groups with which they have had virtually no direct prior contact, history, or knowledge.

This was the situation faced by the Equity Network as we organized ourselves in the late 1990s to undertake a strategic intervention to transform teacher preparation for urban schools serving LI/RCLD students. The stories told in this book speak to the multifaceted effort we made to respond to the conditions in which we were embedded and to the possibilities we could envision. As we have demonstrated, the results were mixed, but show genuine promise. In this next section, we will draw together the lessons from our work within a framework that we call "engaged pedagogy" and then we will outline the direction of our current work as we strive to grapple with the deep challenges of improving the lives of LI/RCLD students and communities.

Lessons from the Equity Network: Engaged Pedagogy and Beyond

We quickly learned that we were confronted with an enormous challenge of creating PDSs that had to be specifically geared into their particular local situations and thus could not have models imposed upon them. While we had the four primary goals as direction finders—strengthening teacher preparation, linking this to in-service professional development, embedding both in action research directed at classroom and school-level reform, all aimed at improving outcomes for LI/RCLD students—we had no road maps; the route had to be discerned as we went along, and even the wisdom of others who had traveled this way before had to be translated afresh into our own programs and schools. We had to give up the false hope of a method; prescribed methods were no more applicable in the invention of structures for deep learning across the professional spectrum than they were in the development of evocative curriculum for the classroom. We had no choice but to engage our situation directly, with all its limits and its few open spaces, to discover what could and should be done to realize our vision. We had no choice but to abandon the constraints of our old roles and institutions, to interrupt the traditions that had shaped us, and then to reinvent our profession and establish new systems that could facilitate the work that needed to be done. The practical realities of these processes coupled with the grounded knowledge that emerged from reflection and research on them, led us to articulate some core principles to guide us, and while these were never fully realized or embodied, they nonetheless provided a touchstone for measuring how far we had come and the distance yet to go.

One of our first realizations was that we were engaged in a profound historical struggle for the just treatment of LI/RCLD people. We were aware of the history of the reform of schools and teacher education previously recounted, but even more acutely we recognized that political forces in California had aligned in ways that threatened the very premises of the Equity Network. In the previous decade, an often cynical agenda had been enacted into law that constituted a virtual assault on low-income, minority, and immigrant groups, whether by denying public schooling and health care to undocumented immigrants and their children (Proposition 187), by virtually ending bilingual education (Proposition 227), or by establishing standards and testing that exclude or devalue their history, culture, language, and experiences. We saw that this political agenda was also an attack on us and the values to which we were committed, and understanding that we were aligned in an historic struggle not only gave us the energy to persevere when we might otherwise have been tempted to give up, it offered us a moral and political foundation for solidarity with the students and families in the Equity Network schools and neighborhoods. It also reaffirmed that the commitment to education for social justice meant a commitment to a way of life, to a struggle over the long haul (Horton, 1998).

Equity Network faculty members, teachers, and schools, together with pupils and their families, found many creative ways to resist the political forces arrayed against the ideals and goals of the PDSs, and to publicly value the language, culture, and experience of students and their families in concrete ways that impacted the curriculum content and instructional practices both in the schools and in the teacher preparation program. *We constructed the core curriculum across the teaching and learning domains of the PDSs on the basis of LI/RCLD students' lives and voices, historical and cultural backgrounds, and their current perspectives and emerging cultural formations.* In order to do this, all the professionals in the PDSs, from university faculty members, to teachers, to teacher candidates, had to grasp the lives of LI/RCLD students in both their intimate detail and their broad outline. As we have described and discussed in section one, our commitment to these principles of engaged pedagogy led to programming that elevated community funds of knowledge in constructing science curriculum in a PDS and addressed community health needs in the science curriculum of another PDS. We also found ways to connect the PDS professionals directly to the community, through such activities as home visits, oral history projects, and participation in community organizations. The development of grounded knowledge of the lives of LI/RCLD students became a central focus of our learning as professionals, and we accepted responsibility for this in the same way that we accepted responsibility for the acquisition of research-based knowledge about cognition or instruction.

As we deepened our understanding of the complex realities faced by LI/RCLD students and their families, we learned that this had to occur in collaboration with them. It was not a case of "studying others" as if their realities were somehow disconnected from our own, but rather it meant grasping that we are all inextricably caught up in a single web of reality that shaped our everyday experiences and understandings in different ways. Thus, our commitment to an engaged pedagogy meant that we pursued *dialogical approaches that ensured the inclusion of students' and families' languages, thoughts, ideas, and perspectives.* Not only did this enable us to more fully subject our own actions to critical evaluation, but the dialogues brought students and families into a more critical understanding of the challenges confronting us as educators and thus made them more capable of effective actions to strengthen learning outcomes. By demonstrating in practical and concrete ways that we had a genuine desire to make equitable connections with the community in order to become partners in the teaching and learning process, we became allies in the larger struggle to make schooling more meaningful and rewarding for LI/RCLD students.

As we examined the ways that schools often gave LI/RCLD students and families the message that they were not valued or respected, we discovered more deeply the often unintended and subtle dynamics of these processes, and how frequently we were implicated in them. While there was little we could do about the testing regimes and the negative messages conveyed by them, we were able to ensure that students and their parents got other forms of positive feedback about their knowledge and skills. *We became more cognizant of the role of schools in identity formation and took steps to ensure that students received support for navigating the often treacherous forces of assimilation that discredit and ignore their rich, complex family journeys.* Too often, educators pay little attention to the gaps between school assumptions, expectations, and identity ascriptions and the family and community realities, concerns, and hopes; too often, educators allow the prevailing ethnic, racial, linguistic, and gender norms of the dominant culture to exercise their influence without concern for the impact on kids who do not and cannot measure up. By bringing these dynamics into the conversation of the classroom and the school, by exploring them in the studies and self-reflections of the PDS professional formation work, we could begin to construct the schools as places that affirm and preserve valuable legacies for their LI/RCLD students while at the same time prepare them for the vicissitudes of everyday life. Identities are shaped in complex interactions among culture, language, ethnicity, race, gender, and social class, and as we became more aware of these processes in our students and our teacher candidates, we also became more aware of them in our own lives and self-understanding.

As we took the initial steps to explore these matters within the discussions of the LENS faculty meetings and in some of the dialogues with the cooperating teachers, we quickly uncovered the difficulty of unpacking the emotionally laden forces that are hidden not far beneath the surface descriptions of who we are. We have far to go, and we have yet to even initiate these important dialogues with administrators, community members, and others less central to the teaching and learning environments of the Equity Network. But there was no escaping the truth that *our commitment to engaged pedagogy meant that we had to confront our own processes of self-actualization and identity formation.* Simply our status as professionals was something we experienced as contested. Maintaining a sense of efficacy in our work in underresourced and so-called underperforming schools is difficult as teachers and teacher educators bear the brunt of the blame for test scores deemed to be substandard. What is substandard in our experience has more to do with teaching/working conditions that complicate our mission. Our voices are dismissed when we petition policymakers to address the mismatches between our LI/RCLD students' needs and the mandated curriculum (Ladson-Billings, 1994). We are caricatured and demeaned in unrelenting ideological attacks promulgated in the media and political debates. The Equity Network took steps to analyze and counter these forces, but, more important, *we built new professional roles and routines that connected us with one another and provided us with the grounded knowledge and experience we needed to succeed with our students* despite the hostile context that surrounded us. We discovered that by working collaboratively and honoring the knowledge that we each brought to our project, we were each enriched and our sense of efficacy solidified and became enhanced. We began to create new traditions for the teacher candidates we were preparing, so that it became taken for granted that we had multiple domains of responsibility that included the formation of the profession, the improvement of schools through action research and community engagement, and the long-term success of LI/RCLD students (not simply raising their test scores).

We wish we could say that it was easy to achieve these transformations, or that we always reached the goals we set. The reality was more mixed, as our case studies show. The context of criticism of LI/RCLD schools and teachers intensified, punitive measures against "program improvement" schools increased, and mandates for the adoption of highly scripted standardized curricula were implemented. The existing conditions of work in the K–16 system could not always be as flexible as we needed, and the extended responsibilities of our reconstituted professional roles had to be met largely through personal sacrifice since few formal accommodations were made to permit this restructuring. These pressures often led to resentment and tendencies to want to regroup around the safety of the traditional mode of doing our work, each professional safely ensconced in his or her cocoon free from the encroachment of the others. Some faced questions from their families about their priorities, and wondered how they could possibly meet all the obligations entailed by the Network PDSs. Administrators in both schools and the university questioned the value added by these expanded professional roles, and challenged the cost-benefit ratios of the time commitments that led teachers and faculty members to be working in one another's domains of practice.

To understand these dynamics, we had to return to the recognition that *race and class matter* not only in the value placed on prioritizing sites for the investment of K–16 resources and in the value placed on supporting the reconstruction of the profession to address the needs of LI/RCLD children and communities, but also in our own professional and personal identities. We had to confront issues of privilege that mark the race and class divides between teachers and university faculty and between all of these educators and the LI/RCLD students and communities they are trying to serve. Our varying senses of privilege and entitlement influenced how we approached the resolution of the pressures we faced just as surely as they influenced our teaching practices and relationships with one another and the students and families. Once again, we learned that *engaged pedagogy means that the work of confronting dominant ideologies was both internal and external*, and that the more we did the internal work necessary to develop a more critical self-understanding, the more we were able to do the external work necessary to build strong connections across race and class lines to struggle for our vision of quality education.

Part of that vision of course focused directly on the classroom, and many of the activities of the Equity Network approach to engaged pedagogy *involved deepening collaborative knowledge construction about teaching and learning and deepening collaborative curriculum construction (and selection)*. We refused to be discouraged by the imposition of standards and test-driven scripted curricula, and we discovered that many niches for innovation remained that could be turned to our advantage. As our stories have conveyed, we created transformative modes of teaching and learning that integrated content reflecting community resources and concerns, methodologies that incorporated research-proven best practices in instruction and assessment, and technologies that prepared both teachers and students for the mediated realities of the twenty-first century. All of the educators in the Network PDSs significantly expanded their repertoire of constructivist, inquiry-based, concept-based, and thematic instructional approaches, and learned more deeply how to differentiate instruction while incorporating scaffolding for English learners and academic language acquisition. We also not only advanced our knowledge of designing authentic assessments for the students, but discovered how these insights could be applied in the design of authentic assessments of the professional knowledge of our teacher candidates. This in turn led to more critical self-reflection by our cooperating teachers and Network faculty members about their own professional development needs.

As we have described, it was important that *we built sturdy yet flexible structures to support these new forms of professional collaboration and practice.* Whether these structures took the form of physically locating university office and classroom space on school grounds, of providing for the concurrent delivery of university methods courses and the school curriculum, of lesson study and praxis groups to critically analyze and transform teaching, or of any of the other ways we grounded our emerging intuitional relationships, the focus was always on making the PDS system responsive to the professional knowledge and practice needs of the Network educators and the social and academic needs of the LI/RCLD students.

It goes without saying, but it is important to emphasize, that the Network PDS approach to teaching and learning across the spectrum required profoundly transformed professional roles but it also required transformed relationships with others having key roles in the lives of LI/RCLD children and youth. Professional borders are often barriers to effective communication, and the Network had to work hard to make them permeable; and even more than simply permeable, we tried to make them actively facilitative of dialogue and collaboration. Time and again, the key to making these new relationships and roles effective was the shared commitment to keeping student needs foremost, and as trust was built across professions and with the larger community and other community agencies, these traditional barriers at closely guarded borders broke down. We established a wide range of new and fruitful collaborations: between universities and schools and communities; between colleges of the university and programs within colleges; between programs and grade levels within schools; between schools and district offices; between teachers associations and universities; between universities, schools, and community organizations; between schools and federal agencies; between the university, schools, communities, and funding sources. Despite the powerful advances we made fostering cross-border cooperation among the educational professionals and among others directly tied to teaching and learning in schools, we had less success overcoming the many obstacles to effective communication with the social workers, probation officers, housing agency workers, adult educators, public health officials, and other professionals who are actively involved with LI/RCLD students and communities. We know that as long as the support for the transformation of the schools and communities of LI/RCLD families remains fragmented, our own work in schools continues to be less effective than could or should be the case.

After more than six years of effort to build the Equity Network and implement its strategies for interrupting the traditions of teacher preparation, of in-service teacher professional development, of reform of LI/RCLD schools, and of instruction and assessment of the LI/RCLD students, *we have learned most of all that to practice engaged pedagogy means to dream big, to act both strategically and focused on making an immediate difference, and to never cease our own critical self-reflection and professional development.* By itself, teaching is a humbling profession. To teach with a commitment to justice for LI/RCLD students and communities is even more humbling. Honesty demands humility as we confront the internal work that comes along with having to give up so many certitudes about who we are and what we know. It demands humility as we confront the persistent inequities and disadvantages heaped upon the children, families, and schools to which we have dedicated ourselves. Honesty demands humility as we confront the limits of our own instructional prowess and the contrastingly huge needs that our students have that must be met for them to be effective learners. Honesty demands humility as we try to remake our profession even as it is being undermined by powerful political and institutional forces that do not share our commitments and values. What sustained us in these seemingly Sisyphian tasks was our relationships, our sense of connection with one another and the children and communities we were working with, and our sense of connection to making a new history that had the power to interrupt the old traditions and establish some new ones.

Engaged pedagogy means a commitment to future generations of teachers and learners to enable them to take their place in the ongoing struggle for a more just and democratic society. Just as we do not expect ourselves, alone or even together, to be able to do all that must be done to transform education for LI/RCLD students and communities, we accept that we must do what we can. Each of us has within the scope of our own reach more than enough opportunity to work to make a difference, enough to last us a lifetime of trying. Part of the attraction of our jobs as educators is that we are naturally tied to the future, and we see our work reflected in the hopes and struggles of those who follow us. What is particularly rewarding for Network educators is to have had the experience of connecting with the students and families themselves in the struggle to make life better in their communities, recognizing that these are, after all, our communities as well. This shared sense of responsibility for the future is the force that moves history, and transcends the traditions of the past to open up new possibilities.

We are not sanguine about what it will take to achieve our vision. We know that the nearly unrelenting effort to reform public schooling in the United States over the past 100 years to make it more responsive to the needs of LI/RCLD communities has little altered schooling's core structures, operations, and purposes. With the basic "grammar" of schooling intact (Tyack & Cuban, 1995), schooling continues to produce distressingly persistent outcomes that reinforce disadvantages for students from LI/RCLD communities. The dominant reforms of recent decades have made little headway in reversing this trend. The efforts to restructure school governance and management have not become rooted in LI/RCLD districts or made substantive impacts on achievement (Cuban & Usdan, 2003), even when the educational and political leadership of the reforms is based in communities of color (Henig, Hula, Orr, & Pedescleaux, 1999). The demands for stronger standards and the implementation of testing regimes have added to the barriers these students face (McNeil, 2000; Orfield & Kornhaber, 2001), and even undermined the limited capacity building that occurs when schools attempt to respond to these pressures (Barnes, 2002). The market-oriented reforms that claim to provide choices to LI/RCLD students and their families, whether through charters, vouchers, or other mechanisms, neither level the educational playing field nor ensure that no child is left behind (Lipman, 2004; Wells, 2002). Overall, several decades of top-down government driven reforms have not changed the life chances of LI/RCLD students or the conditions of life in their communities (Anyon, 1997).

Just as making an impact on LI/RCLD schools is challenging, so it is difficult to make substantive changes in LI/RCLD communities. However, we can see that our work has laid a foundation for a promising approach that does not treat LI/RCLD schools and communities in isolation from one another. Communities can impact school reform when partnerships are created that share basic value commitments, even though experience has shown that the larger social, economic, and political contexts can severely constrain the achievements of these efforts (Baum, 2003; Williams, 1989). Projects aimed at improving LI/RCLD schools by empowering and expanding the social capital of the parent communities, thus linking school reform to broader struggles to address basic community needs (Shirley, 1997), show even more promise. But even these experiments in democracy have had to face certain sobering realities in the profound challenges and complexities in LI/RCLD communities that have limited their success; it has become undeniable that a broad-based effort to build community capacity is necessary (Stone, Henig, Jones, & Pierannunzi, 2001). We join with those who argue that a new social movement is needed to make real differences in the lives of LI/RCLD students and families (Anyon, 2005), and that this may be the social justice issue of the century. Grassroots activism linked to collaborative community-based inquiry has been able to challenge some aspects of the prevailing logics of schooling and of school reform in certain limited contexts (Oakes, Rogers, & Lipton, 2006), and these experiments need to be tried more broadly.

These are the next steps that we are trying to take as the Equity Network moves into the next phase of its work. As we travel into our future, we gather inspiration from Paulo Freire's words:

> We are surrounded by a pragmatic discourse that would have us adapt to the facts of reality. *Dreams*, and *utopia*, are called not only useless, but positively impeding. . . . I do not understand human existence, and the struggle needed to improve it, apart from hope and dream. . . . One of the tasks of the progressive educator, through a serious, correct political analysis, is to unveil opportunities for hope, no matter what the obstacles may be. After all, without hope there is little we can do. (1997, 7–9)

Notes

1. The longtime opponents of the politically progressive Children's Defense Fund (CDF) rather cynically appropriated the CDF motto to title this significantly underfunded act, which most observers believe will cause significant harm to LI/RCLD students for a number of years.

2. Goodlad, Sarason, and others are joined in this agreement by prominent organizations such as the Holmes Partnership affiliate, Urban Network to Improve Teacher Education (UNITE), the Association for Supervision and Curriculum Development, and the Council for Great City Schools.

References

A Casebook on School-based Mentoring. (1989). Secondary Teacher Education Program. East Longmeadow School District, MA: University of Massachusetts, Amherst, School of Education.

Abdal-Haqq, I. (1998). *Professional development schools: Weighing the evidence.* Thousand Oaks, CA: Corwin Press.

Achinstein, B., Ogawa, R., & Speiglman, A. (2004). Are we creating separate and unequal tracks of teachers? The effects of state policy, local conditions and teacher characteristics on new teacher socialization. *American Educational Research Journal, 41*(2), 557–603.

Amrein, A. L., & Berliner, D. C. (2002). High stakes testing, uncertainty, and student learning. [Electronic version]. *Education Policy Analysis Archives, 10*(18). Retrieved on May 9, 2002, from http://epaa.asu.edu/epaa/v10n18/.

Anyon, J. (1997). *Ghetto schooling: A political economy of urban educational reform.* New York: Teachers College Press.

Anyon, J. (2005). *Radical possibilities: Public policy, urban education and a new social movement.* New York: Routledge.

Apple, M. (2000). *Official knowledge: Democratic education in a conservative age.* New York: Routledge.

Apple, M. (2001). *Education the "right" way: Markets, standards, God and inequality.* New York: Routledge.

Apple, M. W., & Beane, J. A. (Eds.). (1995). *Democratic schools.* Alexandria, VA: Association for Supervision and Curriculum Development.

Bailey, K. (1994). *Sociology and the new systems theory: Toward a theoretical synthesis.* Albany: State University of New York Press.

Ball, D., & Cohen, D. (1990). Policy and practice: An overview. *Educational Evaluation and Policy Analysis, 12*(3), 233–239.

Barba, R. H. (1995). *Science in the multicultural classroom.* Boston: Allyn and Bacon.

Barnes, C. (2002). *Standards reform in high-poverty schools.* New York: Teachers College Press.

Bartolomé, L. (1994). Beyond the methods fetish: Toward a humanizing pedagogy. *Harvard Educational Review, 64*, 173–194.

Barton, A. C., & Osborne, M. D. (Eds.). (2001). *Teaching science in diverse settings: Marginalized discourses and classroom practice.* New York: Peter Lang.

Baum, H. (2003). *Community action for school reform.* Albany: State University of New York Press.

Bell, L., Washington, S., Weinstein, G., & Love, B., (2003). Knowing ourselves as instructors. In A. Darder, M. Baltodano, & R. Torres (Eds.), *The critical pedagogy reader* (pp. 464–478). New York: RoutledgeFalmer.

Berliner, D. (2005). *Our impoverished view of education reform.* Presidential Address to the American Educational Research Association, Montreal, Canada.

Borich, G. (1996). *Effective teaching methods.* Englewood Cliffs, NJ: Merrill.

Borthwick, A., Stirling, T., Nauman, A., & Cook, D. (2003). Achieving successful school-university collaboration. *Urban Education, 38*(3), 330–371.

Bowles, S., & Gintis, H. (1976). *Schooling in capitalist America: Educational reform and the contradictions of economic life.* New York: Basic Books.

Boyer, E. (1983). *High school: A report of secondary education in America.* New York: Harper and Row.

Bridges, E. (1982). Research on the school administrator: The state of the art, 1967–1980. *Educational Administration Quarterly, 18*(3), 12–33.

Bridges, M., Fuller, B., Rumberger, R., & Tran, L. (2004). *Preschool for California's children: Promising benefits, unequal access.* Policy Brief 04-9. Berkeley: Policy Analysis for California Education.

Brooks, J. G., & Brooks, M. G. (1993). *The case for constructivist classrooms.* Alexandria, VA: Association for Supervision and Curriculum Development.

Bryant, G. K., Nechie, R., Neapolitan, J. E., Madden, M., & Rifkin, L. (2004). Transforming faculty roles by waving the magic wand. In J. E. Neapolitan, T. D. Proffitt, C. L. Wittmann, & T. R. Berkeley (Eds.), *Traditions, standards, & transformations: A model for professional development school networks* (pp. 107–134). New York: Peter Lang.

Calabrese-Barton, A. (2003). *Teaching science for social justice.* New York: Teachers College Press.

California State University. (2000). *Percentage of CSU freshmen needing remedial education drops for first time.* [Online article]. Retrieved on June 1, 2006, from http://www.calstate.edu/pa/news/2000/RemedialReport.shtml.

Camburn, E., Rowan, B., & Taylor, J. (2003). Distributed leadership in schools: The case of elementary schools adopting comprehensive school reform models. *Educational Evaluation and Policy Analysis, 25*(4), 347–374.

Cantor, J. (2002). Who's teaching the urban poor? Supporting an emerging social justice educator in a professional development school. *Equity and Excellence in Education, 35*(3), 225–235.

Carey, K. (2004). *A matter of degrees: Improving graduation rates in four year colleges and universities.* Washington, DC: The Education Trust.

Carnate, B., Newell, G., Hoffman, S. E., & Moots, R. (2000). The growing of a school/university partnership and the preparation of teachers for the urban context. In M. Johnston, P. Brosnan, D. Cramer, & T. Dove (Eds.), *Collaborative reform and other improbable dreams: The challenges of professional development schools* (pp. 171–188). Albany: State University of New York Press.

Carnoy, M., & Levin, H. (1985). *Schooling and work in the democratic state.* Palo Alto, CA: Stanford University Press.

Carnoy, M., Hannaway, J., Chun, M., Stein, S., & Wong, P. (1995). *Urban and suburban school districts: Are they different kinds of educational producers?* Camden, NJ: Consortium for Policy Research in Education.

Carroll, D. (2006). Developing joint accountability in university-school teacher education partnerships. *Action in Teacher Education, 27*(4), 3–11.

Casserly, M. (2006). *Beating the odds IV. A city-by-city analysis of student performance and achievement gaps on state performance assessments. Results from the 2004–2005 school year.* Washington, DC: Council of Great City Schools.

Castle, S., Fox, R., & Souder, K. (2006). Do PDSs make a difference? A comparative study of PDS and Non-PDS teacher candidates. *Journal of Teacher Education, 57*(1), 65–80.

Center for Research on Education, Diversity & Excellence. (2004). *Houston CREDE: Synthesis Project.* [Online article]. Retrieved on September 16, 2006, from http://www.coe.uh.edu/crede/synthesis.html.

Chang, H. (1992). *Adolescent life and ethos: An ethnography of a U. S. high school.* New York: Falmer Press.

Children's Defense Fund. (2002). *Protect Children Instead of Guns.* Washington, DC: Author.

Children's Defense Fund. (2004a). *Teacher quality: Quick facts.* [Online article]. Retrieved on June 1, 2006, from http://www.childrensdefense.org/education/teacherquality.pdf.

Children's Defense Fund. (2004b). *Educational resource disparities for low-income and minority children: Quick facts.* [Online article]. Retrieved on June 1, 2006, from http://www.childrensdefense.org/education/resource_disparities.pdf.

Chrispeels, J. H. (1997). Educational policy implementation in a shifting political climate. *American Journal of Education Research, 34*(3), 453–481.

Clifford, G. J., & Guthrie, J. W. (1988). *Ed school: A brief for professional education.* Chicago: University of Chicago Press.

Cloud, N., Genesee, F., & Hamayan, E. (2000). *Dual language instruction: A handbook for enriched education.* Boston: Heinle & Heinle.

Cochran-Smith, M. (1991). Learning to teach against the grain. *Harvard Educational Review, 61*(3), 279–309.

Cochran-Smith, M. (2001). Learning to teach against the (new) grain. *Journal of Teacher Education, 52*, 3–4.

Cochran-Smith, M., & Lytle, S. L. (1993). *Inside/Outside: Teacher research and knowledge.* New York: Teachers College Press.

College Board. (2005). *Tuition increases slow at public colleges, according to the College Board's 2005 reports on college pricing and financial aid.* [Online Press Release]. Retrieved on June 1, 2006, from http://www.collegeboard.com/press/releases/48884.html.

Conant, J. B. (1959). *The American high school today.* New York: McGraw-Hill.

Cooner, D., & Tochterman, S. (2004). Life inside a professional development school: What experienced teachers learn. *The Teacher Educator, 39*(3), 184–195.

Corbett, D., & Wilson, B. (2002). What urban kids say about good teaching. *Educational Leadership, 60*(1), 18–22.

Cuban, L., & Usdan, M. (Eds.). (2003). *Powerful reforms with shallow roots: Improving America's urban schools.* New York: Teachers College Press.

Cusick, P. (1973). *Inside high school.* Toronto: Holt, Rinehart and Winston.

Dailey-Dickinson, R. (2000). A clinical educator: Redefining a teacher's role. In M. Johnston, P. Brosnan, D. Cramer, & T. Dove (Eds.), *Collaborative reform and other improbable dreams: The challenges of professional development schools* (pp. 43–52). Albany: State University of New York Press.

Darling-Hammond, L. (1989). Accountability for professional practice. *Teachers College Record, 91*(1), 59–80.

Darling-Hammond, L. (1994). *Professional development schools: Schools for developing a profession.* New York: Teachers College Press.

Darling-Hammond, L., & Youngs, P. (2002). Defining "highly qualified teachers": What does "scientifically-based research" actually tell us? *Educational Researcher, 31*(9), 13–25.

Darling-Hammond, L., Bullmaster, M. L., & Cobb, V. L. (1995). Rethinking teacher leadership through professional development schools. *The Elementary School Journal, 96,* 87–106.

Delpit, L. (1988). The silenced dialogue: Power and pedagogy in educating other people's children. *Harvard Educational Review, 56,* 379–385.

Desimone, L. (1999). Parent involvement and achievement: Do race and income matter? *Journal of Educational Research, 93(*1), 11–30.

Dickens, C. (2000). Too valuable to be rejected, too different to be embraced: A critical review of school/university collaboration. In M. Johnston, P. Brosnan, D. Cramer, & T. Dove (Eds.), *Collaborative reform and other improbable dreams: The challenges of professional development schools* (pp. 21–42). Albany: State University of New York Press.

Doyle, M. (2005, December 16). San Joaquin: The new Appalachia. *The Sacramento Bee,* A1.

Dresner, M., & Worley, E. (2006). Teacher research experiences, partnerships with scientists, and teacher networks sustaining factors from professional development. *Journal of Science Teacher Education, 17*(1), 1–14.

Driver, R., Guesne, E., & Tiberghien, A. (1985). *Children's ideas in science.* Philadelphia: Open University Press.

Ducharme, E. R., & Ducharme, M. K. (1996). Development of the teacher education professoriate. In F. B. Murray (Ed.), *The teacher educator's handbook: Building a knowledge base for the preparation of teachers* (pp. 691–714). San Francisco: Jossey-Bass.

Education Data Partnership. (2007). Fiscal, demographic, and performance data on California's K–12 schools. [Online resource]. Retrieved on August 3, 2007, from http://www.ed-data.k12.ca.us.

Elmore, R., & McLaughlin, M. (1988). *Steady work: Policy, practice, and the reform of American education.* Santa Monica, CA: Rand.

Emery, K., & Ohanian, S. (2004). *Why is corporate America bashing our public schools?* Portsmouth, NH: Heinneman.

Epperly, E. W., & Preus, N. (1989). Teacher empowerment: An unanticipated benefit from a clinical schools approach to teacher education. Proceedings of the National Forum of the Association of Independent Liberal Arts Colleges for Teacher Education.

Epstein, J. (1992). School and family partnerships. In M. Alkin (Ed.), *Encyclopedia of Educational Research* (6th ed., pp. 1139–1151). New York: Macmillan.

Epstein, J. (1995). School/family/community partnerships: Caring for the children we share. *Phi Delta Kappan. 76*(9), 701–712.

Erickson, G., Brandes, G., Mitchell, I., & Mitchell, J. (2005). Collaborative teacher learning: Findings from two professional development projects. *Teaching and Teacher Education. 21*(7): 787–798.

Evans, R. (1996). *The human side of school change: Reform, resistance, and the real-life problems of innovation.* San Francisco: Jossey-Bass.

Fager, P. (1993). Teamed to teach: Integrating teacher training through cooperative teaching at an urban professional development school. *Teacher Education and Special Education, 16*(1), 51–59.

Ferlazzo, L., & McGarvey, C. (2005). Teaching is organizing (or should be). [Online article]. *Social Policy, Summer.* Retrieved on April 2, 2007, from http://www.socialpolicy.org.

Fernandez, C., & Yoshida, M. (2004). *Lesson study: A Japanese approach to improving mathematics teaching and learning.* Mahwah, NJ: Lawrence Erlbaum.

Foley, D. E. (1990). *Learning capitalist culture: Deep in the heart of Tejas.* Philadelphia: University of Pennsylvania Press.

Foster, C. (2005). *Better choices for children: The impact of the 2005–06 federal and state budget decisions on California's children.* [Online article]. Los Angeles: Children's Defense Fund. Retrieved on April 4, 2006, from http://www.cdfca.org/2004/cdfca-better_choices_for_children.htm.

Fountain, C. (1997, February 27). *Collaborative agenda for change: Examining the impact of urban professional development schools.* Paper presented at the Annual Meeting of the American Association of Colleges for Teacher Education, Phoenix, AZ.

Fredericks, L., & Dickson, S. (2003) *Improving academic achievement in urban districts: What policy makers can do.* [Online article]. Retrieved on June 1, 2006, from http://www.ecs.org/html/educationIssues/Urban/urbanpdf/UrbanOverview.pdf.

Freire, P. (1970/1994). *Pedagogy of the oppressed.* New York: Continuum.

Freire, P. (1973). *Education for critical consciousness.* New York: Seabury.

Freire, P. (1993). *Pedagogy of the city.* New York: Continuum.

Freire, P. (1997). *Pedagogy of hope.* New York: Continuum.

Freudenberger, K. (1999). *Rapid rural response appraisal and participatory rural appraisal.* Baltimore, MD: Catholic Relief Services.

Fullan, M. (1982). *The meaning of educational change.* New York: Teachers College Press.

Fullan, M. (1991). *The new meaning of educational change.* New York: Teachers College Press.

Fullan, M. (1993). Change forces: Probing the depths of educational reform. New York: Falmer Press.

Fullan, M. (2001). *The new meaning of educational change.* New York: Teachers College Press.

Futernick, K. (2003). Charts 1–3 and Tables 2–4. [Online resource]. Retrieved on May 3, 2007, from http://www.edfordemocracy.org/tqi/TQI_Charts.htm.

Gandin, L., & Apple, M. (2004). New schools, new knowledge, new teachers: Creating the Citizen Schools in Porto Alegre, Brazil. *Teacher Education Quarterly, 31*(1), 173–198.

Garcia, G. F., & Garcia, M. (1996). Charter schools—another top-down innovation. *Educational Researcher, 25*(8), 34–36.

Gehrke, N. (1991). *Developing teachers' leadership skills.* Washington, DC: ERIC Digest. (ERIC Document No. 330691).

Gettelman, E. (2002). *California youth violence prevention scorecard.* [Online article]. San Francisco: Communications, LLC. Retrieved on June 1, 2006, from http://www.preventviolence.org/download/Score11_8.pdf#search='youth%20 violence%20scorecard'.

Gibboney, R. A. (1994). *The stone trumpet: A story of practical school reform 1960–1990.* Albany: State University of New York.

Gibbons, P. (2003). Mediating language learning: Teacher interactions with ESL students in a content-based classroom. *TESOL Quarterly, 37*(2), 247–273.

Glass, R., & Wong, P. (2003). Engaged pedagogy: Meeting the demand for justice in urban professional development schools. *Teacher Education Quarterly, 30*(2), 69–89.

Goldstein, J. (2003). Making sense of distributed leadership: The case of peer assistance and review. *Educational Evaluation and Policy Analysis, 25*(4), 397–422.

Gonzales, S., & Lambert, L. (2001). Teacher leadership in professional development schools: Emerging conceptions, identities, and practices. *Journal of School Leadership, 11*(1), 6–24.

Gonzalez, N., & Moll, L. (2002). Cruzando el puente: Building bridges to funds of knowledge. *Educational Policy, 16*(4), 623–642.

Gonzalez, N., Moll, L. C., & Amanti, C. (2005). *Funds of knowledge: Theorizing practices in households and classrooms.* Mahwah, NJ: Lawrence Erlbaum.

Goodlad, J. (1984). *A place called school.* San Francisco: McGraw-Hill.

Goodlad, J. (1990). *Teachers for our nation's schools.* San Francisco: Jossey-Bass.

Goodlad, J. (1994). *Educational renewal: Better teachers, better schools.* San Francisco: Jossey-Bass.

Goodlad, J. I., Soder, R., & Sirotnik, K. A. (Eds). (1990). *Places where teachers are taught.* San Francisco: Jossey-Bass.

Grant, G. (1988). *The world we created at Hamilton High.* Cambridge: Harvard University Press.

Groulx, J. (2001). Changing preservice teacher perceptions of minority schools. *Urban Education, 36*(1), 60–92.

Groulx, J., & Thomas, C. (2000). Discomfort zones: Learning about teaching with care and discipline in urban schools. *International Journal of Educational Reform, 9*(1), 59–69.

Haberman, M. (1999). The Milwaukee public schools: How a great city prepares its teachers. *Kappa Delta Pi Record, 36*(27), 27–30.

Haberman, M. (2000). What makes a teacher education program relevant preparation for teaching diverse students in urban poverty schools? *The Milwaukee Teacher Education Center Model.* Washington, DC: ERIC (ERIC Document No. 442745).

Hallinan, M. T. (Ed.). (1987). *The social organization of schools.* New York: Plenum.

Hammond, L. (2001). Notes from California: An anthropological approach to science education. *Journal of Research on Science Teaching, 38*(9), 983–999.

Hampel, R. (1986). *The last little citadel: American high schools since 1940.* Boston: Houghton Mifflin.

Hansen, J. (1994). Applying systems theory to systemic change: A generic model for educational reform. Paper presented at the 1994 Annual Meeting of the American Educational Research Association, New Orleans, LA.

Hanushek, E. (Ed.) (2003). *The economics of schooling and school quality.* Northampton, MA: Edward Elgar.

Hartzler-Miller, C., & Wainwright, T. (2004). Defining our own roles: Professional renewal for teachers and university faculty. In J. E. Neapolitan, T. D. Proffitt, C. L. Wittmann, & T. R. Berkeley (Eds.), *Traditions, standards, & transformations: A model for professional development school networks* (pp. 55–69). New York: Peter Lang.

Hawthorne, R. D. (1997). Impact on colleges of education. In N. E. Hoffman, W. M. Reed, & G. S. Rosenbluth (Eds.), *Lessons from restructuring experiences: Stories of change in professional development schools* (pp. 295–322). Albany: State University of New York Press.

Haycock, K. (1998). Good teaching matters . . . a lot. *Thinking K–16, 3*(2), 1–6.

Hecsh, J. (2001). *Not starting from scratch: Structuring school structure in two comprehensive high schools.* Unpublished dissertation, University of California, Davis.

Henig, J., Hula, R., Orr, M., & Pedescleaux, D. (1999) *The color of school reform: Race, politics, and the challenge of urban education.* Princeton, NJ: Princeton University Press.

Henke, R., Chen, X., & Geis, S. (2000). *Progress through the teacher pipeline: 1992–1993 college graduates and elementary/secondary school teaching as of 1997* (Paper No. NCES 2000152). Washington, DC: National Center for Educational Statistics.

Hess, F. M. (2002). *School boards at the dawn of the 21st century: Conditions and challenges of district governance.* Prepared for the National School Boards Association. Retrieved on January 15, 2006, from http://www.nsba.org/site/docs/1200/1143.pdf.

Hoffman, N. E., Reed, W. M., & Rosenbluth, G. S. (Eds.). (1997). *Lessons from restructuring experiences: Stories of change in professional development schools.* Albany: State University of New York Press.

Holmes Group. (1990). *Tomorrow's schools: Principles for the design of professional development schools.* East Lansing, MI: Holmes Group.

Holmes Group. (1995). *Tomorrow's schools of education.* East Lansing, MI: Holmes Group.

hooks, b. (1994). *Teaching to transgress: Education as the practice of freedom.* New York: Routledge.

Horton, M. (1998). *The long haul: An autobiography.* New York: Teachers College Press.

Horton, M., & Freire, P. (1990). *We make the road by walking: A conversation between Miles Horton and Paulo Freire.* Philadelphia: Temple University Press.

Howey, K. R. (2000). *A review of challenges and innovations in the preparation of teachers for urban contexts.* Washington, DC: National Partnership for Excellence and Accountability in Teaching.

Howey, K. R. (1994). Leadership teams and networking: A strategy for faculty development. In K. R. Howey & N. L. Zimpher (Eds.), *Informing faculty development for teacher educators* (pp. 15–49). Norwood, NJ: Ablex.

Howey, K. R., & Zimpher, N. L. (1994). Introduction. In K. R. Howey & N. L. Zimpher (Eds.), *Informing faculty development for teacher educators* (pp. 1–13). Norwood, NJ: Ablex.

Howey, K., Post, L., & Zimpher, N. (2002). *Recruiting, preparing and retaining teachers for urban schools.* Washington, DC: American Association of Colleges of Teacher Education (AACTE).

Ingersoll, R. (1999). The problem of underqualified teachers in American secondary schools. *Education Researcher, 28*(2), 26–37.

Ingersoll, R. (2004). *Why do high-poverty schools have difficulty staffing their classrooms with qualified teachers?* Washington, DC: Renewing Our Schools, Securing Our Future: A National Task Force on Public Education.

Jacobs, L., Cintrón, J., & Canton, C. (2002). *The politics of survival in academia: Narratives of inequity, resilience, and success.* Lanham, MD: Rowman & Littlefield.

Jansen, J. (2005). The colour of change: The emotional and political dilemmas of leading for social justice in South Africa. Paper presented at the 2005 Annual Meeting of the American Educational Research Association, Montreal, Canada.

Jett-Simpson, M. (1992). Portrait of an urban professional development school. Paper presented at the Annual Meeting of the American Educational Research Association, San Francisco.

Johnston, M., Brosnan, P., Cramer, D., & Dove, T. (Eds). (2000). *Collaborative reform and other improbable dreams: The challenges of professional development schools.* Albany: State University of New York Press.

Jones, C. L., & Hill, C. (1998). Strategy and tactics in subsystem protection: The politics of education reform in Montgomery County, Maryland. In C. N. Stone (Ed.), *Changing urban education* (pp. 139–160). Lawrence: University of Kansas Press.

Jones, M. G., Jones, B. D., & Hargrove, T. Y. (2003). *The unintended consequences of high-stakes testing.* New York: Rowman & Littlefield.

Katznelson, I., & Weir, M. (1985). *Schooling for all.* Berkeley: University of California Press.

Kershaw, C., Cagle, L., Hersh, S., O'Sullivan, M., & Staten, M. (2004). *Voices and reflections: An urban education handbook.* Milwaukee, WI: UNITE: The Urban Network to Improve Teacher Education.

Kim, J. S., & Sunderman, G. L. (2005) Measuring academic proficiency under the No Child Left Behind Act: Implications for educational equity. *Educational Researcher, 34*(8), 3–13.

Kindall-Smith, M. (2004). Teachers teaching teachers: Revitalization in an urban setting. *Music Educators Journal, 91*(2), 41–46.

Kleinheinz, R. A. (2007). *Housing market 2007.* [Online article]. California Association of Realtors. Retrieved on August 20, 2007, from http://www.car.org/library/media/papers/pdf/05-09-07%20Wescom.pdf.

Knight, S., Wiseman, D., & Cooner, D. (2000). Using collaborative teacher research to determine the impact of professional development school activities on elementary students' math and writing outcomes. *Journal of Teacher Education, 51*(1), 26–38.

Kohn, A. (1993). *Punished by rewards: The trouble with gold stars, incentive plans, A's, praise, and other bribes.* Boston: Houghton Mifflin.

Kozol, J. (1967). *Death at an early age.* Boston: Houghton Mifflin.

Kozol, J. (1991). *Savage inequalities: Children in America's schools.* New York: HarperCollins.

Kyle, W. C. (2001). Foreword: Towards a political philosophy of science education. In A. C. Barton & M. D. Osborne (Eds.), *Teaching science in diverse settings* (pp. xi–xvii). New York: Peter Lang.

Ladson-Billings, G. (1994). *The Dreamkeepers: Successful teachers of African American children.* San Francisco: Jossey-Bass.

Ladson-Billings, G. (2001). *Crossing over to Canaan: The journey of new teachers in diverse classrooms.* San Francisco: Jossey-Bass.

Lane, S., Lacefield-Parachini, N., & Isken, J. (2003). Developing novice teachers as change agents: Student teacher placements "against the grain." *Teacher Education Quarterly, 30*(2), 55–68.

Lecos, M. A., Cassella, C., Evans, C., Leahy, C., Liess, E., & Lucas, T. (2000). Empowering teacher leadership in professional development schools. *Teaching and Change, 8*(1), 98–113.

Lee, O., & Fradd, S. (1998). Science for all, including students from non-English language backgrounds. *Educational Researcher, 27*(4), 12–21.

Lee, V., & Burkam, D. (2002). *Inequality at the starting gate: Social background differences in achievement as children begin school.* Washington, DC: Economic Policy Institute.

Leland, C., & Harste, J. (2005). Doing what we want to become: Preparing new urban teachers. *Urban Education, 40*(1), 60–77.

Levin, H., & McEwan, P. (Eds.). (2002). *Cost effectiveness and educational policy.* Larchmont, NY: Eye on Education.

Lewis, C. (2002). What are the essential elements of lesson study? [Online article]. *The California Science Project Connection. 2*(6), 1–4. Retrieved on July 6, 2006, from http://www.lessonresearch.net/newsletter11_2002.pdf.

Lewis, C., & Tsuchida, I. (1998). A lesson is like a swiftly flowing river: Research lessons and the improvement of Japanese education. *American Educator, Winter,* 14–17 and 50–52.

Lewis, C., Perry, R., & Hurd, J. (2004). A deeper look at lesson study. [Online article]. *Educational Leadership, 2*(2), 18–22. Retrieved on July 6, 2006 from http://www.lessonresearch.net/DeeperLookatLS.pdf.

Lightfoot, S. L. (1983). *The good high school.* New York: Basic Books.

Lipman, P. (2004). *High stakes education: Inequality, globalization and urban school reform.* New York: RoutledgeFalmer Press.

Little, J. (1982). Norms of collegiality and experimentation: Workplace conditions of school success. *American Educational Research Journal, 19*(3), 325–340.

Little, J. (1990). The mentor phenomenon and the social organization of teaching. *Review of Research in Education, 16*, 297–351.

Loeb, S., Boyd, D., Lankford, H., & Wyckoff, J. (2005). The draw of home: How teachers' preferences for proximity disadvantage urban schools. *Journal of Policy Analysis and Management, 24*(1), 113–132.

Lortie, D. (2002). *Schoolteacher: A sociological study.* Chicago: University of Chicago Press.

Louis, K. S., & Miles, M. B. (1990). *Improving the urban high school: What works and why.* New York: Teachers College Press.

Lynch, S. (2001). "Science for all" is not equal to "one size fits all": Linguistic and cultural diversity and science education reform. *Journal of Research in Science Teaching, 38*(5), 622–627.

Lyons, N., Stroble, B., & Fischetti, J. (1997). The idea of the university in an age of school reform: The shaping force of professional development schools. In M. Levine & R. Trachtman (Eds.), *Making professional development schools work: Politics, practice, and policy* (pp. 88–111). New York: Teachers College Press.

Mantle-Bromley, C., & Foster, A. (2001). Toward stewardship of democratic ideals: Using students' perspectives to improve school-university collaboration and model democratic practice. *Teaching Education, 12*(2), 213–224.

Marzano, R., Pickering, D., & Pollock, J. (2001). *Classroom instruction that works: Research-based strategies to increase student achievement.* Alexandria, VA: Association for Supervision and Curriculum Development.

McCombs, J., & Carroll, S. (2005). *Ultimate test: Who is accountable for education if everybody fails?* [Online article]. RAND Review. Retrieved on June 1, 2006, from http://www.rand.org/publications/randreview/issues/spring2005/ulttest.html.

McLaughlin, M., & Talbert, J. (2001). *Communities of practice and the work of high school teaching.* Chicago: University of Chicago Press.

McNeil, L. (2000). *Contradictions of school reform: Educational costs of high stakes testing.* New York: Routledge.

Mehan, H. (1978). Structuring school structure. *Harvard Educational Review, 48*(1), 32–64.

Meier, D. (1995). *The power of their ideas.* Boston: Beacon Press.

Melnick, S., & Zeichner, K. (1998). Teacher educator's responsibility to address diversity issues: Enhancing institutional capacity. *Theory into Practice, 37*(2), 88–95.

Menchaca, V., & Battle, J. (1997). Addressing diversity through a field-based center for professional development and technology. *Teacher Education and Practice, 13*(1), 14–21.

Merino, B. J., & Hammond, L. (2001). How do teachers facilitate writing for bilingual learners in "sheltered constructivist" science? *Electronic Journal of Literacy through Science, 1*(1). Retrieved on April 5, 2006, from http://www.sjsu.edu/elementaryed/ejlts/.

Merino, B., & Hammond, L. (2002). Writing to learn: Science in the upper-elementary bilingual classroom. In M. Schleppegrell & M. Colombi (Eds.), *Developing advanced literacy in first and second languages* (pp. 227–243). Mahwah, NJ: Lawrence Erlbaum.

Meyer, J., & Rowan, B. (1977). Institutionalized organizations: Formal structure as myth and ceremony. *American Journal of Sociology, 83*(2), 340–363.

Moll, L. C. (Ed.). (1990). *Vygotsky and education: Instructional implications and applications of sociohistorical psychology.* Cambridge, UK: Cambridge University Press.

Murrell, P. C., Jr. (2001). *The community teacher: A new framework for effective urban teaching.* New York: Teachers College Press.

Murrell, P. C., Jr. (1998). *Like stone soup: The role of the professional development school in the renewal of urban schools.* Washington, DC: American Association of Colleges of Teacher Education.

National Association for Research in Science Teaching. (2001). *Journal of Research in Science Teaching, 38*(8, 9, & 10). East Lansing, MI: Wiley.

National Center for Education Statistics. (2005). *Digest of education statistics tables and figures 2005.* Washington, DC: author.

National Council for the Accreditation of Teacher Education (NCATE). (2001). *Standards for professional development schools.* [Online article]. Retrieved on February 10, 2006, from http://www.ncate.org/public/standards.asp.

Neufeld, J. A., & McGowan, T. M. (1993). Professional development schools: A witness to teacher empowerment. *Contemporary Education, 64*(4), 249–251.

Noel, J. (2002). Diversity and location in students' selections of teacher preparation centers. Paper presented at the 2002 Annual Meeting of the American Educational Studies Association, Pittsburgh, PA.

Noel, J. (2004). From 'learning to teach' to 'becoming a member of an urban education community.' Paper presented at the 2004 Annual Meeting of the American Educational Research Association, San Diego, CA.

Noel, J. (2005). *Factors in pre-service teachers' selections of urban, suburban, and multicultural/multilingual teacher preparation sites.* Unpublished paper, California State University, Sacramento, CA.

Novak, J. D., (Ed.). (1987). *Proceedings of the second international seminar on misconceptions in science and mathematics.* Ithaca, NY: Cornell University Press.

O'Cadiz, P., Wong, P., & Torres, C. (1998). *Education and democracy: Paulo Freire, social movements and education reform in São Paulo.* Boulder, CO: Westview Press.

Oakes, J. (2003). *Teaching to change the world.* Boston: McGraw-Hill.

Oakes, J., Rogers, J., & Lipton, M. (2006). *Learning power: Organizing for education and justice.* New York: Teachers College Press.

Olsen, B., & Anderson, L. (2007). Courses of action: A qualitative investigation into urban teacher retention and career development. *Urban Education, 42*(1), 5–29.

Oplatka, I. (2006). Going beyond role expectations: Toward an understanding of the determinants and components of teacher organizational citizenship behavior. *Educational Administration Quarterly, 42*(3), 385–423.

Orfield, G., & Kornhaber, M. (Eds.). (2001). *Raising standards or raising barriers?: Inequality and high-stakes testing in public education.* New York: Century Foundation Press.

Osborne, R., & Freyberg, P. (1985). *Learning in science: The implications of children's science*. Birkenhead, Auckland: Heinemann Education.

Payne, R. (1996). *Framework for understanding poverty*. Highlands, TX: aha! Process, Inc.

Peske, H., & Haycock, K. (2006). *Teaching inequality: How poor and minority students are shortchanged on teacher quality*. Washington, DC: Education Trust.

Posner, G. J., Hewson, P. W., & Gertzog, W. A. (1982). Accommodation of scientific conception: Towards a theory of conceptual change. *Science Education, 66*(2), 211–227.

Powell, A., Farrar, E., & Cohen, D. (1985). *The shopping mall high school: Winners and losers in the educational marketplace*. Boston: Houghton Mifflin.

Price, J., & Valli, L. (2005). Pre-service teachers becoming agents of change: Pedagogical implications for action research. *Journal of Teacher Education, 56*(1), 57–72.

Quartz, K. H. (2003). Too angry to leave: Supporting new teachers' commitment to transform urban schools. *Journal of Teacher Education, 54*, 99–111.

Quartz, K., & Oakes, J. (2003). Teacher education and social justice. *Teacher Education Quarterly, 30*(2), 7–116.

Reed, W. M., Ayersman, D. J., & Hoffman, N. E. (1997). The story of a changing role: Teacher research in action. In N. E. Hoffman, W. M. Reed, & G. S. Rosenbluth (Eds.), *Lessons from restructuring experiences: Stories of change in professional development schools* (pp. 109–140). Albany: State University of New York Press.

Riches, E. (2004). *Locked out: California's affordable housing crisis*. Sacramento: California Budget Project.

Ridley, S., Hurwitz, S., Hackett, M., & Miller, K. (2005). Comparing PDS and campus-based preservice teacher preparation: Is PDS-based preparation really better? *Journal of Teacher Education, 6*(1), 46–56.

Rodriguez, A. J. (1998). Strategies for counterresistance: Toward sociotransformative constructivism and learning to teach science for diversity and understanding. *Journal of Research in Science Teaching, 35*(6), 589–622.

Rowan, B., & Miskel, C. (1999). Institutional theory and the study of educational organizations (pp. 359–384). In J. Murphy & K. Lewis (Eds.), *Handbook of research on educational administration*. San Francisco: Jossey-Bass.

Sanders, M. (2003). Community involvement in schools: From concept to practice. *Education and Urban Society, 35*(2), 161–180.

Sandholtz, J. H., & Wasserman, K. (2001). Students and cooperating teachers: Contrasting experiences in teacher preparation programs. *Action in Teacher Education, 23*(3), 54–65.

Sarason, S. (1993). *The case for change: Rethinking the preparation of educators*. San Francisco: Jossey-Bass.

Scott, W. R. (1992). *Organizations: Rational, natural, and open systems* (3rd ed.). Upper Saddle River, NJ: Prentice-Hall.

Sergiovanni, T. (1990). *Value-added leadership: How to get extraordinary performance in schools*. San Diego: Harcourt Brace Javonovich.

Sessoms, D. B., Hecsh, J. N., & Wong, P. (2005). Young (i.e. untenured) teacher educators focusing on social justice issues: Fears, compromises and lessons learned. Paper presented at the 3rd Annual International Conference on Teacher Education and Social Justice, Honolulu, HI.

Shirley, D. (1997). *Community organizing for urban school reform.* Austin: University of Texas Press.

Shive, J. (1997). Collaboration between K–12 schools and universities. In N. E. Hoffman, W. M. Reed, & G. S. Rosenbluth (Eds.), *Lessons from restructuring experiences: Stories of change in professional development schools* (pp. 33–50). Albany: State University of New York Press.

Shulman, L. (1986). Those who understand: Knowledge growth in teaching. *Educational Researcher, 15,* 4–14.

Shulman, L. (2004). *The wisdom of practice: Essays on teaching, learning, and learning to teach.* San Francisco: Jossey-Bass.

Simmons, J. (2006). *Breaking through: Transforming urban school districts.* New York: Teachers College Press.

Simmons, J. M., Konecki, L. R., Crowell, R. A., & Gates-Duffield, P. (1999). Dream keepers, weavers, and shape-shifters: Emerging roles of PDS coordinators in educational reform. In D. M. Byrd & D. J. McIntyre (Eds.), *Research on professional development schools: Teacher education yearbook VII* (pp. 29–45). Thousand Oaks, CA: Corwin Press.

Sizer, T. R. (1993). *Horace's school: Redesigning the American high school.* Boston: Houghton Mifflin.

Sizer, T. R. (1996). *Horace's hope: What works for the American high school.* Boston: Houghton Mifflin.

Sleeter, C. (2001). Preparing teachers for culturally diverse schools: Research and the overwhelming presence of whiteness. *Journal of Teacher Education, 52,* 94–106.

Snow-Gerono, J. (2005). Professional development in a culture of inquiry: PDS teachers identify the benefits of professional learning communities. *Teaching and Teacher Education, 21*(3), 241–256.

Spillane, J. (2003). Educational Leadership. *Educational evaluation and policy analysis, 25*(4), 343–346.

Steel, S., Jenkins, R., & Colebank, D. (1997). The story of two changing teachers. In N. E. Hoffman, W. M. Reed, & G. S. Rosenbluth (Eds.), *Lessons from restructuring experiences: Stories of change in professional development schools* (pp. 81–108). Albany: State University of New York Press.

Stein, M., & Nelson, B. (2003). Leadership content knowledge. *Educational Evaluation and Policy Analysis, 25*(4), 423–448.

Stigler, J. W., & Hiebert, J. (1999). *The teaching gap: Best ideas from the world's teachers for improving education in the classroom.* New York: Summit Books.

Stone, C. N. (Ed.). (1998a). *Changing urban education.* Lawrence: University of Kansas Press.

Stone, C. N. (1998b). Urban education in political context. In C. N. Stone (Ed.), *Changing urban education* (pp. 1–22). Lawrence: University of Kansas Press.

Stone, C., Henig, J., Jones, B., & Pierannunzi, C. (2001). *Building civic capacity: The politics of reforming urban schools.* Lawrence: University of Kansas Press.

Tatum, B. (2000). Examining racial and cultural thinking. *Educational leadership, 57,* 54–58.

Teitel, L. (2000). *Assessment: Assessing the impacts of professional development schools.* Washington, DC: American Association of Colleges for Teacher Education Publications.

Thompson, J., Bakken, L., & Mau, W. (1998) Comparing interactions of field-based and campus-based pre-service teachers. *Teaching Education, 10*(1), 67–75.

Timar, T. (1994). Politics, policy and categorical aid: New inequities in California school finance. *Educational Evaluation and Policy Analysis, 16*(2), 143–160.

Timar, T. (2004). *Categorical school finance: Who gains, who loses.* Berkeley, CA: Policy Analysis for California Education.

Tobin, K., & Tippins, D. (1993). Constructivism as a referent for teaching and learning. In K. Tobin (Ed.), *The practice of constructivism in science education* (pp. 3–22). Hillsdale, NJ: Lawrence Erlbaum.

Tyack, D. (1974). *The one best system. A history of American urban education.* Cambridge: Harvard University Press.

Tyack, D., & Cuban, L. (1995). *Tinkering toward utopia: A century of public school reform.* Cambridge: Harvard University Press.

Tyack, D., & Hansot, E. (1982). *Managers of virtue: Public school leadership in America 1820 to 1980.* New York: Basic Books.

U.S. Census Bureau. (2006). *State and county quickfacts.* [Electronic version]. Retrieved on April 25, 2006, from http://quickfacts.census.gov/qfd/states/06000.html.

Urban Network to Improve Teacher Education (UNITE). (2004). *Voices and reflections: An urban education handbook.* Milwaukee, WI: author.

Valdés, G. (1996). *Con respeto: Bridging the distances between culturally diverse families and schools: An ethnographic portrait.* New York: Teachers College Press.

Valenzuela, A. (1999). *Subtractive schooling: U.S.-Mexican youth and the politics of caring.* Albany: State University of New York Press.

Villegas, A. M., & Lucas, T. (2002). Preparing culturally responsive teachers: Rethinking the curriculum. *Journal of Teacher Education, 53*(1), 20–32.

Walsh, K. (2001). *Teacher certification reconsidered: Stumbling for quality.* Baltimore, MD: Abell Foundation.

Wang-Iverson, P. (2002). Why lesson study? Paper presented at the Lesson Study Conference, Stamford, CT.

Warren, M. (2005). Communities and schools: A new view of urban education reform. *Harvard Educational Review, 75,* 133–173.

Weiner, L. (1999). *Urban teaching: The essentials.* New York: Teachers College Press.

Weiner, L. (2000). Research in the 90s: Implications for urban teacher preparation. *Review of Educational Research, 70*(3), 369–406.

Wells, A. (Ed.). (2002). *Where charter school policy fails: The problems of accountability and equity.* New York: Teachers College Press.

West, C. (2000). *The Cornel West Reader.* New York: Basic Civitas.

Wiggins, G., & McTighe, J. (2005). *Understanding by design* (2nd ed.). Alexandria, VA: Association for Supervision and Curriculum Development.

Williams, E. (1998, January). *The Early Literacy Learning Initiative (ELLI) at the Ohio State University Research Report.* Columbus: Ohio State University.

Williams, M. (1989). *Neighborhood organizing for urban school reform.* New York: Teachers College Press.

Wilson, B. L., & Corbett, B. L. (2001). *Listening to urban kids: School reform and the teachers they want.* Albany: State University of New York Press.

Wingfield, M., Nath, J., Henry, C., Tyson, E., & Hutchinson, L. (2000). Professional development site schools: A great place for training elementary language arts preservice teachers. Paper presented at the 2000 Annual Meeting of the American Educational Research Association, New Orleans, LA.

Wiseman, F. (Director). (1970). *High school.* [Motion Picture].

Wong, P., Murai, H., Berta-Avila, M., William-White, L., Baker, S., Arellano, A., & Echandia, A. (2007). The M/M Center: Meeting the demand for multicultural, multilingual teacher preparation. *Teacher Education Quarterly, 34*(40, 9–25.

Zeichner, K., Grant, C., Gay, G., Gillette, M., Valli, L., & Villegas, A. M. (1998). A research informed vision of good practice in multicultural teacher education: Design principles. *Theory into Practice, 37*(2), 163–171.

Contributors

Elizabeth M. Aguirre was a community leader working with Sacramento Valley Organizing Communities and Area Congregations Together prior to becoming a public school teacher. She has been teaching for 15 years, the majority of them at an Equity Network school, where she was recently appointed the Principal.

Susan Baker is an Assistant Professor in the Bilingual/Multicultural Education Department at CSU Sacramento. Her areas of interest in research and teaching are in Multicultural Teacher Education and Academic Language Development of English Learning Students. She was a member of the Language Academy of Sacramento charter development team. She has been the Equity Network Liaison at LAS for five years.

Michael Beus has been an 8th grade English as a Second Language and Spanish teacher at Golden State Middle School for many years. He excels at creating integrated units that teach art and language and incorporate his own work as an artist and musician. Mike has been a mentor to new teachers and CSUS student teachers for many years.

Jane F. Camm was a student teacher during the research process defined in chapter one. She has since become a math teacher at this same Equity Network school: Golden State Middle School in Washington Unified School District.

Mercedes Campa-Rodriguez is a teacher at Bowling Green Charter Complex in the Bilingual Program. She has taught for ten years and plays an instrumental role in the instruction of the science methods courses at her school.

Eduardo de León is currently a middle school teacher and Governing Board member at the Language Academy of Sacramento (LAS). He obtained his B.A. in Sociology and his BCLAD and Administrative credentials at CSU Sacramento, where he is currently completing his M.A. in Education.

Larry Ferlazzo was a student teacher during the research process defined in chapter one. He has made a reputation for himself as an English as a Second Language and Social Studies teacher at Burbank High School in Sacramento, where he started a highly successful home computer project. He received the grand prize from the International Reading Association in 2007 for his work with immigrant students, and has published numerous articles about his work.

Ronald David Glass is an Associate Professor of Philosophy of Education at the University of California, Santa Cruz. He serves as chair of the Social Context and Policy Studies Ph.D. specialization and as Director of the Ed.D. in Collaborative Leadership program. Ron's interests focus on education as a practice of freedom, ideological formation, community-driven school reform, and education and democracy. He collaborated with the Equity Network since its inception in developing its evaluation and research programs.

Lorie Hammond is an Associate Professor of the Department of Teacher Education at CSU Sacramento. She works in community-based teacher education, with an emphasis on multicultural science education and has coordinated several different collaborative teacher preparation programs including Middle Ground. She is also a co-founder and active participant in a masters program centered around integrating the arts in K–12 teachers' classrooms. Lorie's research interests center around community centered approaches to education in general, and to science and arts education in particular.

Kathryn Hayes is a research associate for the Equity Network and a Lecturer in the Department of Teacher Education at CSU Sacramento. She has conducted research in the areas of Ecological Education, Urban Education, and Equity in Education and teaches courses in elementary science methods, gender equity and sex role stereotyping, and educational foundations.

Janet I. Hecsh is an Associate Professor in the Department of Teacher Education and Coordinator of PULSE, a Secondary Urban Teacher Preparation Collaborative at California State University, Sacramento. Before coming to CSUS, she taught at Florin High school for ten years. Her areas of interest in research and teaching are in the anthropology of education, participatory action research, visual studies of schooling and urban education, and the history of California secondary education.

David Jelinek is a professor of science education at CSU Sacramento and Project Director of a Javits grant for gifted and talented students in under-represented populations. He has directed two federally-funded projects incorporating lesson study into inquiry-based instruction, and served as a liaison to two Equity Network schools.

Julita G. Lambating is a Professor in the Department of Teacher Education at CSU Sacramento. She is a liaison to an Equity Network school and teaches a mathematics methods class on-site at this school. Her interests include inquiry approaches to teaching, assessment, and developing problem-solving skills.

Claudya A. Lum, a public school teacher for four years, is currently an Assistant Professor in the Department of Bilingual/Multicultural Education at California State University, Sacramento. Dr. Lum teaches both the elementary and secondary science methods courses. Her teaching and research interests include science education for social justice, multicultural science education, inquiry and science education, science teacher professional development, and teacher change.

Jeanne Malvetti was a public school teacher for 35 years, and for 17 of those years she was and continues to be, a lecturer in the Department of Teacher Education. She was a coordinator of the Sacramento City Unified School District Teacher Preparation Center for seven years, and is currently a liaison to an Equity Network school.

Mario Martín has a B.A. in Chicano Studies and a BCLAD credential. He is in his third year of teaching 6th and 7th graders at the Language Academy of Sacramento.

Ricardo Martinez has been teaching in the bilingual program at Bowling Green Elementary School for nearly a decade. He has been a leader in developing the teacher preparation science methods course for CSU Sacramento's Multilingual/Multicultural Teacher Preparation Program.

Jana Noel is an Associate Professor in the Department of Teacher Education and Coordinator of the Urban Teacher Education Center at California State University, Sacramento. Her areas of interest in research and teaching are in Multicultural Teacher Education, Urban Education, Identity Development, and History of Education related to African Americans and Native Americans in the late 1800s in California and Montana.

William T. Owens Jr. is an Associate Professor in the Department of Teacher Education at CSU Sacramento. He was an elementary teacher for six years and has been a teacher educator for the past 20 years. His interests include

Appalachian studies and social studies education. He coordinates the San Juan Professional Development School Center.

Pam Phelps is currently a middle school teacher at the Language Academy of Sacramento (LAS). She attained a BCLAD credential at California State University, Sacramento (CSUS) and began teaching 14 years ago as a 1st grade teacher. She was a key member of the LAS charter development team. In addition, she has long been associated with the Bilingual/Multicultural Education Department at CSU Sacramento as a cooperating teacher and as an M.A. student.

Jenna Porter was an elementary school teacher for five years and is currently in the Ph.D. program at UC Davis with an emphasis in Educational Psychology. She has worked with the CSUS Teacher Education Department as coordinator of Collaborative Teachers for the Elk Grove Cohort and served as a supervisor for student teachers as well. Her research interests include reflective practices in teacher education, lesson study, sociocultural perspectives on learning, and school–community partnerships.

Deidre B. Sessoms is an Associate Professor in the Department of Teacher Education and Director of the Teacher Preparation and Credentials Office (TPAC) at CSUS. Her areas of interest include foundations of education (philosophical, sociological, anthropological), schooling in a democratic society, and how state and university policies and practices impact culturally and linguistically diverse college students as they pursue higher education. She served as the Coordinator of the Placer County Multiple Subjects Collaborative Teacher Preparation Center and was a Liaison for Equity Network Schools for three years before becoming the director of TPAC.

Cynthia Suarez has been a bilingual teacher for ten years. She currently teaches 3rd grade at the Language Academy of Sacramento, a two-way Spanish immersion charter school in Sacramento's inner city. She is pursuing a master's degree in Multicultural Education from California State University Sacramento.

Rita Ultreras teaches in the primary grades of the bilingual program at Bowling Green Elementary School. She has been active in the implementation of the teacher preparation program science methods course.

Christie Wells-Artman has been an educator for three years. She did her student teaching at Bidwell Elementary School, a distinguished professional development urban school, and continues there as a teacher leader today.

Paul Winckel is a highly creative 7th grade teacher, who incorporates his own abilities as a cartoonist, movie maker, and musician into teaching English learners all subjects. His creative projects—building a rain forest in his classroom and construction of giant pyramids to illustrate geometry principles—have achieved wide acclaim. He was recently featured as the keynote speaker at the California Math Conference.

Pia Lindquist Wong was a professor in the Bilingual/Multicultural Education Department at CSU Sacramento for 12 years and served as the Director of the Equity Network since 2001. Her research interests include urban professional development schools, urban teacher preparation and democratic school reforms in the United States and in Brazil. She is currently the Associate Dean for the CSU Sacramento College of Education.

Index

Prioritizing Urban Children, Teachers, and Schools through Professional Development Schools